Other Titles in This Series

561 **Jane Gilman,** Two-generator discrete subgroups of $PSL(2, R)$, 1995
560 **F. Tomi and A. J. Tromba,** The index theorem for minimal surfaces of higher genus, 1995
559 **Paul S. Muhly and Baruch Solel,** Hilbert modules over operator algebras, 1995
558 **R. Gordon, A. J. Power, and Ross Street,** Coherence for tricategories, 1995
557 **Kenji Matsuki,** Weyl groups and birational transformations among minimal models, 1995
556 **G. Nebe and W. Plesken,** Finite rational matrix groups, 1995
555 **Tomás Feder,** Stable networks and product graphs, 1995
554 **Mauro C. Beltrametti, Michael Schneider, and Andrew J. Sommese,** Some special properties of the adjunction theory for 3-folds in $\mathbb{P}^5$, 1995
553 **Carlos Andradas and Jesús M. Ruiz,** Algebraic and analytic geometry of fans, 1995
552 **C. Krattenthaler,** The major counting of nonintersecting lattice paths and generating functions for tableaux, 1995
551 **Christian Ballot,** Density of prime divisors of linear recurrences, 1995
550 **Huaxin Lin,** C^*-algebra extensions of $C(X)$, 1995
549 **Edwin Perkins,** On the martingale problem for interactive measure-valued branching diffusions, 1995
548 **I-Chiau Huang,** Pseudofunctors on modules with zero dimensional support, 1995
547 **Hongbing Su,** On the classification of C^*-algebras of real rank zero: Inductive limits of matrix algebras over non-Hausdorff graphs, 1995
546 **Masakazu Nasu,** Textile systems for endomorphisms and automorphisms of the shift, 1995
545 **John L. Lewis and Margaret A. M. Murray,** The method of layer potentials for the heat equation on time-varying domains, 1995
544 **Hans-Otto Walther,** The 2-dimensional attractor of $x'(t) = -\mu x(t) + f(x(t-1))$, 1995
543 **J. P. C. Greenlees and J. P. May,** Generalized Tate cohomology, 1995
542 **Alouf Jirari,** Second-order Sturm-Liouville difference equations and orthogonal polynomials, 1995
541 **Peter Cholak,** Automorphisms of the lattice of recursively enumerable sets, 1995
540 **Vladimir Ya. Lin and Yehuda Pinchover,** Manifolds with group actions and elliptic operators, 1994
539 **Lynne M. Butler,** Subgroup lattices and symmetric functions, 1994
538 **P. D. T. A. Elliott,** On the correlation of multiplicative and the sum of additive arithmetic functions, 1994
537 **I. V. Evstigneev and P. E. Greenwood,** Markov fields over countable partially ordered sets: Extrema and splitting, 1994
536 **George A. Hagedorn,** Molecular propagation through electron energy level crossings, 1994
535 **A. L. Levin and D. S. Lubinsky,** Christoffel functions and orthogonal polynomials for exponential weights on [-1,1], 1994
534 **Svante Janson,** Orthogonal decompositions and functional limit theorems for random graph statistics, 1994
533 **Rainer Buckdahn,** Anticipative Girsanov transformations and Skorohod stochastic differential equations, 1994
532 **Hans Plesner Jakobsen,** The full set of unitarizable highest weight modules of basic classical Lie superalgebras, 1994
531 **Alessandro Figà-Talamanca and Tim Steger,** Harmonic analysis for anisotropic random walks on homogeneous trees, 1994

(Continued in the back of this publication)

Memoirs
of the
American Mathematical Society

Number 561

Two-Generator Discrete Subgroups of $PSL(2, R)$

Jane Gilman

American Mathematical Society
Providence, Rhode Island

1991 *Mathematics Subject Classification.*
Primary 30F35, 30F40, 32G15, 20H10, 30F60.

Library of Congress Cataloging-in-Publication Data

Gilman, Jane, 1945– .
 Two-generator discrete subgroups of $PSL(2, R)$ / Jane Gilman.
  p. cm. – (Memoirs of the American Mathematical Society, ISSN 0065-9266; no. 561)
 "September 1995, volume 117, number 561 (fourth of 5 numbers)."
 Includes bibliographical references (p. –).
 ISBN 0-8218-0361-1
  1. Fuchsian groups. 2. Kleinian groups. 3. Teichmüller spaces. I. Title. II. Series.
QA3.A57 no. 561
[QA335]
510 s–dc20
[515′.223]   95-9531
                                                                                                   CIP

Memoirs of the American Mathematical Society

This journal is devoted entirely to research in pure and applied mathematics.

Subscription information. The 1995 subscription begins with Number 541 and consists of six mailings, each containing one or more numbers. Subscription prices for 1995 are $369 list, $295 institutional member. A late charge of 10% of the subscription price will be imposed on orders received from nonmembers after January 1 of the subscription year. Subscribers outside the United States and India must pay a postage surcharge of $25; subscribers in India must pay a postage surcharge of $43. Expedited delivery to destinations in North America $30; elsewhere $92. Each number may be ordered separately; *please specify number* when ordering an individual number. For prices and titles of recently released numbers, see the New Publications sections of the *Notices of the American Mathematical Society*.

Back number information. For back issues see the *AMS Catalog of Publications*.

Subscriptions and orders should be addressed to the American Mathematical Society, P. O. Box 5904, Boston, MA 02206-5904. *All orders must be accompanied by payment.* Other correspondence should be addressed to Box 6248, Providence, RI 02940-6248.

Copying and reprinting. Individual readers of this publication, and nonprofit libraries acting for them, are permitted to make fair use of the material, such as to copy a chapter for use in teaching or research. Permission is granted to quote brief passages from this publication in reviews, provided the customary acknowledgement of the source is given.

Republication, systematic copying, or multiple reproduction of any material in this publication (including abstracts) is permitted only under license from the American Mathematical Society. Requests for such permission should be addressed to the Manager of Editorial Services, American Mathematical Society, P. O. Box 6248, Providence, RI 02940-6248. Requests can also be made by e-mail to `reprint-permission@math.ams.org`.

The owner consents to copying beyond that permitted by Sections 107 or 108 of the U.S. Copyright Law, provided that a fee of $1.00 plus $.25 per page for each copy be paid directly to the Copyright Clearance Center, Inc., 222 Rosewood Dr., Danvers, MA 01923. When paying this fee please use the code 0065-9266/95 to refer to this publication. This consent does not extend to other kinds of copying, such as copying for general distribution, for advertising or promotion purposes, for creating new collective works, or for resale.

Memoirs of the American Mathematical Society is published bimonthly (each volume consisting usually of more than one number) by the American Mathematical Society at 201 Charles Street, Providence, RI 02904-2213. Second-class postage paid at Providence, Rhode Island. Postmaster: Send address changes to Memoirs, American Mathematical Society, P. O. Box 6248, Providence, RI 02940-6248.

© Copyright 1995, American Mathematical Society. All rights reserved.
Printed in the United States of America.
This volume was printed directly from author-prepared copy.
∞ The paper used in this book is acid-free and falls within the guidelines
established to ensure permanence and durability.
♻ Printed on recycled paper.
10 9 8 7 6 5 4 3 2 1   99 98 97 96 95

Contents

I Introduction   1

1 Introduction   **3**
- 1.1 Overview Intersecting Axes 5
- 1.2 Overview of the intertwining cases 8
- 1.3 Why an algorithm is needed 10

2 The Acute Triangle Theorem   **13**
- 2.1 Nielsen equivalence 13
  - 2.1.1 Groups and Triangles 14
  - 2.1.2 The Geometric Description of Trace Minimizing . 15
  - 2.1.3 Groups and pentagons 18
- 2.2 Idea of proof: Acute triangle theorem 19
- 2.3 Labeling Conventions 20
- 2.4 Ascending order conventions 21
- 2.5 The Triangle Algorithm 21
- 2.6 Q and the last triangle along A 25
- 2.7 Combining triangle algorithm steps 28
- 2.8 The sides and heights converge to 0 31
- 2.9 Acute triangle theorem: proof 31

3 Discreteness Theorem Proof Outline   **33**
- 3.1 The Discreteness Theorem 33
- 3.2 Discreteness theorem 35
- 3.3 Geometric equivalence theorems 36

II Preliminaries   39

4 Triangle Groups and their Tilings — 41
- 4.1 Basic facts about triangle groups — 42
- 4.2 Minimal tiling distances — 44
- 4.3 The wedge at a vertex — 46
- 4.4 Proofs of lemmas and theorems — 50
- 4.5 Additional Notation — 55
- 4.6 Distances in the extended wedge — 55

5 Pentagons — 61
- 5.1 Constructing the pentagon, $P_{A,B}$ — 61
- 5.2 Notation — 66
- 5.3 Applying the Poincaré Polygon Theorem — 66
- 5.4 Pentagon Tilings — 67
- 5.5 Distances in the shingling — 68
- 5.6 Distance lemmas in P — 71

6 Hyperbolic Formulae & Geometry — 73
- 6.1 Addition formulas for the hyperbolic sine and cosine — 73
- 6.2 Hyperbolic Triangles — 74
- 6.3 Geometric Corollaries and Lemmas — 75
  - 6.3.1 Consequences of the Hyperbolic Law of Cosines — 75
  - 6.3.2 Geometric corollaries for quadrilaterals and pentagons — 76
  - 6.3.3 The geometry of acute and equilateral triangles — 78

7 Extending Knapp & Poincaré — 81
- 7.1 Extending the Knapp Count — 82
- 7.2 Facts and Notation — 83
- 7.3 Restrict to $P = P_{A,B}$ — 85
- 7.4 Counting the images of vertices — 91

III Geometric Equivalence and the Discreteness Theorem — 95

8 The Standard Acute Triangles — 97
- 8.1 Stact: $(2,3,n) t = 3, k = 3$ — 98

CONTENTS

    8.2   Stact: $(2,4,n)t = 2; k = 2$ 102
    8.3   Stact: $(2,3,7)t = 9; k = 2$ 103
    8.4   Pentagon distances $(2,3,n)t = 3; k = 3$ 107

9 Nielsen Eq: $(2,3,n)t = 3; k = 3$ 109
    9.1   Introduction 109
    9.2   Types of triples: distances 110
    9.3   Locating t_2 and t_3 110

10 Nielsen Eq: $(2,4,n)t = 2; k = 2$ 113
    10.1   Introduction 113
    10.2   Types of triples 114
          10.2.1   Distances in the standard pentagon 115
    10.3   Location of t_1, t_2 and t_3 119

11 Pentagon $t = 9$ & 2-2 Spectrum   121
    11.1   Step 1: Label the wedge 122
    11.2   Step 2: Double and Extend 123
    11.3   Step 3: Drop perpendiculars 126
    11.4   The two-two spectrum 129
    11.5   More distance computations 130
    11.6   Distances to q_0' 132
    11.7   Locate three order two points 140

12 The Seven & Geometric Eq $t = 9$ 141
    12.1   Introduction 141
    12.2   The variation of h and b 142
    12.3   Rule out a seven on the β side 144
    12.4   Rule out a seven on the D side 144
    12.5   Interior sevens 146
    12.6   Notation 148
          12.6.1 $b = T_0$ 148
          12.6.2   Rule out $b = 2T_0 = T_1$ 149
          12.6.3   Rule out $\{\mathbf{q}, \mathbf{A}^{-1}(\mathbf{q}), \mathbf{q}'''\}$ 150
          12.6.4   Rule out $b = T_2$ 151
    12.7   Geometric equivalence $(2,3,7)t = 9; k = 2$ 156

13 Discreteness Theorem Proof — 159
13.1 The Proof of the Discreteness Theorem 159
13.2 The proof of sufficiency 161

IV The Real Number Algorithm and the Turing Machine Algorithm — 165

14 Forms of the Algorithm — 167
14.1 What is an algorithm? 168
    14.1.1 Turing machine Algorithms 170
    14.1.2 Real Number Algorithms 171
14.2 The Elliptic Order Algorithm 173
14.3 Notation and Preliminary Computations 176
    14.3.1 Fixed points and cross-ratios 176
    14.3.2 Computation of p_2 and γ 177
    14.3.3 Positive and Negative Rotations 178
14.4 The Real Number Algorithm 179
14.5 The Turing Machine Algorithm 190

V Appendix — 193

A Verify Matelski-Beardon Count — 195

B A Summary of Notation — 199

ABSTRACT

Two-generator Discrete Subgroups of $PSL(2, \mathbf{R})$

Let A and B be elements of $PSL(2, \mathbf{R})$ and let G be the group they generate. Assume that G is non-elementary. *The discreteness problem* is the problem of finding an algorithm to determine whether G is or is not discrete. This is an old and subtle problem. Historically, papers on the subject have been known for their errors and omissions. In this monograph we provide what one hopes is the definitive solution to the discreteness problem. We present the first complete geometric solution to the discreteness problem building upon the cases done by Gilman and Maskit. We are able to explain exactly why the discreteness problem requires an algorithmic solution. We translate the geometric algorithm into a a purely computational algorithm, one which allows all standard computations with real numbers. We call this the real number algorithm. It is a modified BSS machine. We also provide conditions on the entries of the two matrices that assure that the geometric algorithm and the real number algorithm translate into a Turing machine algorithm, an algorithm that can be implemented on a computer.

Key words: Discrete, $PSL(2, \mathbf{R})$, Fuchsian, Kleinian, Algorithm
AMS Subject Classification: 30F35, 30F40, 32G15, 20H10, and 30F60.

Author address: Department of Mathematics, Rutgers University, Newark, NJ 07102; *e-mail* gilman@andromeda.rutgers.edu

Acknowledgements

A number of people have shared insights with me and offered me guidance during the preparation of this paper and related papers in the area. I want to thank them all. First of all, I am most indebted to Gerhard Rosenberger. In response to a question I asked him at a conference, he introduced me to the literature on the subject. We corresponded during the springs of 1985 and 1986 and he elaborated upon the literature and explained some of the subtleties. The distinction between the geometric and the algebraic algorithm as well as an idea of what was lacking in the literature on the subject emerged in a series of conversations with Alan Beardon at MSRI during the spring of 1986. These conversations began because I had stumbled upon an error in the literature. My coauthor Bernie Maskit has also exerted an important influence upon my thinking. Irwin Kra has given me invaluable advice and moral support, as have Fred Gehring and Troels Jørgensen. Bob Gilman helped me with parts of the exposition on algorithms in chapter 14 and as always supplied unlimited moral support.

I want to thank the referees who made stylistic suggestions and the referee who took the time to read the paper in detail and who made many invaluable suggestions. I also want to thank Peter Shalen for his thoughtfulness, patience and encouragement as the manuscript went through a number of revisions and expansions.

I also must thank the mathematics department at Princeton University for its support. I worked out the proof of the geometric algorithm during the 1988-89 academic year when I was a visitor there and I wrote the first draft of this manuscript when I returned there for the 1990-91 academic year. I am also grateful to the Mittag-Leffler Institute. Some initial portions of the manuscript were written during a visit there.

Part I

Introduction

Chapter 1

Introduction

Let A and B be elements of $PSL(2,\mathbf{R})$ and let $G = \langle A, B \rangle$ be the group they generate. Assume that G is non-elementary. This monograph[1] is devoted to the question of how to determine whether or not G is a discrete group[2].

While Jørgensen's inequality [17] gives an elegant necessary condition for discreteness in $PSL(2,\mathbf{C})$, a sufficient condition even in $PSL(2,\mathbf{R})$ has been elusive. There are numerous papers on the subject (see [20], [22], [27], [29], [30], [31], [19], [32], [34], [35], [36], and [37] and the rest of the bibliography), but many of these papers have errors and omissions.

There are basically two approaches to the problem, one mostly algebraic and the other involving a combination of geometry and algebra. Much of the more algebraic treatment is due to Purzitsky and Rosenberger. Rosenberger gives a summary of the algebraic results in [37]. His paper cites results from more than a dozen other papers. Even though each of the errors or omissions in the cited papers appears to be corrected in a subsequent paper, it is difficult for a nonexpert or even an expert to trace the complete algebraic argument. Matelski [27] began the more geometric treatment of the problem, but his work is incomplete.

We pursue the second approach here. The problem is divided into

---

[1]Supported in part by NSF grants # DMS-9001881 & # DMS-9409115.
[2]Received by the editor December 1991 and in revised form March 1993, March 1994 and May 1994.

seven cases according to the geometric types of the two generators: the cases that A and B are respectively (I) elliptic-elliptic, (II) elliptic-parabolic, (III) elliptic-hyperbolic, (IV) parabolic-parabolic, (V) hyperbolic-parabolic, (VI) hyperbolic-hyperbolic where the axes of the hyperbolics are disjoint and (VII) hyperbolic-hyperbolic where the axes of the hyperbolics intersect.

Maskit and I [15] gave a complete treatment along the lines of Matelski for cases I-VI. These six cases are referred to as the *intertwining cases*.

The main objective of this monograph is to present a complete geometric treatment of case (VII), pairs of hyperbolics with intersecting axes. This case is more complicated than all of the other six cases combined. The main result is the discreteness theorem (theorem 3.1.1).

A second purpose of this monograph is to present a complete result for all seven cases so that the reader can find the solution all in one place (theorem 14.4.1). The complete result is given in the form of a real number algorithm (see chapter 14). We consider an algorithm geometric if the steps of the algorithm include geometric operations such as locating the intersection of two hyperbolic lines, comparing areas or determining rotation angles. By contrast, a real number algorithm is one where the geometrically defined procedures have been reduced to computations with real numbers. We translate both the discreteness theorem for case VII proved in chapter 13 and the more geometrically based algorithm for the intertwining cases derived in [15] into a real number algorithm. We also give sufficient conditions on the input to the real number algorithm that assure the algorithm can be run on a computer (theorem 14.5.1). An algorithm that can be run on a computer is called a Turing machine algorithm.

A third purpose of this monograph is to present an account of the relationship between the geometric and algebraic approaches to the problem and in doing so to provides insight into why the correct solution has been so elusive. The algebraic approach to the problem is to apply what are called trace minimizing Nielsen transformations to a given pair of generators. At times this procedure can be confusing, probably because it is unmotivated. The geometric picture of this procedure gives a conceptual framework which motivates the procedure.

A final goal of this monograph is to clarify the sense in which the discreteness problem requires an algorithmic solution. This requires an elementary introduction to the theory of algorithms and models of computation which is found in the introductary sections of chapter 14 (through sections 14.1 and 14.1.2) along with section 1.3 of this chapter.

Since this monograph has four main goals, readers may consult this manuscript for different reasons. A reader who has a two generator subgroup of $PSL(2, \mathbf{R})$ and wants to know whether or not it is discrete, will only need to look at the real number algorithm or the Turing machine algorithm (theorem 14.4.1 or theorem 14.5.1 of Part IV) or the discreteness theorem (theorem 3.1.1). A reader who wants an overview of the procedure and/or an understanding of the relationship between the algebraic solution and the more geometrically motivated approach will read all of Part I which consists of the introduction (chapter 1), the proof that the triangle algorithm stops (chapter 2) and the outline of the proof of the discreteness theorem (chapter 3). Others may shorten this to the overviews in this introduction, especially the overview of the intertwining case (section 1.2), and the statements of the main theorems in chapters 2 and 3. Still others who want to see the complete proof of the discreteness theorem for hyperbolics with intersecting axes will read all of Parts I, II and III using chapter 3 of Part I as a guide to the contents of Parts II and III. Finally those who want a better understanding of the role that algorithms play will read part IV, especially the introductory sections of chapter 14.

An attempt has been made to organize the material so as to make it accessible to all types of readers. This has required some repetition to assure that certain sections could be read independently. It is hoped that this repetition has been kept to a minimum.

1.1 Overview of hyperbolics with intersecting axes

The discreteness or non-discreteness of the group generated by a pair of hyperbolics with intersecting but distinct axes depends upon the nature of the commutator of the two generators. If one begins with a pair of hyperbolics with intersecting axes, one of three things can happen: either (i) one can tell immediately that the group is discrete, (ii) one can tell immediately that the group is not discrete or (iii) one cannot determine either fact from the given set of generators. It is not difficult to use the Poincaré polygon theorem to show that (i) occurs if the commutator is hyperbolic, parabolic, a primitive rotation or the square of a primitive rotation. If the commutator is elliptic of but not finite order, (ii) occurs. If the commutator is of finite order n and the square of a rotation by an angle of $2k\pi/n$ for some relatively prime integers k and n with $k \neq 1$, then one proves that (ii) occurs when $k \neq 2$ or 3 and that the indeterminate situation, (iii), occurs when $k = 2$ or 3.

The case where the commutator is the square of a non-primitive rotation of finite order is the difficult part of the problem. It involves two main theorems, the acute triangle theorem and the discreteness theorem. The acute triangle theorem is a statement about an algorithm coming to a stopping point. The algorithm is referred to as the triangle algorithm. At its stopping point the triangle algorithm associates to a generating pair (A, B) a triangle, $Act_{A,B}$, all of whose angles are $\leq \pi/2$. The discreteness theorem gives a necessary and sufficient conditions which when applied to the triangle $Act_{A,B}$ determine discreteness.

The triangle algorithm proceeds as follows: Each pair of hyperbolics with intersecting axes determines a hyperbolic triangle and vice-versa. Replacing (A, B) by a Nielsen equivalent pair replaces the triangle with a new triangle and we do so (following a specific recipe) provided the triangle contains an obtuse angle. The algorithm for replacing the triangle by a new one decreases the lengths of the sides of the triangle. Since the lengths of the sides are related to the traces of the generators, this triangle replacement is the geometric equivalent of trace minimizing. We show that after a finite number of steps, the triangle that we arrive at has all angles $\leq \pi/2$. We call this triangle *the acute triangle associated to* (A, B) and denote it by $Act_{A,B}$.

As a consequence of Knapp's Theorem (see [20] or part A of the appendix.) one knows that if G is discrete, it must be either a $(2, 3, n)$ triangle group or a $(2, 4, n)$ triangle group or a subgroup of index two in such a group, G^* and k must be 2 or 3. For each of these groups there is a *standard acute triangle*, *Stact*. In the $(2, 3, n)$ case, $n \neq 7$, *Stact* is an equilateral triangle. For $(2, 4, n)$, *Stact* is a right isosceles

1.1. OVERVIEW INTERSECTING AXES

triangle. For a $(2,3,7)$ group there are two possible standard triangles, the equilateral one described above and another one which we will describe later. Each of these correspond to two distinct Nielsen equivalence classes of generators. The existence of the second triangle contributes to the length of this paper. In the earliest works on two generator discrete groups it was overlooked.

For a given (A, B) one forms $Act_{A,B}$. The discreteness theorem says essentially that $G = <A, B>$ is discrete if and only if $Act_{A,B}$ is one of the standard triangles.

A pair of hyperbolics also determines a pentagon with four right angles. We let $\phi = 2k\pi/n$ be the angle at the fifth vertex, v. When we replace the generators by a Nielsen equivalent pair to obtain a new triangle, the pentagon is replaced by either the same pentagon or a new one, but the area of the pentagon is unchanged. (The area of the pentagon is determined by the vertex angle ϕ which is in turn determined by the trace of the commutator which in turn is unchanged under a Nielsen transformation.) The arguments for the proof of the acute triangle theorem depend upon the fact that if the sequence of triangles is infinite, the lengths of the sides of the triangles and their heights decrease. At the same time the areas of the pentagons, which are also related to the lengths of the sides of the triangles and their heights, remain constant forcing the heights to increase.

The proof of the discreteness theorem depends upon the same idea but requires in addition an analysis of the possible tilings of the hyperbolic plane by triangles and shinglings of the plane by pentagons that occur in the discrete case. (Shinglings are tilings where the tiles are allowed to overlap.) Discreteness says that within any bounded neighborhood of a given point there are only a finite number of points that are fixed by elements of the group and these points can be clearly identified in the shingling pattern. In certain cases one actually computes the early terms of the **two-two spectra**, for certain triangle groups. (The two-two spectra is the set of distances between the fixed points in the hyperbolic plane of the elements of order two of the group.) The analysis of the shingling pattern is used to show that when the group is discrete, $Act_{A,B}$ depends only upon the Nielsen equivalence class of (A, B) and that there is (with the exception of the $(2, 3, 7)$ group) only one such Nielsen equivalence class of generators.

1.2 Overview of the intertwining cases

The treatment assumes a hierarchy of cases. That is, case I is viewed as being *easier* than case II, case II easier than case III, etc. If one begins with a pair of generators in any of cases I-VI, one of three things can happen: (i) one can tell immediately that the group is discrete by using the Poincaré polygon theorem, (ii) one can tell immediately that the group is not discrete by using Jørgensen's inequality, the Shimizu-Leutbecher theorem (p. 19 of [26]), or an area inequality, or (iii) one cannot determine either fact directly from the given set of generators. In the latter case one replaces the given set of generators (A, B) (after some normalization) by the Nielsen equivalent pair (A, AB). Either the new pair lies in an easier case or it remains in the same case. One proves that one can only remain in the same case a finite number of times before one is either forced to move up into an easier case or has a situation of type (i) or (ii).

While pairs of elliptics and pairs of parabolics can be given treatments that do not require moving up into an easier case, to give the full treatment of case (VI) one needs to move through all of the cases (I)-(VI), whence the name *intertwining cases*. Thus (VII) is the only fully self-contained case.

In all seven cases one begins by enlarging the group G to a three generator group, G^*, in which G sits as a subgroup of index at most two. G and G^* are either simultaneously discrete or simultaneously non-discrete. The construction of G^* varies from case to case. When A and B are pairs of hyperbolics with disjoint axes, for example, let L be the common perpendicular to the two axes and let r_L denote reflection in L. Then there are reflections r_A and r_B such that $A = r_A \cdot r_L$ and $B = r_L \cdot r_B$ and G^* is the group generated by the three reflections.

The three possibilities (i), (ii), and (iii) usually correspond to three different algebraic inequalities and geometric configurations. We illustrate this by considering the case of two hyperbolic generators A and B whose axes are disjoint and whose product is hyperbolic. Since this case has been treated erroneously in the literature, the example also serves to illustrate how a point that is subtle from the algebraic point of view is easily understood from the geometric perspective.

We let g and h be elements of $SL(2, \mathbf{R})$ whose images are A and

1.2. OVERVIEW OF THE INTERTWINING CASES

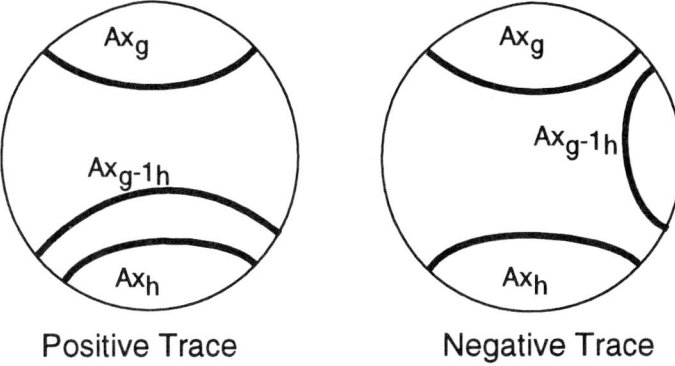

Figure 1.1: The Geometric Picture of Positive and Negative Trace.

B respectively. Replacing g and h by $-g$ and $-h$ if necessary, we may assume that $tr\ g \geq 2$ and $tr\ h \geq 2$. Here tr denotes the trace. After replacing g and h by their inverses if necessary, we may further assume that $tr\ gh > 2$. Then either $tr\ g^{-1}h > 2$ or $tr\ g^{-1}h < -2$. That is, either $tr\ g^{-1}h$ is positive or negative.

Papers in the subject correctly identified the fact that negative trace implied discreteness. However, they sometimes also tried to prove the incorrect statement that positive trace also implied discreteness or that the condition $|tr\ g^n \cdot h| > 2 \ \forall\ n$ implied discreteness.

The geometric picture clarifies the situation. Once one has seen it, one will not make the same mistake for one proves that negative trace implies that the axes of A, B and $A^{-1}B$ bound a region in the hyperbolic plane whereas positive trace implies that one of the three axes separates the other two (see figure 1.1). Further it can be shown that the axes bound a region if and only if the reflection axes, the axes of r_L, r_A and r_B, also bound a region, and that one axis separates the other two if and only if one of the reflection axes separates the other two reflection axes. When the trace is negative, one can apply the Poincaré polygon theorem to the region bounded by the reflection axes to conclude discreteness. On the other hand, in the case of positive trace, when one axis separates the other two, one would not expect to be able to conclude anything about discreteness. In this indeterminate case the algorithm tells one to replace the generators A and B (or g and h by a Nielsen equivalent pair and to begin again.

The two different geometric pictures axes bounding or separating are qualitatively different as the two algebraic statements, $tr\ g^{-1}h > 2$ and $tr\ g^{-1}h < -2$, are quantitatively different. When one adds in the geometric pictures for $-2 \leq tr\ g^{-1}h \leq 2$, one obtains precise numbers that describe how the geometric pictures change qualitatively as the algebra changes quantitatively.

The general method is to understand the relation between the algebraic situation and the geometric pictures in all the indeterminate cases.

1.3 Why an algorithm is needed

We end this introduction with a word about why an algorithm is needed at all and how the algorithm given in this monograph compares with other algorithms.

If there were a necessary and sufficient condition for discreteness that could be applied directly to every set of generators for a two-generator group G, then we would call that a *closed form* discreteness condition. For example, if every set of generators for a discrete two generator group were *geometric generators*, ones to which the Poincaré polygon theorem could be directly applied, then Jørgensen's inequality and the Poincaré polygon theorem would combine to give a closed form condition. An algorithm is needed precisely because not every generating set is a set of geometric generators. One measure of how close to a closed form condition the algorithm comes is the number of generating pairs that the algorithm must consider.

Roughly speaking our discreteness algorithm proceeds by using the Jørgensen/Poincaré dichotomy. That is, if a pair of generators fails to satisfy Jørgensen's inequality, the group is not discrete; if the generators (for the enlarged three-generator group) fulfill the conditions of the Poincaré polygon theorem, the group is discrete; and if neither happens, the algorithm tells how to replace the pair of generators by a Nielsen equivalent pair and assures that after a finite number of re-

1.3. WHY AN ALGORITHM IS NEEDED

placements one obtains a pair where discreteness or non-discreteness can be determined immediately. (We also label a pair of generators for a the two-generator group geometric generators when the corresponding generators for the enlarged three-generator group are geometric generators.) The algorithm sometimes determines discreteness without actually finding the geometric generators, but it is easy to make the geometric generators explicit at each point where the algorithm stops. That is, the algorithm stops when the geometric generators are in sight.

It turns out that one can actually go through the steps in the algorithm and bound the number of replacements it takes before one obtains a pair of generators where the direct determination can be made. This is done in [14].

To simplify the exposition and for ease of comparison with other algorithms, assume for the time being that our original matrices are in $PSL(2, \mathbf{Q})$. This forces elliptic elements of finite order to be either of order two or three. Let T be the maximum of the four initial traces. That is, let $T = \max\{Tr\ A, Tr\ B, Tr\ AB, Tr\ AB^{-1}\}$. It is shown in [14] that the number of pairs of generators that the algorithm must consider is at most $30T+30$. This allows one to formulate the geometric discreteness algorithm as:

Theorem: 1.3.1 *A necessary and sufficient condition for a non-elementary two-generator subgroup $G = \langle A, B \rangle$ of $PSL(2, \mathbf{Q})$ to be discrete is that one of at most $30T + 30$ pairs of generators which are algorithmically obtained from A and B are geometric generators.*

This result which gives a linear bound on the number of generating pairs that the algorithm must consider roughly says that the algorithm is as close to a closed form necessary and sufficient condition for having a pair of geometric generators as one can hope. It can essentially be carried out by hand. The theory of computational complexity can be brought to bear to make this precise ([14]).

The algorithm is this good because in determining discreteness or non-discreteness it uses a wide range of results beyond Jørgensen's inequality and the Poincaré polygon theorem. As a basis for comparison, consider the procedure that Riley developed based solely on the Jørgensen/Poincaré dichotomy ([33]).

Riley's procedure is much more powerful. It applies in a a much more general setting. It is for determining whether or not a finitely generated subgroup of $PSL(2,\mathbf{C})$ is discrete, but it is not an algorithm because it does not always stop. It begins with a set of generators and at iteration n it tests all pairs of words of length less than or equal to n for Jørgensen's inequality and all subsets of words of length less than or equal to n for the hypotheses of the Poincaré polyhedron theorem. When the group is geometrically finite, Riley's procedure is an algorithm. In particular, it is an algorithm for two-generator subgroups of $PSL(2,\mathbf{R})$. Since there is no known upper bound for the number of iterations that Riley's algorithm requires, the most one can say is that the n-th iterate involves considering at least 2^{2^n} sets of generators (all subsets of words in the generators of length $\leq n$). The Riley procedure was not intended to be close to a closed form condition.

Chapter 2

The Triangle Algorithm and the Acute Triangle Theorem

In this chapter we describe the triangle algorithm in detail and prove the acute triangle theorem, that the algorithm stops after a finite number a steps (theorem 2.9.1). In other words, we show how a pair of hyperbolics with intersecting axes determines a triangle; if this triangle contains an obtuse angle, we show how to replace the triangle by a another triangle that corresponds to a Nielsen equivalent set of generators; and finally we prove that this algorithm stops in a finite number of steps, i.e. that after a finite number of applications one obtains an acute or a right triangle.

Throughout this chapter we assume that A and B are hyperbolics with intersecting but distinct axes and that the commutator of A and B, $[A, B]$, is a rotation of finite order.

2.1 Nielsen equivalence

We begin by recalling the definition of Nielsen equivalence.

Definition: 2.1.1 *The elementary* **Nielsen transformations** *of the group G are the transformations which replace the ordered pair of gen-*

erators (A, B) by the ordered pair, (C, D) where either

- $(C, D) = (B, A)$, or
- $(C, D) = (A^s, B^r)$ where $r = \pm 1$ and $s = \pm 1$, or
- $(C, D) = (A^n B, A)$ where $n = \pm 1$, or
- $(C, D) = (ABA^{-1}, A)$.

Definition: 2.1.2 *We say that the pair (A, B) is **Nielsen equivalent** to the pair (C, D) if one can be obtained from the other by a finite sequence of elementary Nielsen transformations and conjugations by elements of the group.*

Let Tr denote the trace of a matrix in $SL(2, \mathbf{R})$. If g and h in $SL(2, \mathbf{R})$ are preimages of A and B respectively, $Tr\,[g, h]$ is independent of which preimages are chosen. Thus it makes sense to speak of $Tr\,[A, B]$. It is easy to calculate that $Tr\,[A, B]$ does not change when an elementary Nielsen transformation is performed on (A, B).

2.1.1 Groups and Triangles

There is a well known correspondence between pairs of hyperbolics with intersecting axes and triangles. If p_2 is the point where the axes of A and B intersect, let E_{p_2} be the *half turn* about p_2. (E_x, the *half turn* about a point x, is the element of order two fixing x.) Let p_1 be a point chosen on the axis of A half the translation length of A from p_2 so that $A = E_{p_1} E_{p_2}$ Similarly choose p_3 on the axis of B so that $B = E_{p_3} E_{p_2}$. The points p_1, p_2, p_3 determine a hyperbolic triangle, T. (See figure 2.1.) We also use $T_{A,B}$ to denote T when we wish to emphasize its relation to the original pair of generators.

The group G^* is defined to be the group generated by the three half-turns. G is of index at most 2 in G^*. If $\gamma = E_{p_1} E_{p_2} E_{p_3}$, then $\gamma^2 = [A, B]$.

If T_A and T_B denote half the translation length of A and B respectively, then two sides of T have these length. Let C be the hyperbolic length of the segment from p_1 to p_3. Let θ be the angle opposite the side corresponding to C.

2.1. NIELSEN EQUIVALENCE

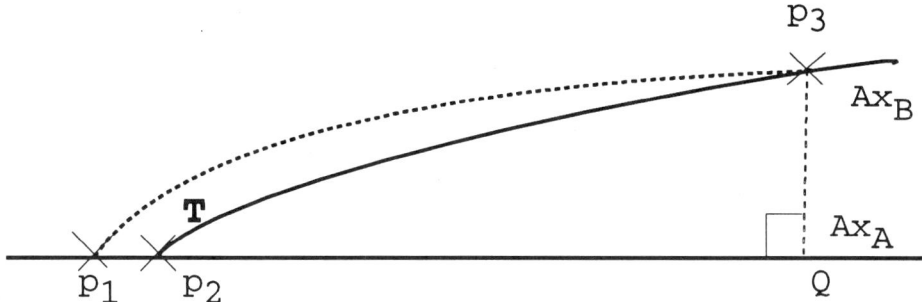

Figure 2.1: The two axes, the perpendicular, and the triangle, T.

Our understanding of this triangle and others obtained from it boils down to the hyperbolic law of cosines (6.9) which says

$$\cosh C = \cosh(T_A)\cosh(T_B) - \sinh(T_A)\sinh(T_B)\cos\theta. \qquad (2.1)$$

Drop a perpendicular from p_3 to the axis of A. Let Q be the point where the perpendicular hits Ax_A. Let h be the hyperbolic segment from Q to p_3. The **height** of T is h. The **base** of T is the segment from p_1 to p_2 and has length T_A.

2.1.2 The Geometric Description of Trace Minimizing

Our definition gives a well-defined triangle T corresponding to the pair of generators (A, B). However, we could also have assigned a triangle to the pair by choosing $E_{p_2}(p_1) = \bar{p}_1$, the other point along the axis of A at a distance of T_A from p_2, instead of p_1. Let D be the hyperbolic length of the geodesic segment connecting p_3 and $\bar{p}_1$ and T' the triangle with vertices $\bar{p}_1$, p_2 and p_3. (See figure 2.2.) The hyperbolic law of cosines also says that

$$\cosh D = \cosh(T_A)\cosh(T_B) - \sinh(T_A)\sinh(T_B)\cos(\pi - \theta). \qquad (2.2)$$

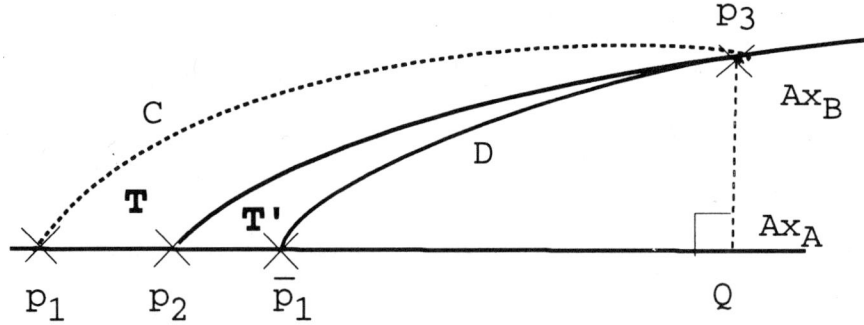

Figure 2.2: T' another choice of triangle.

Combining equation 2.1 and 2.2, we obtain

Theorem: 2.1.3 *$C \geq D$ if and only if $\theta \geq \pi/2$ with equality holding when $\theta = \pi/2$.*

Corollary: 2.1.4 *Either triangle T contains no obtuse angles or $D < C$.*

For a transformation Q, we shorten T_Q to Q and note for future use that equations 2.1 and 2.2 also imply that $2 \cosh A \cosh B = \cosh C + \cosh D$, whence if $\theta \geq \pi/2$,

$$\cosh A \cdot \cosh B \leq \cosh C. \tag{2.3}$$

Roughly speaking the algorithm which we define with full precision in section 2.5 produces a sequence of triangles as follows: Interchange A and B if necessary so that $T_A \leq T_B$. Form triangle T. If $D < C$, form the new triangle T'. We will see that this corresponds to replacing the generating pair (A, B) by the Nielsen equivalent pair (A, BA). Either T' contains no obtuse angles or we can replace it by a new triangle beginning the procedure again. Under this replacement the length of the longest side always decreases and this is then the geometric description of the algebraic operation **trace minimizing**.

2.1. NIELSEN EQUIVALENCE

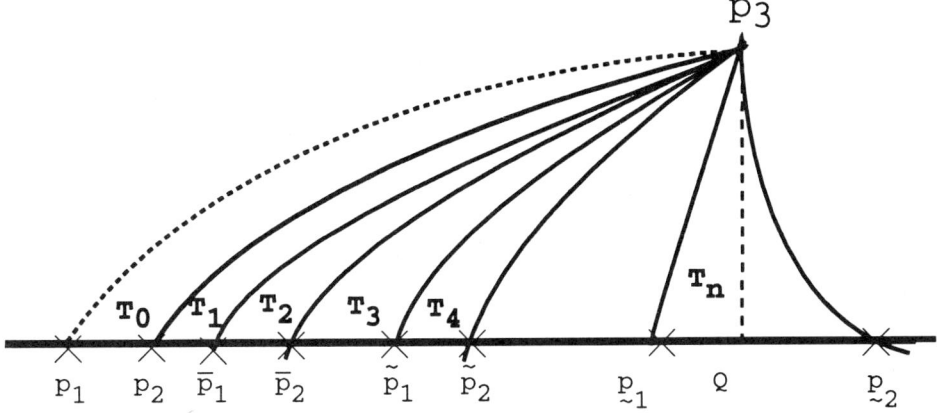

Figure 2.3: Continuing several steps along the axis of A.

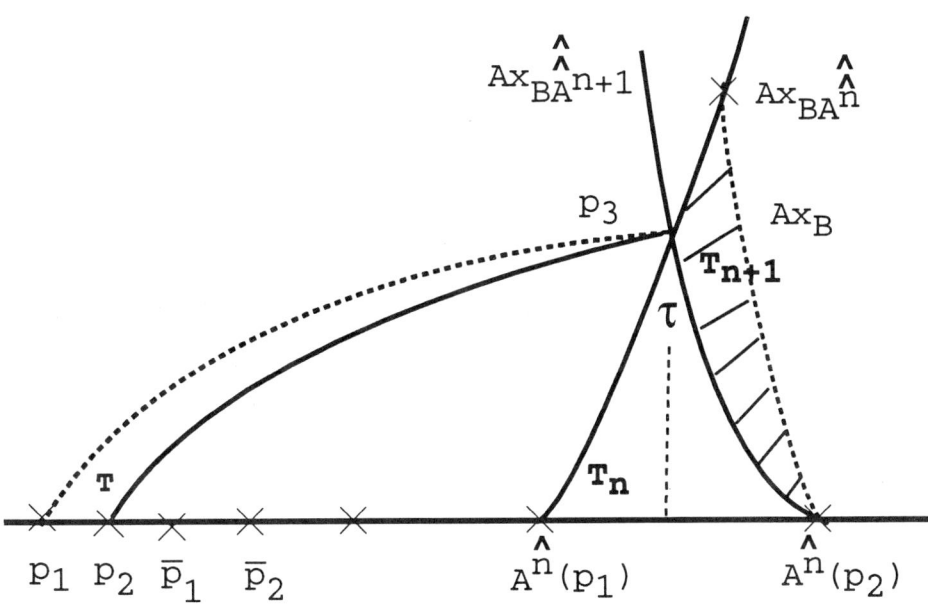

Figure 2.4: Turning a corner: a non-final giant step.

There are essentially two different ways to pass from a given triangle to a new one. Either T_A remains the length of the shortest side in each subsequent triangle or it becomes the length of the longest side. In the first case we **continue along the axis of** A. In the second case we **turn a corner**. The geometric picture is given in figures 2.2, 2.3 and 2.4.

We will show that we can only continue along the axis of A for a finite number of steps before we must turn a corner. The main result that one needs in order to prove that this procedure comes to a stop is that one *cannot turn an infinite number of corners*.

Making all of this precise and proving that one can not turn an infinite number of corners is the major goal of the rest of this chapter.

2.1.3 Groups and pentagons

The pair A, B also determines a pentagon $P_{A,B}$ as follows (see figure 2.5): If h is the perpendicular from p_3 to the axis of A, then $A(h)$ is a segment connecting $A(p_3)$ to $A(Q)$. The perpendicular to h at p_3 and the perpendicular to $A(h)$ at $A(p_3)$ intersect (in the indeterminate cases) in the point v where $\gamma(v) = v$. (See chapter 5 for details.) $P_{A,B}$ is then the pentagon with vertices Q, $A(Q)$, $A(p_3)$, v, and p_3. The angles of $P_{A,B}$ are all right angles except for ϕ, the vertex angle at v, which is determined by the trace of the commutator of A and B. If we replace A and B by a Nielsen equivalent pair, we obtain either the same pentagon or a new one, but in either case the vertex angle v remains the same because the trace of the commutator is not changed by a Nielsen transformation.

We call the length of the segment h the **height of the pentagon** and one half of the length of the segment from Q to $A(Q)$ which is T_A the **base of the pentagon**. Our understanding of the pentagon comes from the formula (see 6.14)

$$\sinh T_A \sinh h = cos(\phi/2) \tag{2.4}$$

The importance of this equation is that for a fixed Nielsen equivalence class of generators, the lengths and heights of the pentagons vary inversely.

2.2. IDEA OF PROOF: ACUTE TRIANGLE THEOREM

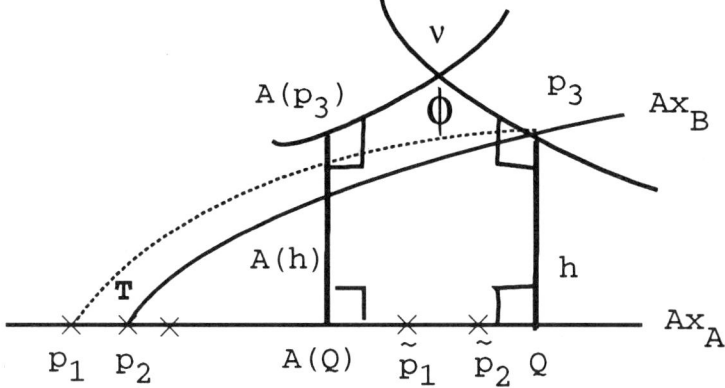

Figure 2.5: The pentagon

We note that the lengths of the height and the base of the pentagon determined by A and B are the same as the lengths of the height and base for the triangle determined by A and B.

2.2 The idea of the proof of the acute triangle theorem

The proof by contradiction proceeds along the following lines. We assume that we turn an infinite number of corners so that we have an infinite sequence of triangles. Corresponding to the sequence of triangle we have a sequence of pairs of generators, a sequence of heights, a non-increasing sequence of bases and a sequence of pentagons. For each pentagon in the sequence, ϕ remains fixed, so that equation 2.4 tells us that the sequence of heights must be non-decreasing. We prove that whenever we turn a corner, the smallest side of a triangle (at one stage) become the largest side (at another stage) so that the sequence of longest sides of the triangles converges to the same limit as the sequence of shortest sides. We use equation 2.3 to show that the bases actually converge to 0. Since the height of a triangle to its smallest side is smaller than its longest side, if we turn an infinite number of corners, any given height is dominated by the length of some base. This forces the heights also to converge to 0 and gives a contradiction.

2.3 Labeling Conventions

To make the algorithm precise, we need additional notation and naming conventions. The algorithm will not merely produce sequences of pairs of generators, triangles, and pentagons. It will produce sequences of ordered pairs of generators, triangles with ordered sides, and ordered triples of fixed points of the group G^* of order two.

We saw how an ordered pair of generators determined three ordered points in the hyperbolic plane. Conversely, any three non-collinear ordered points in the hyperbolic plane, q_1, q_2, q_3, determine an ordered pair of hyperbolic transformations with intersecting axes, $A = E_{q_1} E_{q_2}$ and $B = E_{q_3} E_{q_2}$.

We denote the hyperbolic triangle, T, by $\triangle(q_1, q_2, q_3)$ when we wish to emphasize the points q_i and by $T_{A,B}$ when we wish to emphasize the pair of generators.

We need to understand how the ordered pairs of generators, the ordered triples of sides and the ordered triples of points changes as we pass from T to T'.

For any two points a and b in the hyperbolic plane, let $[a, b]$ be the geodesic segment connecting a and b and $[a, b]_d$ its non-euclidean length. Let $\triangle(p_1, p_2, p_3)$ be a triangle. Set $A = E_{p_1} E_{p_2}$, $B = E_{p_3} E_{p_2}$ and $C = E_{p_3} E_{p_1}$. By abuse of notation we name the side of a triangle after the transformation along whose axis it lies. That is, **side-**$A = [p_1, p_2]$, **side-**$B = [p_3, p_2]$ and **side-**$C = [p_3, p_1]$. We write $A = [p_1, p_2]$, $B = [p_3, p_2]$ and $C = [p_3, p_1]$. Under this convention, the axis of the transformation along which side $[a, b]$ lies is the axis of $E_a E_b$ and the length of the side $[a, b]$ is one-half the translation length of $E_a E_b$. Using T_X to denote half the translation length of the transformation X, we have $T_A = [p_1, p_2]_d$, $T_B = [p_3, p_2]_d$, and $T_C = [p_3, p_1]_d$. Further, since $C = E_{p_3} E_{p_1}$, we have $C = BA^{-1}$.

We apply these conventions to the triangle $T' = \triangle(p_2, \bar{p}_1, p_3)$. Note that $E_{\bar{p}_1} = E_{p_2} E_{p_1} E_{p_2}^{-1}$ and recall that $D = BA$. The sides of T' are $[p_2, \bar{p}_1]$, $[p_3, \bar{p}_1]$, and $[p_3, p_2]$. The transformations on whose axes the

2.4. ASCENDING ORDER CONVENTIONS

sides lie are respectively $E_{p_2} E_{\bar{p}_1} = E_{p_1} E_{p_2} = A$, $E_{p_3} E_{\bar{p}_1} = BA = D$, and $E_{p_3} E_{p_2} = B$. As we pass from T to T' we replace the ordered triple (p_1, p_2, p_3) by the ordered triple $(p_2, \bar{p}_1, p_3)$ and the pair of generators A and B by the **Nielsen equivalent** pair A and BA.

2.4 Ascending order conventions

We can also name a triangle by listing its sides. That is, since the pair (A, B) determines the triangle with third side C, we let $T(A, B, C)$ also denote T.

We adopt the convention that unless otherwise stated when we name a triangle by its sides, we name the sides in ascending order of length. That is, $T(A, B, C)$ implies that $T_A \leq T_B \leq T_C$; and $T(p_1, p_2, p_3)$ implies that $[p_1, p_2]_d \leq [p_2, p_3]_d \leq [p_3, p_1]_d$. Finally, if $T_A \leq T_B$ we write $A \leq B$ for short.

In summary, when we write the triple $\triangle(a, b, c)$, the notation implies that $[a, b] \leq [b, c] \leq [a, c]$. The corresponding sides are $A = [a, b]$, $B = [b, c]$ and $C = [a, c]$. The corresponding transformations are $A = E_a E_b$, $B = E_c E_b$, and $C = E_c E_a$ with the corresponding ordered pair of generators (A, B). The group determined by $\triangle(a, b, c)$ is $\langle A, B \rangle$ and is denoted by $G(a, b, c)$ or just by G when no confusion is apt to arise.

To illustrate the notation assume that $T_A \leq T_B$. The pair (A, B) determines a triangle with sides $A, B,$ and C, where $C = BA^{-1}$. However, the triangle will either be $T(A, B, C)$, $T(A, C, B)$ or $T(C, A, B)$ depending upon the relative length of C. Here the corresponding pair of generators would be respectively (A, B), (A^{-1}, BA^{-1}), or (BA^{-1}, A^{-1}).

As another illustration assume that $T_A \leq T_B \leq T_C$. The pair (A, B) will determine the triangle $\triangle(p_1, p_2, p_3)$ while the pair (A^{-1}, B) determines the triangle $\triangle(\bar{p}_1, p_2, p_3)$ where $\bar{p}_1 = E_{p_2}(p_1)$.

2.5 The Triangle Algorithm

- **Step #1: the first triangle** We begin with the pair (A, B). After applying a Nielsen transformation and replacing A by A^{-1} and B by B^{-1} if necessary, we may assume that $T_A \leq T_B$ and that

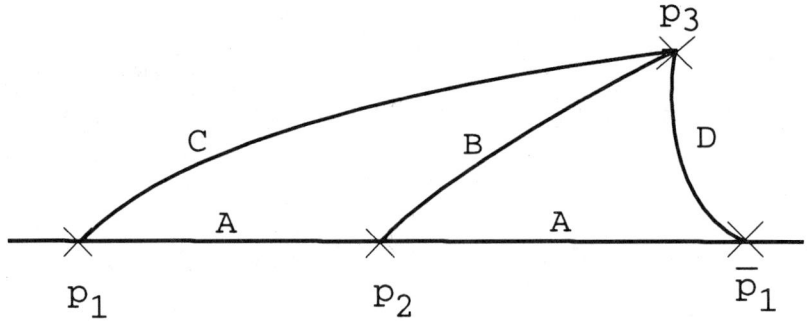

Figure 2.6: The next triangle, $\triangle(A, B, D)$, when $A \leq B \leq D$.

$T_B \leq T_C$ where $C = BA^{-1}$ and that the triangle with sides A, B, and C is actually $\triangle(A, B, C)$. We define $T_1 = \triangle(p_1, p_2, p_3) = \triangle(A, B, C)$.

- **Do we stop?** We determine whether $C = AB^{-1} \leq D = BA$. Equivalently we determine whether $\theta \leq \pi/2$. If $C \leq D$ (or $\theta \leq \pi/2$), then we stop.

- **Step #2: the next triangle.** If $C > D$ so that $\theta > \pi/2$, then we replace $\triangle(A, B, C)$ by the triangle with sides A, B, and D. However, we must do this carefully. There are three basic possibilities for a triangle with sides A, B and D and each of the three has a very different geometric meaning:

$A \leq B \leq D$: We replace T_1 by $T_2 = \triangle(A, B, D)$. See figure 2.6.

We see that in this case T_2 contains no obtuse angle so that the algorithm stops with T_2. Namely, a triangle is acute triangle or a right triangle if the angle opposite its longest side is at most $\pi/2$. Here since $\theta \geq \pi/2$, the angle opposite the longest side, D, is $\pi - \theta$ and is at most $\pi/2$.

$A \leq D \leq B$: In this case, we replace $\triangle(A, B, C)$ with $\triangle(A, D, B)$. The new triangle still has its smallest side along the axis of A and corresponds to the points $\triangle(p_2, \bar{p}_1, p_3)$. and the generators A and BA.

2.5. THE TRIANGLE ALGORITHM

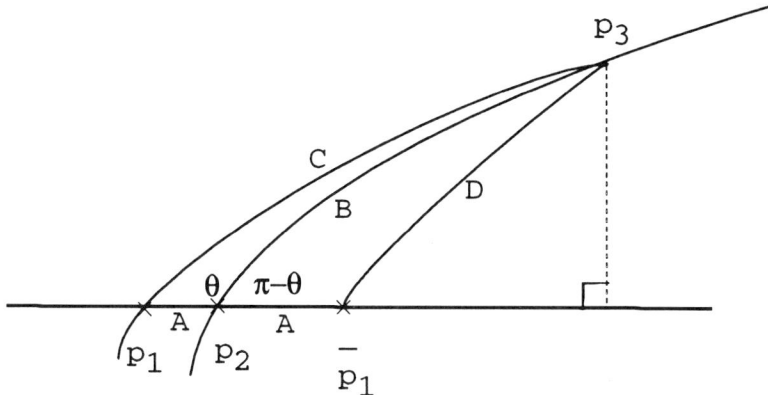

Figure 2.7: Moving a small step along the axis of A: The next triangle, $\triangle(A, D, B)$, when $A \leq D \leq B$.

We call such a step: moving a **small step along the axis of** A. See figures 2.7 and 2.10.

$D \leq A \leq B$: In this case, the vertices of the triangle are p_2, $\bar{p}_1$ and p_3. Let the ordered vertices be q_1, q_2, q_3. Since $D \leq A$, $q_2 = \bar{p}_1$. Since $A = E_{p_2} E_{\bar{p}_1}$, $q_3 = p_2$. Finally, since $D = E_{p_3} E_{\bar{p}_1}$, $q_1 = p_3$. Thus we replace T_1 by T_2 where $T_2 = \triangle(D, A, B) = \triangle(p_3, \bar{p}_1, p_2)$. We call such a replacement preparing to **turn a corner**. The reason for this name will become apparent when we look at the next step. (See figure 2.8.)

This procedure thus gives us a sequence of triangles $T_i = \triangle(A_i, B_i, C_i)$ as well as a sequence of **next sides**, $D_i = B_i A_i$ and angles θ_i.

This description of how to find the **next** triangle is sufficient for determining a well defined algorithm. However, since we want to prove that after a finite number of steps the procedure leads us to an acute triangle, we need to further examine what happens when we follow the various possible types of steps by one another.

It turns out that the key to understanding this lies in locating Q, the point where the perpendicular from p_3 to the axis of A hits the axis of A.

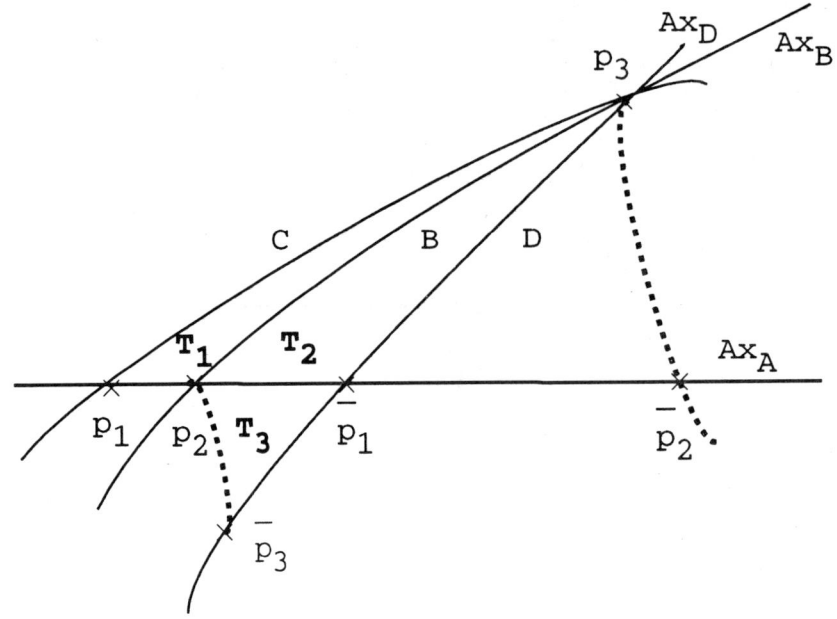

Figure 2.8: The next triangle, $\triangle(D, A, B)$, when $D \leq A \leq B$ or preparing to turning a corner: $T_1 = \triangle(A, B, C)$, $T_2 = \triangle(D, A, B)$ and T_3 lies along Ax_D.

2.6. Q AND THE LAST TRIANGLE ALONG A

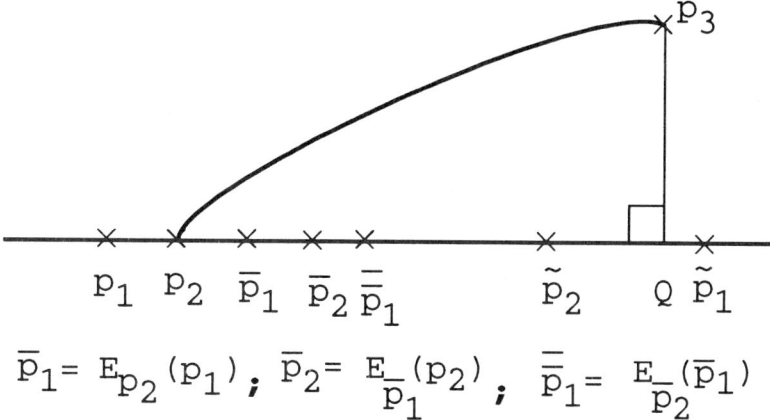

Figure 2.9: The images of p_1 and p_2 along the axis of A.

2.6 Finding Q and the last triangle along the axis of A

In what follows we assume that some triangle in the sequence has its smallest side on the axis of A. We want to understand how long the algorithm moves along the axis of A and when it turns a corner. It turns out that whether we turn a corner or move along the axis of A is governed by where Q lies in relation to p_1 and p_2. The axis of A is filled with images of p_1 and p_2 under successive applications of the half turns E_{p_1} and E_{p_2}. (Figure 2.9.) There is a smallest integer m such that $m \cdot T_A \geq [p_1, Q]_d$. Thus Q lies between some image of p_1, call it $\tilde{p}_1$ and some image of p_2, call it $\tilde{p}_2$ on the axis of A under $E_{p_1}^{s_1} E_{p_2}^{t_1} \cdots E_{p_1}^{s_n} E_{p_2}^{t_n} = A^n$ for some appropriate 2n-tuple $(s_1, ..., s_n, t_1, ..., t_n)$ where each $s_i = \pm 1$ and each $t_i = \pm 1$. As we move along the axis of A from p_2 towards Q, we either encounter $\tilde{p}_1$ first and then $\tilde{p}_2$ or vice-versa. The arguments are the same in either case. For ease of exposition we assume that we always encounter $\tilde{p}_2$ first, so that if $\tilde{p}_1 = A^n(p_1)$, then $\tilde{p}_2 = A^{n-1}(p_2)$. Thus we may assume that $E_{p_3} E_{\tilde{p}_2} = BA^{r-1}$ and $E_{p_3} E_{\tilde{p}_1} = BA^r$ where

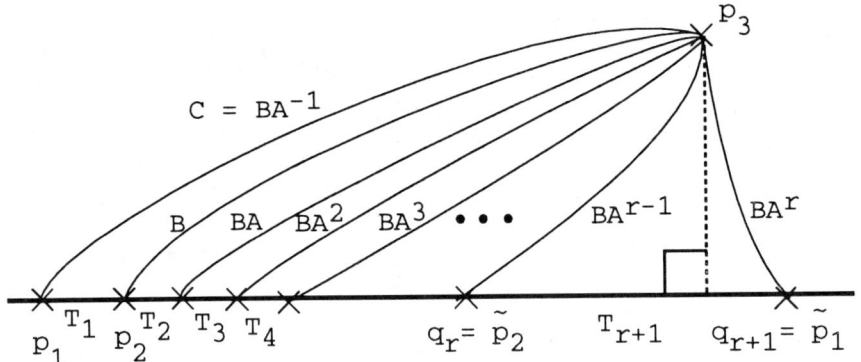

Figure 2.10: Triangles along the axis of A.

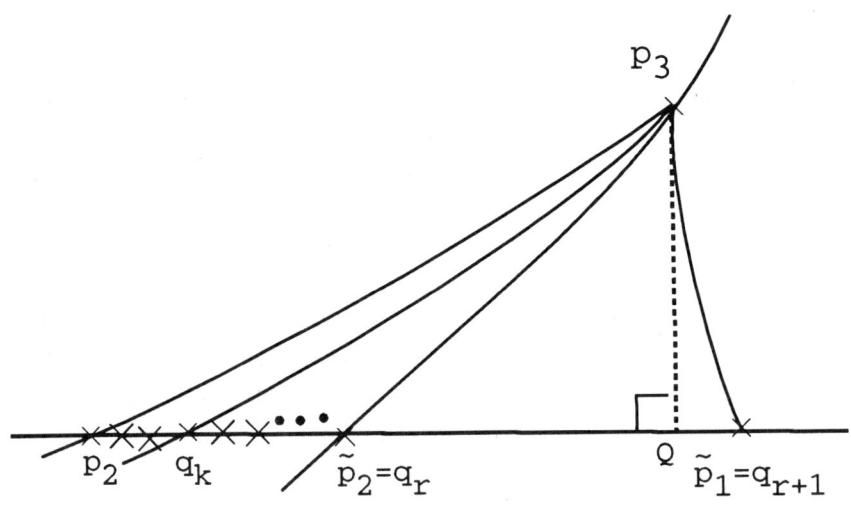

Figure 2.11: $\triangle(q_k, Q, p_3)$, $\triangle(q_r, Q, p_3)$ and $LT_A = \triangle(\tilde{p}_2, \tilde{p}_1, p_3)$, the last triangle along the axis of A.

2.6. Q AND THE LAST TRIANGLE ALONG A

$r = 2n-1$. To simplify our discussion we let $\{q_i\}$ denote the nsuccessive images of both p_1 and p_2 along the axis of A setting $q_1 = p_2$, $q_2 = \bar{p}_1$, $q_3 = E_{\bar{p}_1}(p_2)$, etc. so that Q lies between q_r and q_{r+1}. We name the series of triangles along the axis of A so that $\triangle(A, BA^i, BA^{i+1}) = T_{i+2}$ as long as $1 \leq (i+2) \leq 2n$. (Figure 2.10.) This nomenclature will be in accord with our naming convention if we can establish

Lemma: 2.6.1 *Assume that Q lies strictly between $q_r = \tilde{p}_2$ and $q_{r+1} = \tilde{p}_1$. If $k \neq r-1$ or r, $BA^k > A$ and $BA^k \geq BA^{k+1}$ for $k = -1, 0, ...r-1$. If $k = r-1$ or r, then no information can be inferred, so that any order relation among A, BA^r and BA^{r+1} is possible.*

Proof: We first note that $q_r = \tilde{p}_2$ and $q_{r+1} = \tilde{p}_1$ and $BA^k = [q_{k+1}, p_3]$. If $t < r$, then $[q_t, Q]_d \geq [q_t, q_r]_d \geq A$. In the right triangle $\triangle(q_t, Q, p_3)$ the hypotenuse which is $[q_t, p_3]$ must be longer than the base which is $[q_t, Q]$. Thus $BA^k = [q_{k+1}, p_3]_d \geq [q_{k+1}, Q]_d \geq [q_{r-1}, q_r]_d = A$ if $k+1 < r$. A similar argument shows that $BA^k \geq A$ if $k > r+1$. If $k = r$ or $r+1$, let $D = BA^{r-1}$ and $E = BA^r$. Then all order relations are possible among the sides of $\triangle(\tilde{p}_2, \tilde{p}_1, p_3)$. (Figure 2.11.) Finally apply the hyperbolic law of cosines to the right triangle $\triangle(p_3, Q, q_k)$ to obtain $\cosh[p_3, q_k] = \cosh[p_3, Q] \cosh[q_k, Q]$. Now $BA^{k-1} = [p_3, q_k]$. Since $[q_k, Q] \geq [q_{k+1}, Q]$, conclude that $BA^{k-1} \geq BA^k$ if $k \leq r-1$ (whence $BA^k \geq BA^{k+1}$ if $k \leq r-2$). □

It may turn out that Q coincides with $\tilde{p}_2$ or $\tilde{p}_1$. In that case the triangle is already a right triangle and the algorithm has come to a stopping point. Therefore, in what follows we may assume that Q is strictly between q_r and q_{r+1}.

Definition: 2.6.2 *We call $\triangle(\tilde{p}_2, \tilde{p}_1, p_3)$ the **last triangle along the axis of** A and denote it by LT_A.(Figure 2.11.)*

Note that LT_A has both angles along the axis of A acute. LT_A may or may not actually be a triangle that arises in our sequence. To understand when it is and when it is not, let $LT_A(j+1)$ and $LT_A(j)$, be the two triangles along the axis of A just prior to LT_A. $LT_A(j+1)$

has sides A, BA^{r-2} and BA^{r-1} while $LT_A(j)$ has sides A, BA^{r-3} and BA^{r-2}.

It is possible that $T_1 = LT_A$ or $LT_A(j+1)$. If the former occurs, then since $T_1 = \triangle(A, E, D)$ and the angles along the axis of A in LT_A are acute, T_1 is acute and the algorithm stopped after one step.

If $T_1 = LT_A(j+1)$, then $T_1 = \triangle(A, D, B)$ and either $T_2 = \triangle(A, D, E)$ or $\triangle(A, E, D)$ or $\triangle(E, A, D)$. In all of these cases, either D or E is the longest side and this forces T_2 to be acute.

Thus we may assume that T_1 is neither LT_A or $LT_A(j+1)$. Then Lemma 2.6.1 tells us that $LT_A(j) = T(A, BA^{r-2}, BA^{r-3}) = T_{r-2}$, but that while T_{r-1} and T_r have sides the same lengths as the sides of $LT_A(j+1)$ and LT_A respectively, the ordering of the lengths of the sides may prevent these triangles from actually coinciding. It is this phenomenon that we must understand.

2.7 More Algorithm: combining two types of steps

The purpose of this section is to prove that either the algorithm stops or at some point the length of the smallest side becomes the length of the longest side in a future triangle. To be more precise our aim is to show

Lemma: 2.7.1 *The sequence of small steps along the axis of A terminates either at LT_A or $LT_A(j+1)$. If the sequence includes LT_A, then LT_A is acute and the sequence stops here. Otherwise the triangle sequence turns a corner at $LT_A(j+1)$ and the next triangle in the sequence has longest side of length A, whence all subsequent sides have longest side shorter than A.*

In particular, if the sequence of triangles is infinite, then for each integer i there is an integer k_i such that $C_k \leq A_i$ whenever $k \geq k_i$.

Proof: The proof requires that we consider all the ways in which the two types of steps can be combined.

Beginning with triangle T_1, we move along the axis of A until we get to the last triangle along the axis of A, LT_A. Since Q lies interior to

2.7. COMBINING TRIANGLE ALGORITHM STEPS

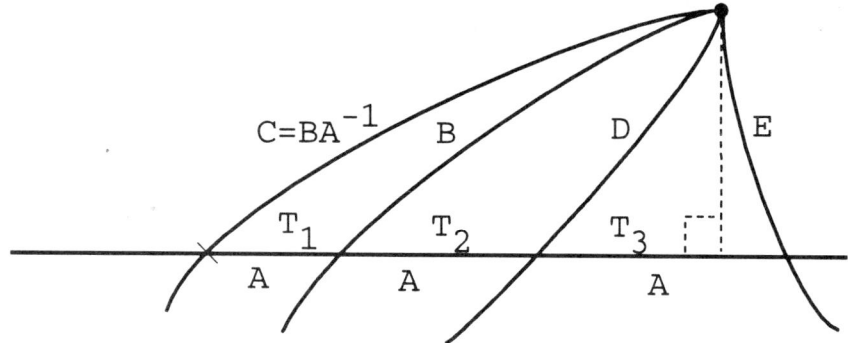

Figure 2.12: Combining two steps: $T_1 = LT_A(j)$, $T_2 = LT_A(j+1)$, and T_3 when $A \le D$ or $A \le E$.

LT_A, both angles along the axis of A in this triangle are acute angles. What is happening here is, therefore, determined by the angle at p_3 which we will call τ. In terms of the length of the three sides A, D and E, one of three things can happen and each possibility is related to the possibilities for τ. For example, we cannot tell a prior which of D and E is larger. Either possibility can occur. Now j is chosen so that $LT_A(j) = T_{r-1} = \triangle(A_{r-1}, B_{r-1}, C_{r-1})$. For each T_k, we have $D_k = B_k A_k$ and θ_k is the angle between sides A_k and B_k. We want to trace the next two triangles in the algorithm T_{k+1} and T_{k+2}.

Now $T_k = \triangle(A, BA^{k-2}, BA^{k-1})$ has sides $BA^{k-2} = [p_3, q_{k-1}]$ and $BA^{k-1} = [p_3, q_k]$ and vertices q_{k-1}, q_k, and p_3. By lemma 2.7.1 since $BA^{k-2} \ge BA^{k-1}$, moving from T_i to T_{i+1} for $i = 1, ..., r-2$ consists of taking small steps along the axis of A. Thus $T_1, ..., T_{r-1}$ are all part of the sequence of triangles obtained from the triangle algorithm. Thus we only need analyze what happens in moving from T_{r-1} to the next triangle given by the algorithm. That is, we may assume that $r = 2$ or equivalently that $LT_A(j) = T_1 = T_{r-1}$ and $LT_A(j+1) = T_2 = T_r$. Thus $C = BA^{r-3} = BA^{-1}$ and $B = BA^{r-2}$. (See Figure 2.12.)

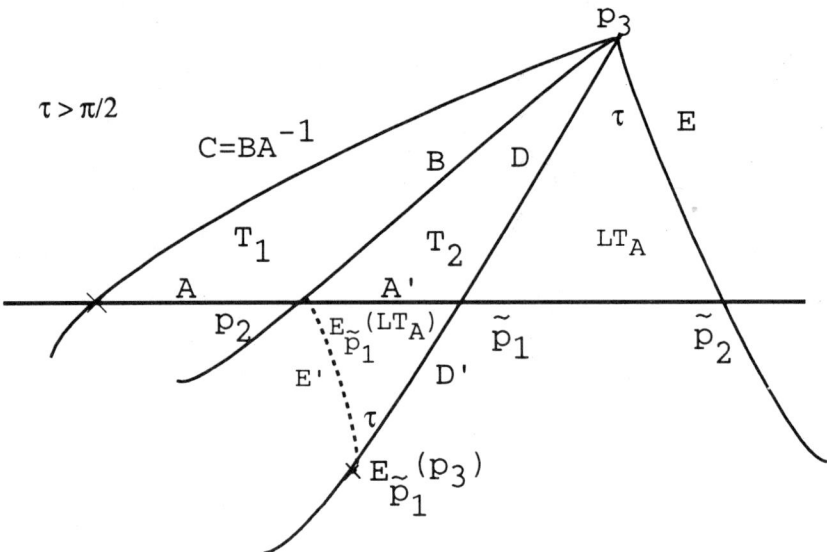

Figure 2.13: Combining two steps: $T_3 = E_{\tilde{p}_1}(LT_A)$.

Since $T_2 = \triangle(A_2, B_2, C_2)$ has sides of length $A_2 = A$, $B_2 = B$ and $D = BA$. We consider each of the three possibilities:

- $A \leq B \leq D$. In this case T_2 is an acute triangle and the algorithm stops.

- $A \leq D \leq B$. In this case T_3 has sides A, D and $E = BA^2$. Either $T_3 = \triangle(A, D, E)$ or $\triangle(A, E, D)$ or $\triangle(E, A, D)$. In all of these cases, either side E or D is the longest side. Since the angles opposite sides E and D are both acute, the triangle T_3 is an acute triangle and the algorithm stops. (I.e. $LT_A = T_3$ and LT_A is in the chain and has acute angles.)

- $D \leq A \leq B$. Here D_2 has the same length as E and $T_3 = E_{\tilde{p}_1}(LT_A)$ so that the angle opposite side $E_{\tilde{p}_1}(A) = A'$ is again τ. Let $D' = E_{\tilde{p}_1}(D)$ and $E' = E_{\tilde{p}_1}(E)$ The three possibilities for T_3 are: $(A_3, B_3, C_3) = (D', A', E')$, $(A_3, B_3, C_3) = (D', E', A')$, and $(A_3, B_3, C_3) = (E', D', A')$. In the first case, the triangle is acute since $LT_A = E_{\tilde{p}_1}(D', A', E')$ has E as its longest side and the angle opposite E is acute. (See figure 2.13.)

In the latter two cases, side A has now become the largest side. If $\tau \leq \pi/2$, the algorithm stops. Otherwise, the algorithm continues

2.8. THE SIDES AND HEIGHTS CONVERGE TO 0

after turning a corner moving along either the axis of E' or the axis of D depending upon which one is shorter.

This shows that either the algorithm stops or at some point the length of the smallest side has become the length of the longest side in a future triangle. This also shows that we move along the axis of A for at most r steps before we must turn a corner. □

2.8 The sides and heights converge to 0

We have now seen how to produce a series of triangles T_i that have a series of sides $T(A_i, B_i, C_i)$ where $A_i \leq B_i \leq C_i$. Further we have shown that either the algorithm stops at an acute or a right triangle in a finite number of steps or we turn an infinite number of corners. In the latter case the three sequences of sides $\{A_i\}$, $\{B_i\}$, $\{C_i\}$ are all non-increasing bounded sequences and thus all converge. Lemma 2.7.1 says that if any one of them converges to a limit, say A_0, then they all converge to the same limit.

Lemma: 2.8.1 *The sequence $\{A_i\}$ converges to 0.*

Proof: If the sequence is infinite, then at each step $\cosh A_i \cdot \cosh B_i \leq \cosh C_i$ (2.3). In the limit this becomes $\cosh A_0 \leq 1$ so that $A_0 = 0$. □

Along with the sequence of triangles and sides, we obtain a sequence of heights. We let h_i be the height of triangle T_i to side A_i.

Corollary: 2.8.2 *The sequence of heights also converges to 0.*

Proof: For each triangle T_i, the height to the shortest side A_i is always less than or equal to each of the other two sides, (ie. $h_i \leq B_i \leq C_i \ \forall i$). Since $\{B_i\}$ is a positive sequence converging to 0, so is $\{h_i\}$. □

2.9 The proof of the acute triangle theorem

Theorem: 2.9.1 The Acute Triangle Theorem. *Let A and B be hyperbolics with intersecting axes whose commutator is a rotation of* *finite order. After applying the triangle algorithm for a finite number of steps one obtains a pair of generators R and S which are Nielsen equivalent to the original generators where $T_{R,S}$, the triangle determined by R and S, contains no obtuse angles.*

Proof: Assume to the contrary that the sequence of triangles is infinite. Corresponding to the sequence of triangles $T_0, T_1, T_2, ...$, we obtain a sequence of heights $h_{T_0}, h_{T_1}, h_{T_2}, ...$ and a sequence of bases $\{b_{T_i}\}$, where b_{T_i} is the length of the shortest side of the triangle T_i. We also have corresponding to the sequence of triangles, a sequence of pentagons $\{P_i\}$ and a sequence of pentagon heights and pentagon bases. However, the pentagon heights are precisely the same as the corresponding triangle heights and the length of the bases (which are by definition half the length of the side opposite the vertex) are precisely the triangle bases, namely the length of the shortest side of the triangle. Since the sequence $\{b_{T_i}\}$ is non-increasing, the sequence $\{h_{T_i}\}$ must non-decreasing since 2.4 holds for each pentagon and ϕ does not change. If the sequence of triangles is infinite, we have seen that the sequence of heights will converge to zero. This gives a contradiction so that some T_i must be an acute or a right triangle. □

Definition: 2.9.2 *The acute or right triangle at which the triangle algorithm stops is called* **the acute triangle determined by A and B** *and is denoted* $Act_{A,B}$.

Note that in some cases **the acute triangle determined by A and B** is actually a right triangle. Note also that for some pair of generators it will happen that $T_{R,S} = Act_{R,S}$. In other words, after replacing A and B by a Nielsen equivalent pair of generators, we may assume that $T_{A,B}$ is an acute or right triangle so that $Act_{A,B} = T_{A,B}$.

Chapter 3

The Discreteness Theorem

In this chapter we state the discreteness theorem and outline its proof. Since the *geometric equivalence* theorem is one of the main ingredients in the proof of the discreteness theorem, its proof is also outlined here. The actual proofs use results from almost all of the subsequent chapters. Part II (chapters 4-7) develops preliminary material needed for the proof and Part III (chapters 8-13) is devoted to the proof of the geometric equivalence and discreteness theorems. The outlines of the proofs can serve as a partial guide to the contents of the subsequent chapters.

3.1 The Discreteness Theorem

In order to state the discreteness theorem, we recall some terminology and notation.

A (geometrically) *primitive rotation* is a rotation by an angle of $\pm 2\pi/n$ for some integer n. If a transformation with matrix X rotates by an angle of $\pm 2\theta$, then $(Tr\ X)^2 = 4\cos^2\theta$. As noted in chapter 2, $Tr\ [A, B]$ is well defined even though A and B are in $PSL(2, \mathbf{R})$. Recall also from chapter 2 that if p_2 is the intersection point of the axes of A and B, then p_1 and p_3 are chosen so that $A = E_{p_1} E_{p_2}$ and $B = E_{p_3} E_{p_2}$. Here E_d denotes the half-turn with fixed point d. By definition $\gamma = E_{p_1} E_{p_2} E_{p_3}$ so that $\gamma^2 = [A, B]$.

We can now state the theorem:

34 CHAPTER 3. DISCRETENESS THEOREM PROOF OUTLINE

Theorem: 3.1.1 Discreteness Theorem. *Let A and B be hyperbolic transformations with intersecting but distinct axes. Let $G = \langle A, B \rangle$.*

1. *If $[A, B]$ is hyperbolic, parabolic, or finite elliptic with γ primitive, then G is discrete.*

2. *If $[A, B]$ is a rotation of infinite order, G is not discrete.*

3. *It never happens that $Tr\,[A, B] = +2\cos k2\pi/n$ where k and n are integers with $1 \leq k < n/2$.*

4. *If $Tr\,[A, B] = -2\cos k2\pi/n$ where k and n are integers with $1 < k < n/2$, let $Act_{A,B}$ be the acute triangle determined by A and B.*

    If $k \neq 2$ or 3, then G is not discrete.

    If $k = 2$ or 3, then G is discrete if and only if one of the following holds:

    $Act_{A,B}$ is a equilateral triangle;

    $Act_{A,B}$ is a right isosceles triangle; or

    $Act_{A,B}$ is an isosceles triangle with sides of length T_0, T_3 and T_3

    where
    $$\cosh T_0 = \cosh^2 D_0 - \sinh^2 D_0 \cos 2\pi/7,$$
    $$\cosh T_3 = \cosh^2 D_0 - \sinh^2 D_0 \cos 3 \cdot 2\pi/7,$$
    $$\text{and } \cosh D_0 = \frac{1}{2\sin \pi/7}.$$

In proving theorem 3.1.1, we actually prove more.

Theorem: 3.1.2 *Under the hypotheses of theorem 3.1.1 when $Act_{A,B}$ is an equilateral triangle, $k = 3$ and G^* is a $(2,3,n)$ triangle group; when $Act_{A,B}$ is a right isosceles triangle, $k = 2$ and G^* is a $(2,4,n)$ triangle group; and when $Act_{A,B}$ is the non-right isosceles triangle, $k = 2$ and G^* is a $(2,3,7)$ triangle group.*

A major tool in the proof of the Discreteness theorem is the Geometric Equivalence theorem.

Theorem: 3.1.3 Geometric Equivalence Theorem. *Let $G = \langle A, B \rangle$ be discrete and assume that $[A, B]$ is a rotation that is not the square of a primitive rotation.*

1. *Let R and S be any other pair of generators for G. Then $Tr\,[A, B] = Tr\,[R, S]$ if and only if $Act_{R,S} = h(Act_{A,B})$ for some $h \in G^*$.*

2. *$Act_{A,B}$ is one of the three standard triangles types listed in theorem 3.1.1.*

Since $Act_{R,S} = h(Act_{A,B})$ implies that (R, S) is Nielsen equivalent to (A, B), a corollary is

Theorem: 3.1.4 Nielsen Equivalence Theorem *Assume that G is discrete and that (A, B) and (R, S) each generate G with $[A, B]$ and $[R, S]$ rotations neither of which are squares of a primitive rotation. Then (A, B) and (R, S) are Nielsen equivalent if and only if $Tr\,[A, B] = Tr\,[R, S]$.*

3.2 Outline proof of the discreteness theorem

We assume that $[A, B]$ is not a rotation of infinite order and construct the pentagon associated to A and B. (This is done in chapter 5.) Lemma 5.3.1 uses the Poincaré polygon theorem to give case 1. A straightforward argument will rule out case 3. Thus we assume that we are in case 4. We apply the Matelski-Beardon area count (theorem A.0.2) to conclude that either $k = 2$ or 3 or G is not discrete. Conclude further by the same theorem that if G is discrete, then either G^* is

- a $(2, 3, n)$ triangle group with $k = 3$ and $t = 3$,
- a $(2, 4, n)$ triangle group with $k = 2$ and $t = 2$, or
- a $(2, 3, 7)$ triangle group with $k = 2$ and $t = 9$.

Here t is the covering number defined in chapter 7. Construct a standard acute triangle, *Stact*, in each of these cases (chapter 8). The standard triangles are respectively the equilateral triangle, the right isosceles triangle, and the non-right isosceles triangle. Next assume that G is discrete and apply the geometric equivalence theorem to conclude Act is one of these standard triangles. For the converse, use theorem 13.2.1 which (via the Poincaré polygon theorem) says that if $Act_{A,B}$ is any one of the three triangle types with $k = 2$ or $k = 3$, then G is discrete.

3.3 Outline proof of geometric equivalence theorems:

Assume that $Tr\,[A,B] = Tr\,[R,S]$. Replacing each pair of generators by a Nielsen equivalent pair, we may assume that $T_{A,B} = Act_{A,B}$ and that $T_{R,S} = Act_{R,S}$. Each triangle corresponds to a triple of points. $Act_{R,S} = \triangle(p_1, p_2, p_3)$ and $Act_{A,B} = \triangle(t_1, t_2, t_3)$. We let $h_{R,S}$ and $h_{A,B}$ be the heights of the respective triangles and $b_{R,S}$ and $b_{A,B}$ their respective bases. If d denotes hyperbolic distance, the length of $b_{R,S}$ is $d(p_1, p_2)$ and that of $b_{A,B}$ is $d(t_1, t_2)$.

When G is discrete, we show that there is an $h \in G^*$ with $h(Act_{A,B}) = Act_{R,S}$ where $Act_{R,S}$ is one of the three standard acute triangles. Which of the three depends upon the trace of the commutator of A and B. This simultaneously proves the forward implication of part 1 and part 2. Each of the three possible standard triangles is treated separately. We outline the ideas common to all three cases.

The constructions of the standard acute triangles in chapter 8 show that the length of the base in each case is either the smallest possible distance between any fixed points of elements of order two in the group under consideration or between an element of order two and an element of order four. In either case this implies $b_{R,S} \leq b_{A,B}$. By (2.4), the inverse variation for the pentagon, $h_{R,S} \geq h_{A,B}$. This says that the height of $h_{A,B}$ is bounded. The bound on $h_{A,B}$ can be used to put a bound on $d(t_3, t_2)$. Other arguments allow us to also put a bound on $d(t_1, t_2)$. Discreteness tells us that there are only a finite number of fixed points of elements of order two within a bounded distance of t_2.

We construct the shingling of the plane by the images of the pen-

3.3. GEOMETRIC EQUIVALENCE THEOREMS

tagon under G^* in order to locate all of the points of order two within a bounded distance of t_2. We then consider the finite number of possibilities for t_1 and t_3 and use various standard and not so standard facts about hyperbolic triangles to rule out those that give an obtuse triangle. For each of the remaining possibilities we produce an $h \in G^*$ with $h(t_i) = p_i, i = 1, 2, 3$.

For the converse of part 1, if $hE_{t_i}h^{-1} = E_{p_i}$ for each i, then h conjugates the pair (A, B) to the pair (R, S) showing that the pairs of generators are actually Nielsen equivalent and that $h[A, B]h^{-1} = [R, S]$ whence $Tr\,[A, B] = Tr\,[R, S]$. This completes the outline of the proof.

As a guide to reading the full proof we note that in order to locate the images of the fixed points of order two in the shingling we need to extend a theorem of Knapp's that counts the number of fixed points of the group both interior to the pentagon and on the boundary of the pentagon. This extension is proved in chapters 7 and applied in chapters 11 and 12.

The geometric and Nielsen equivalence theorems which are proved separately for each of the three possible cases are theorems 9.1.2, and 9.1.1 of chapter 9, theorems 10.1.1 and 10.1.2 of chapter 10, and theorems 12.1.2 and 12.1.4 of chapter 12. The proof of the discreteness theorem is given in chapter 13.

Part II

Preliminaries

Chapter 4

Triangle Groups and their Tilings

In this chapter we begin with a review some of the basic properties of triangle groups and the tilings of the hyperbolic plane that they determine. These are all properties that we will need later. We then establish a number of lemmas about distances in these tilings that we will use in subsequent sections. More specifically, a triangle group has a fundamental domain that consists of the union of two triangles. The images of the fundamental domain under the elements of the group fill up the hyperbolic plane without overlap and thus *tile* the plane. The images of the fixed points of the elliptic generators are the vertices of the triangles and the distances between vertices satisfy certain uniqueness and minimality conditions. These uniqueness and minimality conditions will be an important tool in our investigation of triangle groups. We compute the minimal distances between any two fixed points of order n and m in the tiling. Further we calculate the first few terms in what we will eventually call the $2-2$ **spectrum** in a $(2,3,7)$ triangle group, the set of distances between fixed points of order two in the tiling.

Throughout this chapter we are very fussy and detailed about the notation because we want to carefully tie the algebra to the geometric picture.

4.1 Basic facts about triangle groups

We begin by recalling some of the basic facts about triangle groups and establishing notation and a few conventions.

Definition: 4.1.1 *A group G is called a (p,q,r)-triangle group if it has the presentation*

$$\langle\, x, y, z \mid x^p = y^q = z^r = 1,\ xy = z\,\rangle.$$

The following facts are well-known. The complete proofs are sometimes more complicated than one might expect. We cite references giving the location of complete proofs in the literature.

Fact: 4.1.2 *One can construct a hyperbolic triangle with angles α, β, and γ if and only if*

$$\alpha + \beta + \gamma < \pi. \tag{4.1}$$

A proof that uses the hyperbolic law of cosines can be found in [7] (see page 100). Magnus provides a complete proof of how to construct a triangle with given angles provided that one angle is a right angle (see page 87 of [23]). Beardon (p. 155 of [2]) provides a corresponding construction for polygons with n sides with $n \geq 3$ assuming that one can construct any given right triangle.

Fact: 4.1.3 *If p, q, and r are all integers greater than or equal to 2, then there is a non-euclidean triangle whose angles are $\frac{\pi}{p}$, $\frac{\pi}{q}$ and $\frac{\pi}{r}$ if and only if*

$$\frac{1}{p} + \frac{1}{q} + \frac{1}{r} < 1. \tag{4.2}$$

We will write $\Delta(p,q,r)$ to denote a non-euclidean triangle with angles $\frac{\pi}{p}$, $\frac{\pi}{q}$ and $\frac{\pi}{r}$; $G^*(p,q,r)$ to denote the group generated by reflections in the sides of $\Delta(p,q,r)$; and $G(p,q,r)$ the subgroup of index two in $G^*(p,q,r)$ consisting of orientation preserving transformations. We let v_a denote the vertex of the triangle which subtends an angle of π/a, $[v_a, v_b]$ denote the side connecting the vertices v_a and v_b, and $\widetilde{[v_a, v_b]}$ denote the complete non-euclidean geodesic passing through v_a and v_b. Further, we let R_{ab} denote reflection in the side $[v_a, v_b]$.

Proofs of the following facts can be found in Chapter II.5 of [23]:

4.1. BASIC FACTS ABOUT TRIANGLE GROUPS

Fact: 4.1.4 *The images of $\triangle(p,q,r)$ under the action of $G^*(p,q,r)$ fill the hyperbolic plane without gaps and overlappings. $G^*(p,q,r)$ is discrete and is defined by the relations*

$$R_{pq}^2 = R_{qr}^2 = R_{rp}^2 = 1 \text{ and } (R_{rq}R_{pr})^r = (R_{pr}R_{qp})^p = (R_{qp}R_{rq})^q = 1. \tag{4.3}$$

In what follows, let $R_p = R_{pr}R_{qp}$, $R_q = R_{qp}R_{rq}$ and let $R_r = R_{rq}R_{pr}$, so that $R_a^a = 1 \forall a$ and each R_a is a **counterclockwise** rotation about the vertex v_a by an angle of $2\pi/a$ (except when $a = 2$). Then (see page 86 of [23]) it can further be shown that

Fact: 4.1.5 *The group $G(p,q,r)$ is discrete, is generated by R_p, R_q, R_r, and has defining relations*

$$R_p^p = R_q^q = R_r^r = R_pR_qR_r = 1. \tag{4.4}$$

Any element of finite order in $G(p,q,r)$ is conjugate to a power of R_p, R_q or R_r.

We continue to set the notation with the aim of keeping the connection between the algebra and the geometry clear. We adopt the convention that triangles are named **counterclockwise**. This means that as we move counterclockwise around the boundary of the triangle $\triangle(p,q,r)$ we encounter the vertices v_p, v_q, v_r in that order (and not in the order v_p, v_r, v_q). (Note that the order in which we encounter the vertices affects the direction of the rotation at the vertices when we translate to the algebra.)

Continuing with notation, for arbitrary p,q, and r we let $T_{pq} = \triangle(p,q,r) \cup R_{pq}(\triangle(p,q,r))$. Then it also follows from [23] that T_{pq} is a fundamental domain for $G(p,q,r)$ and that the only points in T_{pq} that are fixed by an element of the group are v_p, v_q, v_r and $R_{pq}(v_r)$.

Fact: 4.1.6 *In particular the interiors of $\triangle(p,q,r)$ and T_{pq} do not contain the images of any fixed points of $G(p,q,r)$.*

Fact: 4.1.7 *If x is any point in the hyperbolic plane that is fixed by some element of the group $G(p,q,r)$, then G_x, the stabilizer of x, is cyclic of order p, q, or r.*

Proof: Let x be any point in the hyperbolic plane that is fixed by some element g in $G(p,q,r)$. Then we know that g is conjugate to a power of R_p, R_q or R_r. To see that x is actually fixed by a conjugate of R_p, R_q or R_r note that after replacing x by an image under the group $G(p,q,r)$ and g by a conjugate if necessary, we may assume that x is in T_{pq} so that $x \in \{v_p, v_q, v_r, R_{pq}(v_r)\}$. □

This allows us to make the following definition:

Definition: 4.1.8 *A point x in the hyperbolic plane which is fixed by an element of the group $G(p,q,r)$ will be called a **point of order** n if its stabilizer is of order n.*

We further adopt the convention that when considering $\triangle(p,q,r)$ we assume that $p \leq q \leq r$. This forces the angle relations $\frac{\pi}{r} \leq \frac{\pi}{q} \leq \frac{\pi}{p}$ and, therefore, the relation among the lengths of the sides in $\triangle(p,q,r)$, $[v_p, v_q] \leq [v_r, v_p] \leq [v_r, v_q]$. Because $[v_a, v_b]$ is the (length of the) side opposite the angle at the vertex v_c where $v_c \notin \{v_a, v_b\}$, it will sometimes be more convenient to write S_c for $[v_a, v_b]$. By convention we will have, therefore, $S_r \leq S_q \leq S_p$.

4.2 Minimal tiling distances

In what follows we will assume that $p = 2$ and $q \neq r$. Results similar to the ones we obtain in this section can be obtained for arbitrary p, q and r. However, we will not need these more general results and the arguments are somewhat less cumbersome when $p = 2$ and $q \neq r$. The images of $\triangle(2,q,r)$ under $G^*(2,q,r)$ tile the plane and the images of the vertices of the triangle are the points of finite order of the tiling. We will prove a series of lemmas about the distances in the hyperbolic plane between arbitrary fixed points of order n and m that essentially formalize what seems obvious: the vertices in $\triangle(2,q,r)$ are the *closest* vertices of the given orders in the tiling. The results are stated in this section. The proofs appear in section 4.4. To be more precise we define $D_0(a,b)$ to be the shortest distance between any two distinct points of order a and b in the tiling. The fact that G is discrete makes $D_0(a,b)$ well defined.

4.2. MINIMAL TILING DISTANCES

Let d denote the distance in the hyperbolic metric.

The length of the hyperbolic segment $[x, y]$ is $d(x, y)$. We will also write S_d or $[x, y]_d$ to denote the length of the hyperbolic segment S or $[x, y]$. However, since it often will be clear from the context whether we are referring to a given hyperbolic segment or the length of the given hyperbolic segment, we will not always distinguish notationally between the name for a hyperbolic segment and its length and will use S or $[x, y]$ for both except when clarity demands the distinction.

We will show (section 4.4)

Lemma: 4.2.1 *When $a \neq b$, $D_0(a, b) = [v_a, v_b]_d$.*

This will follow from

Lemma: 4.2.2 *Let v'_a be any fixed point of order a and v'_b any fixed point of order b with $a \neq b$. Then*

$$d(v'_a, v'_b) \geq [v_a, v_b]_d \qquad (4.5)$$

with equality holding precisely when $\exists g \in G$ with $g(v'_a) = v_a$ and $g(v'_b) = g(v_b)$.

Our labeling convention forces an order on these lengths: $D_0(2, q) \leq D_0(2, r) \leq D_0(r, q)$.

We will obtain as a corollary

Corollary: 4.2.3

- *For any fixed point of order 2 in a tiling determined by a $(2, 3, 7)$ triangle group, there are precisely two fixed points of order 7 at a distance $D_0(2, 7)$ from it and no closer fixed points of order 7. There are also precisely two fixed points of order 3 at a distance of $D_0(2, 3)$ and no closer fixed points of order 3.*

- *For any fixed point of order 3 in a tiling determined by a $(2, 3, 7)$ triangle group, there are precisely three fixed points of order 7 at a distance $D_0(3, 7)$ from it and no closer fixed points of order 7. There are also precisely 3 fixed points of order 2 at a distance of $D_0(2, 3)$ and no closer fixed points of order 2.*

- For any fixed point of order 7 in a tiling determined by a $(2,3,7)$ triangle group, there are precisely seven fixed points of order 3 at a distance $D_0(3,7)$ from it and no closer fixed points of order 3. There are precisely seven fixed points of order 2 at a distance of $D_0(2,7)$ and no closer fixed points of order 2. The ray from any of the seven fixed points of order two to the fixed point of order seven meets any other such ray at an angle of $n2\pi/7$ for some integer n.

We will also need to show for later use that

Lemma: 4.2.4 *In any $(2,q,r)$ tiling There is no fixed point of order 2 closer to v_2 than $R_r(v_2)$ and $R_r^{-1}(v_2)$.*

Let a, b, c be any three points. Then the segments $[a, b]$ and $[b, c]$ form an angle and we write $\prec (a, b, c)$ to denote the angle. When no confusion is apt to arise, we shorten this to $\prec b$. In particular, we can conclude that two points of the same order at a minimal distance from a given fixed point are images of one another under the rotation at the fixed point and which images they are is determined by the angle that they form at the fixed point. To be more precise:

Theorem: 4.2.5 *Let x and y be two points of order two in a tiling determined by a $(2,3,7)$-triangle group, m and n two points of order 3 and v a point of order 7. Assume that $D_0(2,7) = d(x,v) = d(y,v)$ and that $D_0(3,7) = d(m,v) = d(n,v)$. Let k and f be integers such that $\prec (m,v,n) = k2\pi/7$ and $\prec (x,v,y) = f2\pi/7$. Then $R_v^k(m) = n$ and $R_v^f(x) = y$.*

4.3 The wedge at a vertex

Before proving the results listed in section 4.2, we introduce some more terminology and simplify our notation.

When no confusion is apt to arise we drop the (p, q, r) in naming groups and triangles, etc. Thus $\triangle$ is short for $\triangle(p, q, r)$ and G and G^*, etc. have the obvious meaning.

4.3. THE WEDGE AT A VERTEX   47

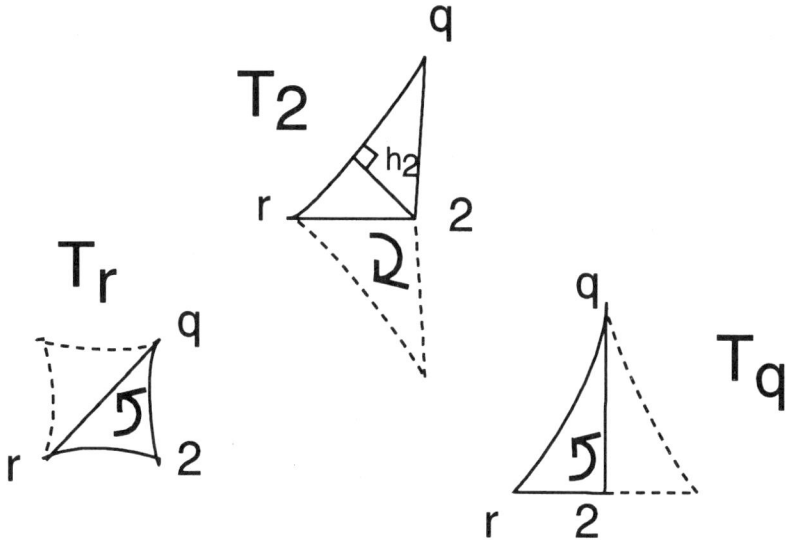

Figure 4.1: The tiles at r, q and 2.

Definition: 4.3.1 *(See figure 4.1.) If v is a vertex of $\triangle(p, q, r)$, define the tile at v, T_v by*

$$T_v = \begin{cases} T_{pr} = \triangle \cup R_{pr}(\triangle) & \text{if } v = v_p, \\ T_{pq} = \triangle \cup R_{pq}(\triangle) & \text{if } v = v_q, \\ T_{rq} = \triangle \cup R_{rq}(\triangle) & \text{if } v = v_r. \end{cases}$$

Definition: 4.3.2 *Further define the boundary of the tile, BT_v by*

$$BT_v = \begin{cases} [v_q, v_r] \cup R_{pr}([v_q, v_r]) & \text{if } v = v_p, \\ [v_r, v_p] \cup R_{pq}([v_r, v_p]) & \text{if } v = v_q, \\ [v_p, v_q] \cup R_{rq}([v_p, v_q]) & \text{if } v = v_r. \end{cases}$$

We can extend all of these definitions to apply to arbitrary fixed points v of G by $T_v = g(T_{v_x})$ and $BT_v = g(BT_{v_x})$ when $g \in G$ is chosen so that $g(v_x) = v$.

Definition: 4.3.3 *By the **wedge at a vertex** v we mean the union of T_v and all of its images under the powers of the rotation about v (figure 4.2).*

48   CHAPTER 4. TRIANGLE GROUPS AND THEIR TILINGS

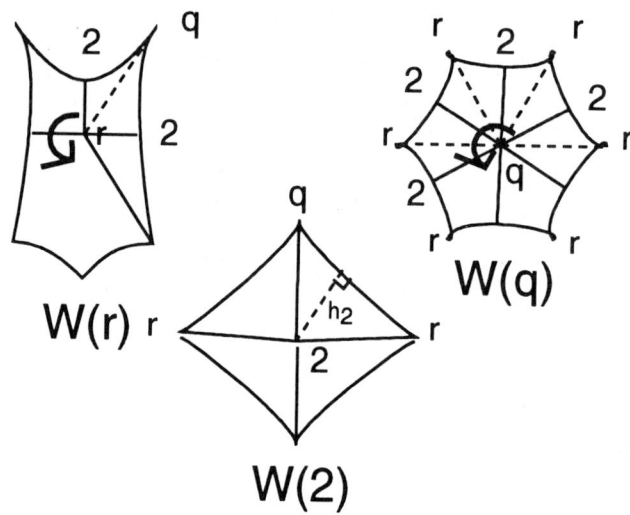

Figure 4.2: The wedges at r, q and 2

We write W or $W(v)$ to denote the wedge at v. Thus

$$W(v_x) = \bigcup_{n=0}^{x} R_x^n(T_{v_x}). \tag{4.6}$$

Definition: 4.3.4 *If v is a fixed point of order x, we define* **the boundary of the wedge at v**, $B(v)$, *by*

$$B(v) = \cup_{n=0}^{x} R_v^n(BT(v)).$$

Remark: 4.3.5 *Note that for any vertex v, the wedge at v is a convex set.*

To see this note that by construction $W(v)$ is a polygon each of whose interior angles is $\leq \pi$ and apply Theorem 7.16.1 page 154 of [2].
  We will show

Lemma: 4.3.6 *Let v be a fixed point of order x.*

- $W(v)$ *contains no images under G of v other than v itself.*

4.3. THE WEDGE AT A VERTEX

- $W(v)$ contains precisely x distinct images of v_y for $y \in \{p,q,r\}$ and $y \neq x$. None of these images lie interior to $W(v)$.

- Assume that w and v are distinct fixed points of G and that their wedges are not disjoint.

    If the interiors of $W(v)$ and $W(w)$ have a non-empty intersection, then the intersection of the wedges contains $g(\triangle(p,q,r))$ for some $g \in G^*$.

    If the interiors of the wedges are also disjoint, the intersection of the wedges contains a vertex or the image of a side of $\triangle(p,q,r)$ or the images of two sides that both lie on the same geodesic.

Proof: Since the interior of $\triangle$ contains no fixed point of G, the proof of the first two parts is clear. Each wedge is the union of some images of $\triangle(p,q,r) = \triangle$ under the group G. Since the images of $\triangle$ tile the plane as they are a fundamental domain for G^*, any two whose interiors have a non-empty intersection must be equal. This leaves only the case where the two wedges intersect only on their boundary. Each boundary is the union of some finite number of non-euclidean geodesic segments. If the boundaries are not disjoint, then at least two of the geodesic segments intersect. Since any two geodesics either are disjoint or coincide, any two geodesic segments which intersect must either agree or intersect in an end point. □

We want to establish that for fixed points of G there is a well-defined minimal distance from the wedge to its boundary and that this minimum distance depends only on the order of the fixed point. To see this we let τ be any geodesic connecting v to some point outside of $W(v)$, let τ_v be the intersection of τ with the wedge at v and let $x_{B(v)}$ be the point of intersection of τ with the boundary of the wedge. (Since the wedge is convex, τ will only intersect its boundary once.)

Lemma: 4.3.7 Let v be a fixed point of G of order x.

- If $x = q$ or r, then $(\tau_v)_d \geq d(v_2, v_x)$.

- If $x = 2$, then $(\tau_v)_d \geq h_2$ where h_2 is the height from the fixed point of order two to the hypotenuse of $\triangle(2,p,q)$. (See figures 4.1 and 4.2.)

Proof: Since G is a group of isometries, $(\tau_v)_d = (g(\tau_v))_d$. Therefore, it suffices to consider the cases where $v = v_2, v_q$, or v_r. The non-euclidean triangle $\triangle$ is convex because all of its interior angles are less than π (see Lemma 1.27 of [23]). Thus each of the images of $\triangle$ under G^* is convex and contains v. The point $x_B(v)$ lies on the boundary of one of these convex triangles. Therefore, τ_v, which is a geodesic connecting v and $x_B(v)$, lies in some one image of $\triangle$. Replacing τ_v by one of its images under the rotation R_v and/or the reflections R_{v2} or $R_{vy}y \neq x$ if necessary, we may assume that τ_v lies entirely in $\triangle$ and is thus a geodesic connecting one vertex in a right triangle with a point on the side opposite that vertex. The lemma follows. (See figures 4.1 and 4.2.) □

Definition: 4.3.8 *The* **minimum wedge length,** $M_{W(v)}$, *of the wedge* $W(v)$ *is defined to be*

$$= \begin{cases} d(v_2, v_r) & \text{if } v = v_r, \\ d(v_2, v_q) & \text{if } v = v_q, \\ h_2 & \text{if } v = v_2. \end{cases}$$

Lemma: 4.3.9 *If w and v are distinct fixed points of G with disjoint wedges, then $d(v, w) > M_{W(v)} + M_{W(w)}$.*

Proof: Let τ be a geodesic connecting v and w. The segments $\tau_v = [v, x_{B(v)}]$, $\tau_w = [w, x_{B(w)}]$, and $[x_{B(v)}, x_{B(w)}]$ are subsegments of τ whose interior are disjoint and whose union if τ. Since τ is a geodesic, its length is the sum of lengths of the three subsegments, all of which are positive. Thus $\tau_d \geq (\tau_v)_d + (\tau_w)_d$. Apply lemma 4.3.7 to obtain the lemma. □

4.4 Proofs of lemmas and theorems

Proof:(lemmas 4.2.2 and 4.2.1)
 We assume that v'_a and v'_b are images of vertices v_a and v_b in $\triangle(2, q, r)$. If τ is the non-euclidean geodesic connecting v'_a and v'_b, then the length of τ is $d(v'_a, v'_b)$. Conjugating by an element of the group G if necessary, we may assume that $v'_a = v_a$.

4.4. PROOFS OF LEMMAS AND THEOREMS

We consider the wedge at v_a, $W(v_a)$ and the wedge at v_b', $W(v_b')$.

We treat first the case that these wedges are disjoint. We apply lemma 4.3.9 for the various possible values of a and b to obtain

$$d(v_2', v_r') > d(v_2, v_r) + h_2$$
$$d(v_2', v_q') > d(v_2, v_q) + h_2$$
$$d(v_q', v_r') > d(v_q, v_2) + d(v_r, v_2).$$

Use the triangle inequality which says that $[v_q, v_2]_d + [v_r, v_2]_d \geq [v_q, v_r]_d$ to obtain the conclusion of the lemma in this case.

We note that if we allow $a = b$ and write v_a'' for v_b, we can also conclude that

$$d(v_q', v_q'') > 2d(v_2, v_q)$$
$$d(v_r', v_r'') > 2d(v_2, v_r) \quad \text{and}$$
$$d(v_2', v_2'') > 2h_c.$$

We next consider the cases where the wedges are not disjoint. Assume first that the interiors of the wedges intersect. The wedges contain a common image of Δ. Since $W(v_a)$ contains only one image of v_a under the group and $W(v_b')$ contains only one image of v_b' under the group, both v_a and v_b' must be in this common image of Δ. If $a = b$, we obtain a contradiction. If $a \neq b$, then $v_b' = R_v^n(v_b)$ for some integer n, so that $d(v_a, v_b') = d(v_a, v_b) =$ the length of τ and we obtain the desired conclusion.

Therefore, the two wedges either share one common vertex or a common boundary segment (and thus two common vertices). Again if $v_b' = R_v^n(v_b)$ for any n, we are done. Therefore, we may assume that $v_b' \neq R_v^n(v_b)$ for any n. Assume $a \neq b$. If the wedges share a common boundary segment, they share an image of $[v_c, v_b]$ where v_c is the vertex of Δ not equivalent to v_a or v_b. This again says that $v_b' = R_v^n(v_b)$ for some integer n contrary to assumption. Therefore, the two wedges must intersect in a single vertex, v_c', an image of v_c. Thus

$$d(v_a, v_b') \leq d(v_a, v_c') + d(v_c', v_b') = d(v_a, v_c) + d(v_c, v_b).$$

Returning to our geodesic τ either

$v_c' \neq x_{B(v_a)}$ or $v_c' \neq x_{B(v_b')}$ in which case $d(v_a, v_b') > M_{W(v_a)} + M_{W(v_b')}$ or

$v'_c = x_{B(v_a)} = x_{B(v'_b)}$ in which case $d(v_a, v'_b) = d(v_c, v_a) + d(v_c, v_b)$.
Consider all of the possibilities for a and b using the triangle inequality as needed to conclude that $d(v_a, v'_b) > d(v_a, v_b)$ in all of these cases. For example, if $a = r$ and $b = 2$, $M_{v_r} + M_{v_2} = d(v_2, v_r) + h_2 > d(v_2, v_r)$. Lemma 4.2.1 follows from lemma 4.2.2 □

Corollary 4.2.3 follows from lemmas 4.2.2 and 4.2.1 when combined with lemma 4.3.6. Theorem 4.2.5 follows from corollary 4.2.3 together with lemma 4.3.6. Lemma 4.2.4 will follow from the next proposition. (Note that a simpler proof of the lemma is possible, but we will use the proposition in other contexts as well.)

Proposition: 4.4.1 *In a $(2, q, r)$ triangle group, we have:*

$$\cosh D_0(2,2) = \cosh 2h_2 = \cosh^2 D_0(2,r) - sinh^2 D_0(2,r) cos 2\pi/r$$

$$= \cosh^2 D_0(2,q) - sinh^2 D_0(2,q) \cdot \cos 2\pi/q.$$

$$D_0(q,q) = 2D_0(2,q).$$

$$D_0(r,r) = 2D_0(2,r).$$

Proof: If v and w are fixed points of the same order and their wedges are disjoint, we saw that $d(v, w) > 2h_2, 2D_0(2,q)$ or $2D_0(2,r)$ depending upon whether the points are of order $2, q$ or r.

If the wedges are not disjoint, then either they coincide or they intersect in a subset of their boundaries. In the latter case, their boundaries must either contain a whole segment $[v'_a, v'_b]$ in common or merely one vertex, v_x where the order of v is not x, a or b and $a \neq b$. Assume first that the intersection is more than a single point. After conjugating $W(w)$ by some power of R_w if necessary, we may assume that the geodesic τ between v and w lies entirely in $\triangle \cup R_{ab}(\triangle)$ and that $w = R_{ab}(v)$. From this configuration (see figure 4.3), one can obtain the desired formulae by applying the hyperbolic law of cosine 6.9 to the triangles $\triangle(v, v_a, w)$ and $\triangle(w, v_b, v)$ and noting that the angles at the vertices v_a and v_b in these triangles are $2\pi/a$ and $2\pi/b$ respectively. Here if the angle at v is $\pi/2$, then τ must be perpendicular to $[v_a, v_b]$ so that $\tau = h_2 \cup R_{ab}(h_2)$. Here we obtain the formulae of the proposition unless we find a smaller distance when the wedges intersect in a point.

4.4. PROOFS OF LEMMAS AND THEOREMS

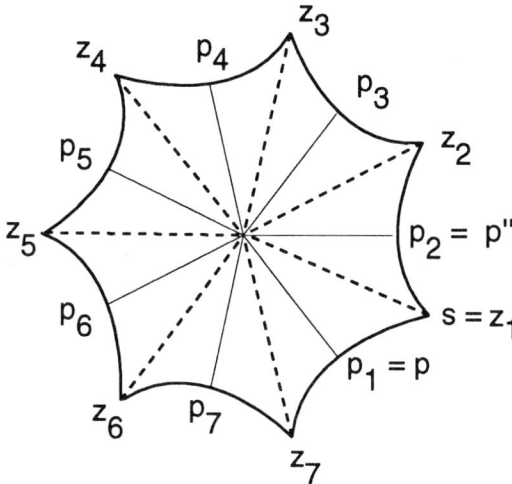

Figure 4.3: The wedge at 7 in a $(2, 3, 7)$ triangle group.

We first remark that

$$d(v_q, R_{v_r}(v_q)) = d(v_q, R_{v_2}(v_q)) = 2D_0(2, q) \text{ and} \tag{4.7}$$

$$d(v_r, R_{v_q}(v_r)) = d(v_r, R_{v_2}(v_r)) = 2D_0(2, r). \tag{4.8}$$

To see this note that $R_{v_r}(v_q) = R_{q2}(v_q) = R_{v_2}(v_q)$ and the similar statement holds with the roles of q and r interchanged.

If the intersection of the wedges consists of a single point, that point must be a vertex. Call it u. Then v and w both lie in $W(u)$. Let $D = d(u, v) = d(u, w)$. Assume that u is a point of order x so that the angle of the basic tile at u is $2\pi/x$. Then any two images of v in the tile v' and v'' lie in a triangle with two sides D and included angle $k2\pi/x$ for some integer k where $2k\pi/x \leq \pi$. The third side has length $d(v', v'')$ which satisfies (by the hyperbolic law of cosines again)

$$\cosh d(v', v'') = \cosh^2 D - \sinh^2 D \cos k2\pi/x.$$

which is smallest when $k = 1$. The proof will be complete once we note that equation 4.7 says that this when $k = 1$, $d(v', v'')$ is precisely $2D$.
□

We obtain the following corollary

Corollary: 4.4.2 *In a $(2,3,7)$ triangle group*

$$D_0(2,3) \leq D_0(2,2) \text{ and } D_0(2,7) \leq 2D_0(2,2).$$

In a $(2,4,n)$ triangle group

$$D_0(2,4) < D_0(2,2) < 2D_0(2,4)$$

Proof: Since $2\pi/3 > \pi/2$, its cosine is negative. Thus

$$\cosh D_0(2,2) = \cosh^2 D_0(2,3) - \sinh^2 D_0(2,3) \cdot \cos 2\pi/3$$

implies

$$\cosh D_0(2,2) \geq \cosh^2 D_0(2,3) \geq \cosh D_0(2,3).$$

Similarly, since $4\pi/7 > \pi/2$,

$$\cosh d(x, R_7^2(x)) = \cosh^2 D_0(2,7) - \sinh^2 D_0(2,7) \cdot \cos 4\pi/7$$

implies that $d(x, R_7^2(x)) \geq D_0(2,7)$. But

$$d(x, R_7^2(x)) \leq d(x, R_7(x)) + d(R_7(x), R_7^2(x)) \leq 2D_0(2,2).$$

Finally

$$\cosh D_0(2,2) = \cosh^2 D_0(2,4) - \sinh^2 D_0(2,4) \cdot \cos 2\pi/4$$

implies

$$\cosh D_0(2,2) \geq \cosh^2 D_0(2,4) > \cosh D_0(2,4).$$

We also have

$$\cosh D_0(2,2) < \cosh^2 D_0(2,4) + \sinh^2 D_0(2,4) = \cosh 2D_0(2,4).$$

The last equality is merely the double angle formula for hyperbolic cosines 6.3. □

4.5 Additional Notation

Let a, b, and c be any three non-collinear points in the unit disc. Then they determine a triangle which we denoted $\triangle(a,b,c)$ in chapter 2. When we write $\triangle(p,q,r)$ it will generally be clear from the context whether p, q and r refer to the vertices of the triangle or to the angles at the vertices (i.e. $\pi/p, \pi/q$, and π/r). Given any three points, they may actually determine a straight line rather than a triangle.

Definition: 4.5.1 *We say $[a, b, c]$ is a **geodesic** to mean that the three points a, b, and c all lie on a single geodesic. More generally, we say $[a_1, a_2, ..., a_n]$ is a **geodesic** when $a_1, ..., a_n$ all lie on a single geodesic.*

Definition: 4.5.2 *If p is any point in the hyperbolic plane, we define the **half-turn at** p to be the elliptic element of order two fixing p and denote it by E_p.*

Definition: 4.5.3 *A hyperbolic segment connecting two points a and b extends to a geodesic that separates the hyperbolic plane into two disjoint subsets. If c is any point in the hyperbolic plane not on the geodesic determined by a and b, we can, therefore, talk about the c-**side** of $[a, b]$ and the **non-c side**.*

4.6 Distances in the extended wedge

Our next task is to enlarge the wedge at a point by first enlarging the tile at a point. We will define the extended tile and the extended wedge. The definition could be made for any $(2, p, q)$ triangle group. However, our primary use will be in the case of a $(2, 3, 7)$ triangle group. So to simplify the exposition we restrict ourselves to the $(2, 3, 7)$.

Recall that the tile at 7, is the tile $T_7 = \triangle \cup R_{37}(\triangle)$ and the wedge at 7, $W(7)$ is $\cup_{n=0}^{6} R_7^n(T_7)$. The wedge $W(7) = W(v)$ has the four vertices, v, p, S, and $p'' = R_{37}(p) = R_7(p)$. Let $p' = R_3(p)$ so that R_3 permutes the set $\{p, p', p''\}$.

Definition: 4.6.1 *We define the **extended tile at** 7 which we denote by $ET(7)$ or $ET(v)$ by*

$$ET(7) = T_7 \cup \triangle(p, S, p') \cup \triangle(p', S, p'').$$

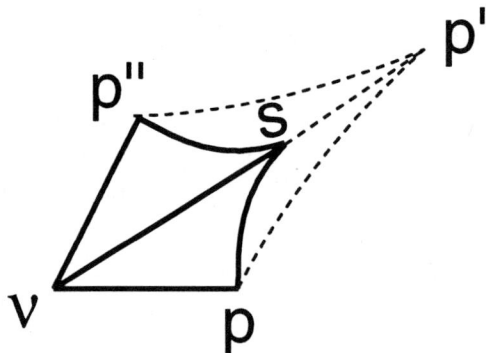

Figure 4.4: The extended tile at 7

See figure 4.4

Notation: 4.6.2 *An extended tile has four vertices and contains a unique fixed point of order three. We write $ET(v) = \{v, p, p', p''\}$ and contains S to indicate that the extended tile has the fixed point v of order 7 and the three fixed points of order two p, p', and p'' which are permuted among themselves by the rotation of order three which fixes S.*

Definition: 4.6.3 *We define the* **extended wedge at 7** *which we denote by $EW(7)$ or $EW(v)$ by*

$$EW(7) = \cup_{n=0}^{6} R_7^n(ET(v)).$$

We label the fixed points of the elements of the group lying in $EW(v)$ about v as follows: $z_i = R_7^{i-1}(S)$, $p_i = R_7^{i-1}(p)$, and $q_i = R_7^{i-1}(p')$. Note that $E_{p_{i+1}}(z_i) = z_{i+1}$. (Subscripts are taken modulo 7, of course.) (See figure 4.5.) And, E_{p_2} must, therefore, map the three points of order two closest to z_2 into those closest to z_1. Therefore, $E_{p_2}(\{q_2, p_2, p_3\}) = \{q_1, p_2, p_1\}$. Since E_{p_2} fixes p_2 and maps points on

4.6. DISTANCES IN THE EXTENDED WEDGE

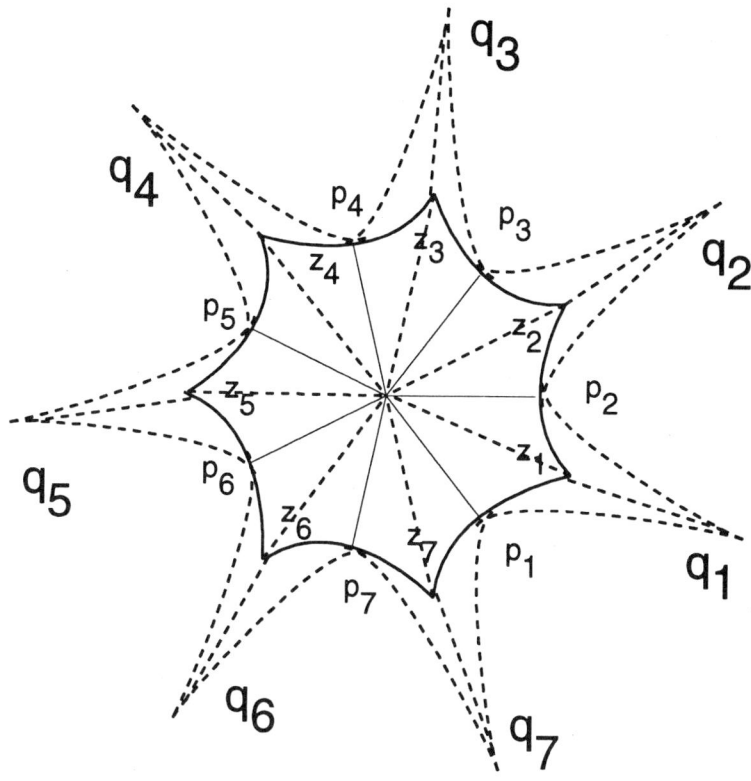

Figure 4.5: The extended wedge at 7

the v side of $[z_2, z_1]$ onto the non-v side, it must map p_3 to q_1 and q_2 to p_1. This tells us that the segment $[q_2, p_2] \cup [p_2, p_1]$ is actually a geodesic. Since $[p_2, p_1]_d = D_0(2,2)$, we have $[q_2, p_2] = D_0(2,2) = [p_2, q_1]$ and $d(q_2, p_1) = 2D_0(2,2)$. Since $E_{p_2}(p_3) = q_1$, $d(p_3, q_1) = 2D_0(2,2)$.

We fix some more notation

Definition: 4.6.4
$$\mathbf{T_0} = D_0(2, 2).$$
$$\mathbf{D_0} = D_0(2, 7).$$
$$\mathbf{Z_1} = D_0(2, 3) + D_0(3, 7).$$

Finally since z_i lies on the same geodesic as $[v, q_i]$, $d(z_i, v) = d(z_i, q_i) + d(q_i, v) = Z_1$.

Lemma: 4.6.5 *Let $k\pi/7$ be the acute angle between $[v, p_i]$ and $[v, q_j]$. Then*

- $\cosh(d(p_i, p_j)) = \cosh^2 D_0 - \sinh^2 D_0 \cdot \cos 2|i - j|\pi/7$.

- $\cosh(d(q_i, q_j)) = \cosh^2 Z_1 - \sinh^2 Z_1 \cdot \cos 2|i - j|\pi/7$.

- $\cosh(d(p_i, q_{j+1})) = \cosh D_0 \cdot \cosh Z_1 - \sinh D_0 \cdot \sinh Z_1 \cdot \cos k\pi/7$

Proof: Apply the hyperbolic law of cosines (6.9). □

Definition: 4.6.6 $\mathbf{T_2} = d(p_1, p_3)$ *and* $\mathbf{T_3} = d(p_1, p_4)$.

We note that the distance between any two p_i and p_j is either T_0, T_2, or T_3.

Lemma: 4.6.7
$$d(p_i, q_i) = T_0.$$
$$d(p_i, q_{i+1}) = 2T_0.$$

For all other i and j, $d(p_i, q_j) > 2T_0$.

4.6. DISTANCES IN THE EXTENDED WEDGE

Proof: First of all, we have $d(p_i, q_i) = d(p_1, q_1) = T_0$ and we have seen that $d(p_1, q_2) = 2T_0$. We have $d(p_i, q_j) = d(p_1, q_{j-i+1})$. Also $d(p_1, q_1) = d(p_1, q_7)$, $d(p_1, q_2) = d(p_1, q_6)$ and $d(p_1, q_3) = d(p_1, q_5)$. Thus we need only consider the cases $i = 1$ and $j = 1, 2, 3$, or 4. We compute that $\cosh d(p_1, q_2) - \cosh d(p_1, q_j) = -\sinh D_0 \cdot \sinh Z_1 \cdot \cos 3 \cdot \pi/7 + \sinh D_0 \cdot \sinh Z_1 \cdot \cos k \cdot \pi/7 = -\sinh D_0 \sinh Z_1 (\cos 3 \cdot \pi/7 - \cos k \cdot \pi/7)$. We need only consider $j = 3$, $k = 5$ and $j = 4$, $k = 7$. If $k = 5$ or 7, $\cos k\pi/7$ is negative so that $\cos 3\pi/7 - \cos k\pi/7$ is positive. Thus $\cosh d(p_1, q_2) - \cosh d(p_1, q_j)$ is negative. Whence the lemma follows.
□

Remark: 4.6.8 *If p_0 and p_0' are any points of order two in $W(v)$ and the acute angle between $[v, p_0']$ and $[v, p_0]$ is $k \cdot 2\pi/7$, then there is an element of the group that maps $\{p_0, p_0'\}$ into $\{p_1, p_{1+k}\}$. Namely, if the acute angle begins (moving counterclockwise) at p_0 it is the rotation that maps p_0 into p_1 and if it begins at p_0' it is the rotation that maps p_0' into p_1.*

Remark: 4.6.9 *If p_0 and q_0 are any two points of order two in $EW(7)$ and the acute angle between $[7, p_0]$ and $[7, q_0]$ is $\pi/7$, then there is an element of the group that maps them into $\{p_1, p_2\}$. To see this we may assume that $p_0 \in W(v)$, but q_0 is not. Since both p_0 and q_0 lie in the same extended tile, some power of R_7 moves the pair either into $\{p_1, q_1\}$ or the pair $\{q_1, p_2\}$. Then R_{z_1} or $R_{z_1}^2$ maps them into the pair $\{p_1, p_2\}$.*

We notice in the extended wedge at v, $[p_1, v, z_4, q_4]$ is a geodesic. This is because the angle $\prec (p_1, v, z_1)$ is $2\pi/7$ and the angle $\prec (z_1, v, z_4)$ is $3 \cdot 2\pi/7$. Further the geodesic $[p_1, q_4]$ encounters the fixed points of the group p_1, v, z_4, and q_4 in that order in moving from p_1 to q_4 and no others. Thus the geodesic $[p_1, E_{q_4}(v)]$ encounters the fixed points $p_1, v, z_4, q_4, E_{q_4}(z_4)$ and $E_{q_4}(v)$ in that order and no others.

Proposition: 4.6.10 *Let p, v, S and q be fixed points of orders respectively 2, 7, 3, and 2 such that $[p, v, S, q]$ is a geodesic lying in $EW(v)$ where p and S are separated by v. Let v' be any fixed point of order seven lying on $\widetilde{[p, v]}$ but separated from p by v. Then $d(p, v') \geq 2D_0(2, 7) + 2D_0(3, 7) + 2D_0(2, 3)$.*

Proof: Since $E_{q_4}(v)$ is the only seven that $[p_1, E_{q_4}(v)]$ encounters other than v itself, we have $d(v', p_1) \geq d(E_{q_4}(v), p_1) = d(p_1, v) + d(v, z_4) + d(z_4, q_4) + d(q_4, E_{q_4}(z_4)) + d(E_{q_4}(z_4), E_{q_4}(v))$. □

Remark: 4.6.11 *The results of this last section extend in a straight forward manner to $(2,3,n)$ triangle groups and $(2,4,n)$ triangle groups. We do not need the more general results for the purposes of this paper, so we do not prove them here. We will, however, refer to the extended tile and wedge at a vertex v in an arbitrary $(2,3,n)$ triangle group.*

Chapter 5

Pentagons

In this chapter we will show that each pair of hyperbolics, A and B with intersecting but distinct axes determines a pentagon with four right angles. If the commutator of A and B is not elliptic, then the pentagon only has the four right angle vertices in the upper half plane, **U**. This construction is due to Matelski [27]. In the cases where the commutator of A and B is hyperbolic, parabolic, or a primitive elliptic element, one can use the Poincaré polygon theorem to conclude that $G = \langle A, B \rangle$ (or possibly G^*) is discrete and that the images of this pentagon under the action of the group *tile* the plane. When the commutator is a non-primitive elliptic element, G and G^* may or may not be discrete. If G^* is discrete, the images of the pentagon will not tile the plane but will form a *shingling*. In order to understand when such a group is and is not discrete, one needs to understand what the images of the pentagon look like under the action of G^*. In particular, one tries to understand these images in as simple a manner as possible by trying to understand how close to a tiling the images are. For this reason, we study the **fundamental tiling strip** of the pentagon and prove a number of lemmas about distances in and across this strip.

5.1 Constructing the pentagon, $P_{A,B}$

The following discussion refers to Figure 5.1 (see also Figure 2.5).

If A and B are hyperbolics with intersecting but distinct axes, we

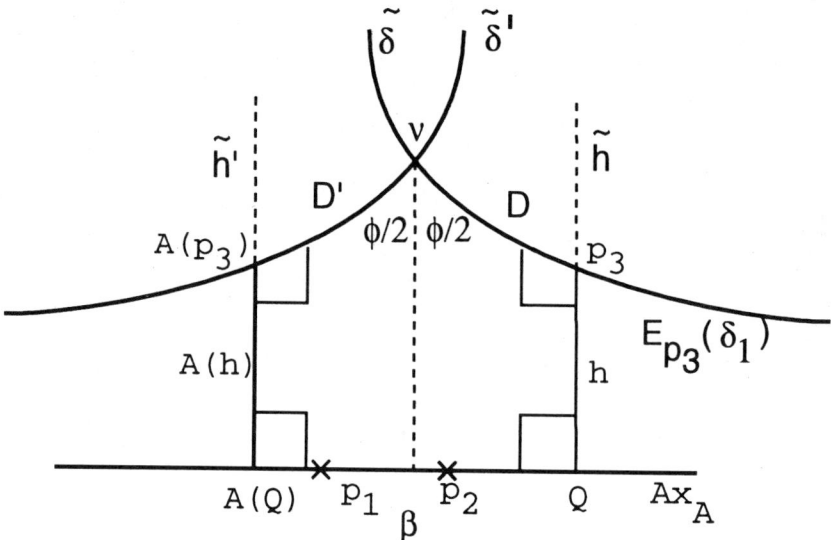

Figure 5.1: The pentagon determined by A and B

next construct the **pentagon associated to A and B**. We will denote this pentagon by $P_{A,B}$ or merely by P when the pair (A, B) is clear from the context.

Recall that p_2 is the point of intersection of Ax_A and Ax_B and that p_1 and p_3 are chosen so that $A = E_{p_1}E_{p_2}$ and $B = E_{p_3}E_{p_2}$. We let h be the perpendicular from p_3 to the axis of A. Assume that h intersects Ax_A at a point Q. Then $A(h)$ is a perpendicular from $A(p_3)$ to the axis of A intersecting the axis of A at $A(Q)$.

Three of the sides of the pentagon will be h, $A(h)$ and the segment $[A(Q), Q]$. The fourth and fifth sides are the segments δ and $E_{p_1}E_{p_2}E_{p_3}(\delta)$, where δ is defined as follows:

First let $\gamma = E_{p_1}E_{p_2}E_{p_3}$ and notice that $\gamma^2 = [A, B]$.

Let $\tilde{\delta}$ be a line perpendicular to h through p_3. Let $\tilde{\delta}' = A(\tilde{\delta})$ be the perpendicular to $A(h)$ through $A(p_3)$. We let $\tilde{h}$ be the complete hyperbolic line of which h is a subsegment. We note that $\tilde{h}$ also contains the segment $E_{p_3}(h)$ which goes from p_3 to $E_{p_3}(Q)$. We also let $\tilde{h}'$ be the complete geodesic of which $h' = A(h)$ is a segment. Then $\tilde{h}'$ also contains the segment $E_{A(p_3)}(h') = A(E_{p_3}(h)) = \gamma(h)$, which has the end points $A(p_3) = \gamma(p_3)$ and $A(E_{p_3}(Q)) = \gamma(Q)$. Since $\gamma(h)$ lies on $\tilde{h}'$, we

5.1. CONSTRUCTING THE PENTAGON, $P_{A,B}$

also have $\gamma(\tilde{h}) = \tilde{h}'$.

The point p_3 divides $\tilde{\delta}$ into two subsegments, one of which contains points from the region between $\tilde{h}'$ and $\tilde{h}$ and the other one of which does not. We let δ_1 be the segment which intersects the region between $\tilde{h}$ and $\tilde{h}'$. Then the other segment is $E_{p_3}(\delta_1)$.

Similarly, the point $A(p_3)$ divides $\tilde{\delta}'$ into two subsegments, one of which contains points from the region between $\tilde{h}'$ and $\tilde{h}$ and the other one of which does not. We let δ_2 be the segment which intersects the region between $\tilde{h}$ and $\tilde{h}'$. Then the other segment is $E_{A(p_3)}(\delta_2)$.

Now either $\gamma(\delta_1) = \delta_2$ or $\gamma(\delta_1) = E_{A(p_3)}(\delta_1)$.

Lemma: 5.1.1 $\gamma(\delta_1) = \delta_2$.

Proof: Since γ and A are orientation preserving isometries, they each must map a pair of perpendicular geodesics through p_3 to a pair of perpendicular geodesics through $A(p_3) = \gamma(p_3)$ and preserve the orientation of the pair. That is, they map the pair $(\tilde{h}, \tilde{\delta})$ to a pair of perpendicular geodesics though $A(p_3)$. By construction $A(\tilde{h}) = \tilde{h}' = \gamma(h)$. So that $\gamma(\tilde{\delta})$ must be perpendicular to $\tilde{h}'$ and pass through $\gamma(p_3) = A(p_3)$ as must $A(\tilde{\delta})$. Therefore, $\gamma(\tilde{\delta}) = \tilde{\delta}'$. To decide whether $\gamma(\delta_1) = \delta_2'$ or $E_{A(p_3)}(\delta_2')$ note that we chose δ_1 to have non-empty intersection with the region bounded by $\tilde{h}$ and $\tilde{h}'$. An equivalent way to describe this is to give $\tilde{h}'$ an orientation with moving from Q to p_3 or from p_3 to $E_{p_3}(Q)$ being positive and choosing δ_1 to lie to the *left* of $\tilde{h}$ when moving in the positive direction. Since $\gamma(h) = [A(p_3), \gamma(Q)]$, $\gamma(\delta_1)$ is that portion of $\tilde{\delta}'$ lying to the *left* of $\gamma(\tilde{h})$, so it must be that $\gamma(\delta_1) = \delta_2$. $\square$

We need the following lemma:

Lemma: 5.1.2
- $\tilde{\delta}$ and $\tilde{\delta}'$ intersect interior to **U** precisely when $[A, B]$ is elliptic and the point of intersection v is the fixed point of $[A, B]$.

- $\tilde{\delta}$ and $\tilde{\delta}'$ intersect on the boundary of **U** precisely when $[A, B]$ is parabolic

- $\tilde{\delta}$ and $\tilde{\delta}'$ are disjoint precisely when $[A, B]$ is hyperbolic.

Proof: If γ^2 is parabolic or elliptic, then so is γ and for any point v in the hyperbolic plane or on its boundary, $\gamma(v) = v$ if and only if $\gamma^2(v) = v$. If γ is elliptic or parabolic, let v be its fixed point so that $\gamma(v) = v$.

The geodesics $\tilde{h}$ and $\tilde{h}'$ divide the plane into three regions: the region to the left of $\tilde{h}'$ where motion from $A(Q)$ to $A(p_3)$ is motion in the positive direction; the region between the two geodesics; and the region to the right of $\tilde{h}$ again using Q to p_3 as the positive direction. We denote these regions $\hat{R}_1$, $\hat{R}_2$, and $\hat{R}_3$. Further, the axis of A divides each of these regions into two subregion, $\hat{R}_i^+$ and $\hat{R}_i^-$ where the positive region is the one which contains h or h'. The geodesics $\tilde{\delta}$ and $\tilde{\delta}'$ further subdivide the region $\hat{R}_2^+$ between $\tilde{h}$ and $\tilde{h}'$ into three subregions, S_1, S_2 and S_3. Here S_1 denotes that portion of $\hat{R}_1^+$ above $\tilde{\delta}'$, S_3 that portion above $\tilde{\delta}$, and S_2 that portion below both $\tilde{\delta}$ and $\tilde{\delta}'$. Here *above $\tilde{\delta}'$* means containing the segment $[A(p_3), \gamma(Q)]$ and *above $\tilde{\delta}$* means containing the segment $[p_3, E_{p_3}(Q)]$. Note that S_1 and S_3 are not necessarily disjoint.

If $\tilde{\delta}$ and $\tilde{\delta}'$ intersect, let q be their point of intersection. We note the following:

- $d(v, p_3) = d(v, A(p_3))$.
- $d(v, \tilde{\delta}) = d(v, \tilde{\delta}')$.
- If δ and δ' intersect, then $d(q, p_3) = d(q, A(p_3))$.

These facts imply that if the curves intersect, then $\gamma(q) = q$. For if the two geodesics do intersect in q, then $E_{p_3}(q)$ is a point on $E_{p_3}(\delta_1)$ at a distance $[q, p_3]_d$ from p_3 and $A(E_{p_3})(q))$ is a point on $A(E_{p_3}(\delta_1)) = \delta_2$ at a distance $[q, p_3]_d$ from $A(p_3)$. This is precisely q.

We will see in a moment that these facts imply that if the commutator is elliptic and the curves intersect, then $q = v$. However, first we want to establish that these facts are true.

Note that since $\gamma(p_3) = A(p_3)$, γ will map the geodesic connecting v and p_3 to that connecting v and $A(p_3)$ and a perpendicular from v to $\tilde{\delta}$ to a perpendicular from v to $\tilde{\delta}'$. To see the last property, let H be a perpendicular from q to the axis of A and let T be its point of intersection with the axis of A. Consider the two quadrilaterals each with three right angles: q, p_3, Q, T and $q, A(p_3), A(Q), T$. They

5.1. CONSTRUCTING THE PENTAGON, $P_{A,B}$

both have opposite sides of length H_d and h_d. Apply corollary 6.3.4 to conclude that these are similar quadrilaterals so that the corresponding sides $[q, p_3]$ and $[q, A(p_3)]$ are of equal length. (Note that $[q, p_3] = [q, A(p_3)]$ implies that $q \in \hat{R}_2$).

We note that if x is any point interior to S_2, then $\gamma(x)$ must lie in S_1. Namely, E_{p_3} interchanges the half-planes above and below $\tilde{\delta}$ and A maps the half-plane above $\tilde{\delta}$ to the half-plane above $\tilde{\delta}$. (See Figure 5.1.) Thus $E_{p_3}(S_2) \subset S_3 \cup A(S_1)$ and $AE_{p_3}(S_2) = \gamma(S_2) \subset A(S_3) \cup S_1$. Thus the interior of S_2 is disjoint from its image so that S_2 cannot contain any fixed point of γ in its interior.

If γ has a fixed point, it is equidistant from p_3 and $A(p_3)$ and thus lies in R_2. Therefore, if γ has a fixed point, it must lie either in S_1 or S_3 or on $\tilde{\delta}$ or $\tilde{\delta}'$. Assume that it lies in S_1 and that $\tilde{\delta}$ and $\tilde{\delta}'$ are disjoint. Let P_δ be a perpendicular from v to $\tilde{\delta}$ and let $\underline{T}$ be the point where this geodesic crosses $\tilde{\delta}$. Let $P_{\delta'}$ be a perpendicular from v to $\tilde{\delta}'$ and let T_0 be the point where the geodesic crosses $\tilde{\delta}$ and T' the point where it crosses $\tilde{\delta}'$. Then $[v, \underline{T}]_d \leq [v, T_0]_d \leq [v, T']$ with equality holding precisely when $\underline{T} = T'$. However, we know that v must be equidistant from $\tilde{\delta}$ and $\tilde{\delta}'$. Thus $\underline{T}$ must equal T' and the geodesics must intersect.

In a similar manner, conclude that v cannot be interior to S_3. Thus if γ has a fixed point, it must lie on $\tilde{\delta}$ or $\tilde{\delta}'$. Now v cannot lie on one geodesic but not the other because v is equidistant from both geodesics. Thus if γ has a fixed point, it must lie on the intersection of the two geodesics. We have shown that the geodesics intersect if and only if γ has a fixed point and in that case they intersect in the fixed point. Minor modifications of these arguments show that the geodesics intersect on the boundary if and only if $[A, B]$ is parabolic and fixes the point of intersection on the boundary of **U**. □

Now we can define δ and δ':

Definition: 5.1.3 *If $[A,B]$ is hyperbolic or parabolic, set $\delta = \delta_1$ and $\delta' = \delta_2$. If $[A, B]$ is elliptic with fixed point v, let $\delta = [p_3, v]$ and $\delta' = \gamma(\delta) = [A(p_3), v]$.*

Definition: 5.1.4 *The **pentagon associated to** (A, B), $P_{A,B}$, is the pentagon with sides h, $A(h)$, δ, $\gamma(\delta)$ and $\beta = [Q, A(Q)]$.*

5.2 Notation

The notation we have established here will remain fixed. Note that Q and T are defined. See Figure 5.1.

To simplify the discussion, we adopt some conventions. The pentagon P has five vertices, but four of them subtend right angles. Therefore, we single out the vertex v and refer to it as **the** vertex of the pentagon. Similarly we call the angle, ϕ at the vertex v **the** angle of the pentagon and the sides D and $D' = \gamma(D)$ are called **the vertex sides**. Sides h and $A(h)$ are referred to as the height of the pentagon and $\beta = [Q, A(Q)]$ as the base. We define the lengths of the sides of $P_{A,B}$ as follows: We let D be the (possibly infinite) length of δ, h the length of side $h = [Q, p_3]$, H the length of the segment $[v, T]$ and b the length of the segment $[Q, T] = T_A$. (Recall that T_A denotes half the translation length of A chapter 2.) Note also that $b = [Q, T] = [T, A(Q)] = [p_1, p_2] = [p_2, E_{p_2}(p_1)]$. (See figure 5.1.)

We refer to h as the **height** of the pentagon and b as the **base**. (Note that the **actual base** is the segment $[Q, A(Q)]$, this is referred to as **the β side of the pentagon**). When we apply standard formulas about lengths and sides of pentagons to this situation 6.14 we obtain the following formula which is one of the essential tools in understanding pentagons and their relations to the generating pair (A, B).

$$\sinh b \sinh h = \cos(\phi/2) \tag{5.1}$$

5.3 Applying the Poincaré Polygon Theorem

Recall that the Poincaré polygon theorem [25] says that if one has a finite sided polygon whose side are identified in pairs, then under certain conditions one can conclude that the group generated by the side pairings is discrete. We want to apply the Poincaré polygon theorem to $P_{A,B}$. If we are being precise, we actually apply the theorem to an eight sided figure because the actual base is the union of four sides: $[A(Q), p_1]$, $[p_1, E_{p_1} A(Q)] = E_{p_1}([A(Q), p_1])$, $[E_{p_1} A(Q), p_2]$, and $[p_2, Q] = E_{p_2}([E_{p_1}(A(Q)), p_2])$.

5.4. PENTAGON TILINGS

Recall that a primitive rotation rotates by $\pm 2\pi/n$ and a non-primitive one by $\pm k2\pi/n$ where k and n are integers with $1 < k < n/2$. Note that when γ is elliptic, the vertex angle must be less than π. Thus our construction forces the rotation angle of γ and the interior angle of the pentagon to coincide. Following Matelski we apply the Poincaré polygon theorem and conclude

Lemma: 5.3.1 *If $[A, B]$ is hyperbolic, parabolic or elliptic with γ a primitive rotation, then P is a polygon with side pairing group $G^* = \langle E_{p_1}, E_{p_2}, E_{p_3} \rangle$ and this satisfies the conditions of the Poincaré polygon theorem so that G^* (and thus also its subgroup of index two $G = \langle A, B \rangle$) is discrete.*

In determining the discreteness of G in the case where γ is a non-primitive rotation, we proceed as follows.

5.4 Pentagon Tilings

Because G and G^* do not satisfy the cycle condition at v, the images of P under G^* do not tile the hyperbolic plane. Since the images of P overlap, they form what is called a shingling of the plane (see chapter 7). Even though they do not tile the plane, we can still seek to understand where the images of P lie under the action of elements of G trying to view the images as being as close to a tiling as possible.

We first note that under powers of A the images move up and down the axis of A and the images of P under the powers of A do not overlap. (See figure 5.2. We refer to the axis of A as the A-axis and in order to make our diagrams less cluttered we draw it as a euclidean straight line. The axis of A has well defined positive and negative sides, namely the half-plane containing p_3 is the positive side of the axis of A.

Also E_{p_1} maps P into a pentagon $\tilde{P}$ on the other side of the axis of A from $\{\cup_{n \in \mathbb{Z}} A^n(P)\}$ and powers of A map $\tilde{P}$ up and down the A-axis without overlap.

If $P_n = A^n(P)$ and $\tilde{P}_n = A^n(\tilde{P})$, we let $\mathcal{P} = \cup_{j \in \mathbb{Z}} (P_j \cup \tilde{P}_j)$ and call $\mathcal{P}$ **the fundamental tiling strip** (figure 5.3). Our aim is to understand the shingling as much as possible through understanding the fundamental tiling strip $\mathcal{P}$.

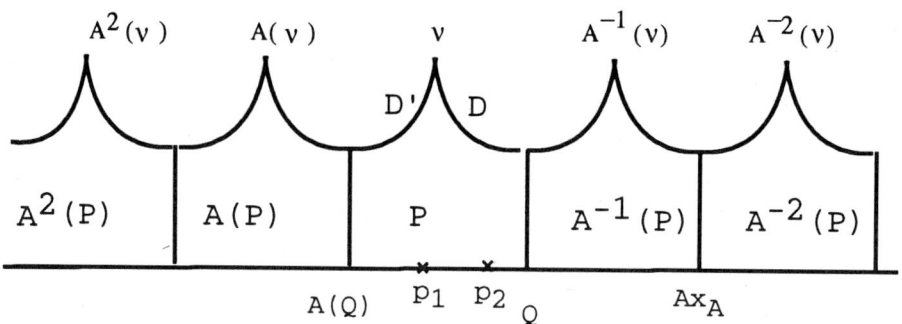

Figure 5.2: Fundamental tile strip **above** the axis of A

5.5 Distances in the shingling

We first note that distances from points on the axis of A to points outside $\mathcal{P}$ are all *large*. To make this precise, we prove

Lemma: 5.5.1 *Let x be any point in β and y any point in $\mathbf{U} - \mathcal{P}$ with τ the non-euclidean segment connecting x and y. Then $D(x,y) \geq h_d$.*

In particular the lemma says that if y is any point in $\mathbf{U} - \mathcal{P}$, then $d(y, Ax_A) \geq h_d$.

Proof: Let $D_i = A^i(D)$, $D' = \gamma(D)$, $d'_i = A^i(D')$, $h_i = A^i(h)$ and $\beta_i = A^i(\beta)$.

Then τ either intersects $\mathcal{D} = \cup_{j \in \mathbb{Z}}(D_j \cup D'_j)$ or $E_{p_1}(\mathcal{D})$.

We first treat the case that τ intersects $\mathcal{D}$. Drop a perpendicular from y to the A-axis and call this segment ρ. Let ρ intersect the A-axis at m. Then m, x, and y determine a right triangle with hypotenuse τ. Therefore, $\tau_d \geq \rho_d$. We claim $\rho_d \geq h_d$.

5.5. DISTANCES IN THE SHINGLING

To see this let i and s be such that ρ crosses $\mathcal{D}$ at s in $A^i(D)$. (If ρ crosses $\mathcal{D}$ at $A^i(D')$, argue in a similar manner.) We first prove a sublemma.

Sublemma: 5.5.2 *Let M be any point on a vertex side of D_i or D'_i, respectively. Then the perpendicular ρ from M to the axis of A lies entirely inside P_i or P'_i, respectively.*

Proof: (of sublemma) Replacing M by $A^{-i}(M)$ we may assume that $M \in D$ or D'. If ρ does not lie entirely in P, then ρ intersects either h or $A(h)$. Now $\mathcal{D}$ is a convex set, so any geodesic connecting two points of $\mathcal{D}$ lies entirely inside $\mathcal{D}$. Thus ρ cannot intersect a vertex side.

Similarly, the set $\cup_{n \in \mathbb{Z}} A^n(P)$ is also convex. Thus any geodesic connecting two points in this set also lies entirely in this set. Thus ρ cannot intersect β unless ρ is already entirely in P. Let k be the point where ρ intersects h or $A(h)$. If m is the point where ρ intersects the axis of A, then either $\{k, m, Q\}$ or $\{k, m, A(Q)\}$ determine a triangle with two right angles. This cannot happen.

Thus ρ lies entirely inside P and intersects either D and Ax_A or D' and Ax_A. But h is a common perpendicular to Ax_A and $D \cup E_{p_3}(D)$ and $A(h)$ is a common perpendicular to Ax_A and $D' \cup E_{A(p_3)}(D')$. Thus $h_d = (A(h))_d \leq \rho_d$. $\square$

The proof of the lemma follows from this sublemma. Finally if τ intersects $E_{p_1}(\mathcal{D})$, replace y and x by their images under E_{p_1}. Then we have just shown that $d(E_{p_1}(y), z) \geq h_d$ for any $z \in \beta$. In particular, it is true if $z = E_{p_1}(x)$. $\square$

Following the notation of the earlier section we let $\mathbf{U} - \mathcal{P}^+$ denote points not in the fundamental tiling strip lying on the positive side of the axis of A and $\mathbf{U} - \mathcal{P}^-$ points on the negative side of the axis of A.

If y is any point in $\mathbf{U} - \mathcal{P}^+$, we let **the pentagon of** y be the P_i which τ_y, the perpendicular from y to the A-axis, intersects. Further, let ρ_y be the segment of τ_y contained in $\mathcal{P}$, x_y the point where τ_y intersects the axis of A, and i_y the i with ρ_y in P_i.

Proposition: 5.5.3 *Let $y \in \mathbf{U} - \mathcal{P}^+$. Let $\tilde{y} = A^{-i_y}(y)$. Let $m_0 = \min\{d(\tilde{y}, p_1), d(\tilde{y}, p_2)\}$. Then $d(y, p_1) \geq m_0$ and $d(y, p_2) \geq m_0$ with strict inequality holding unless $i_y = 1, 0,$ or -1.*

The proposition will follow from the following lemma:

Lemma: 5.5.4

- (i) If $i_y \neq 1, 0$, or -1, then $d(y, p_1) > 2b$ and $d(y, p_2) > 2b$.

- (ii) If $i_y = 0$, $d(y, p_1) \geq d(y, p_2)$ if and only if $d(x_y, p_1) \geq d(x_y, p_2)$.

- (iii) If $i_y = 1$ or -1, then $d(y, p_1) \geq m_0$ and $d(y, p_2) \geq m_0$.

Proof: In (i) the triangle with vertices y, x_y, and p_1 is a right triangle and $d(y, x_y) > 0$ since $y \notin \mathcal{P}$. Thus $d(y, p_1) > d(x_y, p_1)$. The latter is greater than $2b$ if $|i_y| \geq 2$. The proof for p_2 is the same. In (ii) the triangles $\triangle(y, x_y, p_1)$ and $\triangle(y, x_y, p_2)$ are both right triangles with the same height. The one with the longer hypotenuse is, therefore, the one with the longer base. We treat the case that $i_y = 1$. The case $i_y = -1$ is similar. Subdivide $A(\beta)$ into four subintervals, $[A^2(Q), A(p_1)]$, $[A(p_1), A(T)]$, $[A(T), A(p_2)]$ and $[A(p_2), A(Q)]$. If x_y is in one of the first two intervals, $d(x_y, A(p_1)) < d(x_y, p_1)$ so that $d(y, p_1) > d(A^{-1}(y), p_1)$. If x_y is in one of the four intervals, $d(x_y, A(p_2)) < d(x_y, p_2)$ so that $d(y, A(p_2)) = d(A^{-1}(y), p_2) < d(y, p_2)$.

If $x_y \in [A(p_2), A(Q)]$, then $d(y, A(p_2)) \leq d(y, p_1)$ if and only if $d(x_y, A(p_2)) \leq d(x_y, p_1)$. But $d(y, A(p_2)) = d(A^{-1}(y), p_2)$.

If $x_y \in [A(T), A(p_2)]$, then $d(y, p_1) > d(A^{-1}(y), p_1)$ since $d(x_y, p_1) > b > d(p_1, A^{-1}(x_y))$ A similar argument gives $d(y, p_2) > d(A^{-1}(y), p_2)$. □

Note that we have also shown

Proposition: 5.5.5 *If the pentagon is symmetric (i.e. if Q bisects $[p_2, E_{p_2}(p_1)]$), let $\tilde{p}$ be the p_i that is closest to $x_{\tilde{y}}$. Then $d(y, p_i) \geq d(x_{\tilde{y}}, \tilde{p})$ for $i = 1$ or $i = 2$.*

Proof: If the pentagon had been constructed so that Q bisected $[p_2, E_{p_2}(p_1)]$, then we would have $d(\tilde{y}, p_1) \leq d(\tilde{y}, p_2)$ if and only if $x_{\tilde{y}} \in [A(Q), T]$. □

5.6. DISTANCE LEMMAS IN P

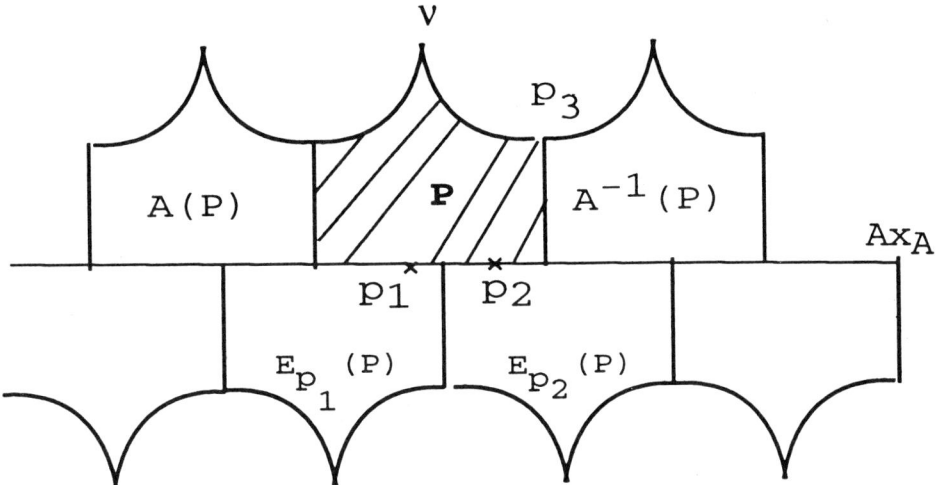

Figure 5.3: Fundamental tile strip along the axis of A

5.6 Distance lemmas in P

We will need to estimate distances between two points inside $\mathcal{P}$.

We adopt the following notation:

If X and Y denote any two sides of P, then $Min(X, Y)$ will denote the minimum distance between any point on X and any point on Y.

Lemma: 5.6.1 *The minimal distances in P are given by*

- $Min(D, \beta) = Min(D', \beta) = h_d$

- $Min(h, A(h)) = 2b$

- $Min(A(h), D) = Min(h, D') = b$

- $Min(X, Y) = 0$ if X and Y are adjacent sides of P.

Proof: The quadrilateral with vertices v, p_3, Q, and T and the quadrilateral with vertices $v, A(p_3), A(Q)$, and T each have three right angles with opposite sides H_d and h_d. Thus by corollary 6.3.4 they are similar. Thus $[A(Q), T]_d = [Q, T]_d = b$. Since $[A(Q), T]$ is a common perpendicular to $A(h)$ and H, $Min(A(h), D) \geq Min(A(h), H) \geq [A(Q), T] = b$. The other parts of the lemma follow easily from the fact that β is the common perpendicular to $\tilde{h}$ and $\tilde{A}(h)$ and h is the common perpendicular to β and $\tilde{D}$. □

We also have

Lemma: 5.6.2 *If x is any point in P_i and y is any point in P_j where $i \neq j$, then $d(x, y) \geq (|i - j| - 1) \cdot 2b$.*

Proof: The distance across one copy of P is at least $2b$. One then only needs to count how many copies of P lie between x and y. □

Finally, we prove one last proposition that we will need when G turns out to be a $(2, 4, n)$ triangle group.

Proposition: 5.6.3 *Assume that $p_1 = p$ is equidistant from Q and $A(Q)$, that $p_2 = Q$, and that $d(Q, p) = D_0(2, 4)$. Then $d(y, p) > d(A^{i_y}(y), p)$ when $i_y \neq 0$.*

Proof: Let τ be the geodesic connecting y to p and y_D the point where τ crosses $\mathcal{D}$. By 5.5.3, we may assume that y_D is either in $P, A(P)$ or $A^{-1}(P)$. Suppose y_D lies on $A(D)$ or $A(D')$. We claim that $d(y, A(p)) > d(A^{-1}(y), p)$. To see this let m be the point where τ hits the axis of A. Now m is in one of two intervals, $[A^2(Q), A(p)]$, $[A(p), A(Q)]$. If the former occurs $[y, p]$ is the hypotenuse of a right triangle with one leg of length at least $2D_0(2, 4)$, so $d(y, p) > 2D_0(2, 4)$. If the latter occurs, consider the two right triangles $\triangle(y, m, p)$ and $\triangle(A(y), A(m), p)$. They both have sides $[y, m]$ and $[A(y), A(m)]$ of equal length. Since $[m, p] > [A(m), p]$, the hypotenuse $[y, p]$ is strictly greater than $[A(y), p]$. A similar argument holds when $y_D \in A^{-1}(D)$ or $A^{-1}(D')$. □

Chapter 6

A Summary of formulas for the hyperbolic trigonometric functions and some geometric corollaries

We begin this chapter by summarizing some basic formulas involving the hyperbolic trigonometric functions and basic formulas from hyperbolic trigonometry. Most of these can be found in [2]. The summary is followed by the derivation of a a number of geometric corollaries. As presented here, the corollaries drawn may seem completely unmotivated. We will use each corollary in some other part of the paper where the motivation for discovering the corollary will become apparent.

6.1 Addition formulas for the hyperbolic sine and cosine

We begin by recalling the addition formulas and double angle formulas for the hyperbolic sine and cosine. These formulas can be derived directly from the definitions of the hyperbolic sine and cosine.

$$\cosh(x \pm y) = \cosh x \cosh y \pm \sinh x \sinh y \tag{6.1}$$

$$\sinh(x \pm y) = \sinh x \cosh y \pm \cosh x \sinh y \tag{6.2}$$

$$\cosh 2x = \cosh^2 x + \sinh^2 x = 2\cosh^2 x - 1 \qquad (6.3)$$

$$\sinh 2x = 2\sinh x \cdot \cosh x \qquad (6.4)$$

6.2 Hyperbolic Triangles

Let $\triangle(A, B, C)$ be a triangle with sides A, B and C. Assume that the angle at the vertex opposite side A is α, opposite side B is β and side C is γ. Then

Fact: 6.2.1 *If γ is a right angle, we have* **the hyperbolic law of cosines for right triangles**

$$\cosh C = \cosh A \cdot \cosh B \qquad (6.5)$$

and **the hyperbolic law of sines for right triangles**

$$\sinh B = \sinh A \cdot \tan \beta. \qquad (6.6)$$

Also

$$\cosh A \cdot \sin \beta = \cos \alpha. \qquad (6.7)$$

$$\cosh B \cdot \sin \alpha = \cos \beta \qquad (6.8)$$

For arbitrary triangles, we have

Fact: 6.2.2 the hyperbolic law of cosines *[2]*

$$\cosh C = \cosh A \cdot \cosh B - \sinh A \cdot \sinh B \cdot \cos \gamma \qquad (6.9)$$

and **the hyperbolic law of sines**

$$\frac{\sinh A}{\sin \alpha} = \frac{\sinh B}{\sin \beta} = \frac{\sinh C}{\sin \gamma}. \qquad (6.10)$$

Fact: 6.2.3 *(See p. 157 of [2].) For a quadrilateral with three right angles and sides A, B, C, and D where ϕ, the non-right angle, is between sides B and C (see figure 6.1), we have*

$$\sinh D \cdot \sinh A = \cos \phi \qquad (6.11)$$

$$\cosh D = \cosh B \cdot \sin \phi \qquad (6.12)$$

$$\cosh A = \cosh C \cdot \sin \phi. \qquad (6.13)$$

6.3. GEOMETRIC COROLLARIES AND LEMMAS

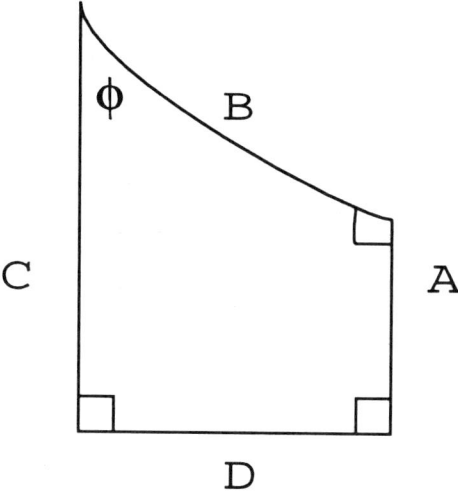

Figure 6.1: Quadrilateral with three right angles

Fact: 6.2.4 *Finally if g is a hyperbolic transformation and T_g denotes is translation length and $tr(g)$ its trace, then*

$$\cosh^2 \frac{T_g}{2} = \frac{tr^2(g)}{4}$$

or

$$\frac{1}{2} \cdot |tr(g)| = \cosh \frac{T_g}{2}.$$

6.3 Geometric Corollaries and Lemmas

6.3.1 Consequences of the Hyperbolic Law of Cosines

There is a relationship between the angle γ and the length of the side C. Namely,

Corollary: 6.3.1

$$\begin{aligned}
\cosh C &> \cosh A \cdot \cosh B &&\text{if } \gamma < \pi/2 \\
&= \cosh A \cdot \cosh B &&\text{if } \gamma = \pi/2 \\
&< \cosh A \cdot \cosh B &&\text{if } \gamma > \pi/2
\end{aligned}$$

Proof: This is an immediate consequence of the hyperbolic law of cosines. □

Given $\triangle(A, B, C)$ with γ the angle opposite side C, let $\triangle(A, B, D)$ be the triangle with sides A, B and D where the angle opposite side D is $\pi - \gamma$. Then the last corollary implies that

Corollary: 6.3.2 $\cosh C \geq \cosh D$ *if and only if* $\gamma \geq \pi/2$.

Further, putting together these two applications of the hyperbolic law of cosines we obtain the adjacent law of hyperbolic cosines.

Corollary: 6.3.3 The adjacent law of hyperbolic cosines.

$$\cosh D = 2 \cosh A \cosh B - \cosh C$$

Further, if $\gamma \geq \pi/2$, *then*

$$\cosh D = 2 \cosh A \cosh B - \cosh C \leq \cosh C.$$

6.3.2 Geometric corollaries for quadrilaterals and pentagons

By the angle of the quadrilateral with three right angles, we mean, of course, the fourth angle. A side is either adjacent to the angle or nonadjacent. It is easy to see that fact 6.2.3 gives the following two corollaries.

Corollary: 6.3.4 *A quadrilateral with three right angles is determined by any of the following*

- *Any side together with the angle.*
- *Two opposite sides.*

Corollary: 6.3.5 *Let P be a pentagon with four right angles and vertex angle ϕ. As customary, we call the vertex with non-right angle **the vertex** of P. Let s be the side opposite **the** vertex, h the lengths of the sides adjacent to s, D the lengths of the sides adjacent to the vertex,*

6.3. GEOMETRIC COROLLARIES AND LEMMAS

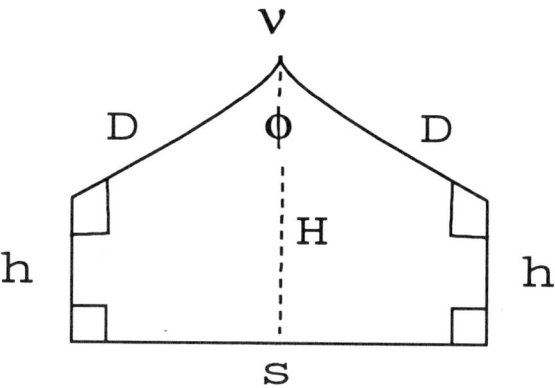

Figure 6.2: A pentagon with four right angles and some symmetry

and H the length of the perpendicular from the vertex to s. (See figure 6.2.)

$$\sinh h \cdot \sinh \frac{s}{2} = \cos(\phi/2) \qquad (6.14)$$

$$\cosh h = \cosh H \cdot \sin(\phi/2) \qquad (6.15)$$

and

$$\cosh \frac{s}{2} = \cosh D \cdot \sin(\phi/2). \qquad (6.16)$$

In particular, if the angle of the pentagon is chosen, the length of the base and height vary inversely. We call half of the length of the side opposite the vertex the **base** of the pentagon. We obtain the following corollary which will prove crucial.

Corollary: 6.3.6 Pentagon variation. *For a fixed angle ϕ, the base s is a decreasing function of the height h.*

Finally, we prove a lemma about quadrilaterals with two right angles.

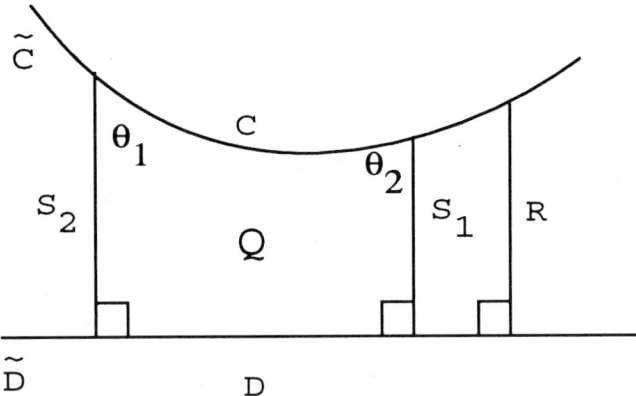

Figure 6.3: One possible location of R

Lemma: 6.3.7 *Let Q be a quadrilateral with two right angles. Let θ_1 and θ_2 be the other two angles with S_1 the side opposite θ_1 and S_2 the side opposite θ_2. Then $\theta_1 \geq \theta_2$ if and only if $S_1 \geq S_2$.*

Proof: Let C and D be the two other sides of Q and let R be the common perpendicular to $\tilde{C}$ and $\tilde{D}$. Then R and S_1 are opposite sides on a quadrilateral with three right angles and fourth angle θ_2 or $\pi - \theta_2$. Similarly, R and S_2 are opposite sides of a quadrilateral with three right angles and fourth angle θ_1 or $\pi - \theta_1$. Figure 6.3 illustrates the configuration for one of the possible locations of R. Since $\sin \alpha = \sin \pi - \alpha$ for any angle α, we can apply fact 6.2.3 to see that $\cosh R = \cosh S_1 \cdot \sin \theta_2$ and $\cosh R = \cosh S_2 \cdot \sin \theta_1$. The conclusion follows once we notice that $\theta_1 + \theta_2 < \pi$ so that if $\theta_1 \leq \theta_2$, $\theta_1 \leq \pi - \theta_2$ and if $\theta_2 \leq \theta_1$, $\theta_2 \leq \pi - \theta_1$. □

6.3.3 The geometry of acute and equilateral triangles

For any $\triangle(A, B, C)$ we let h_X denote the height to side X. If $\triangle$ is an equilateral triangle with side of length t, we let h_{teq} denote its height. We will see that

Lemma: 6.3.8 *If $\triangle(A, B, C)$ is an acute triangle and $A \leq B \leq C$, then $h_A \geq h_{Aeq}$.*

6.3. GEOMETRIC COROLLARIES AND LEMMAS

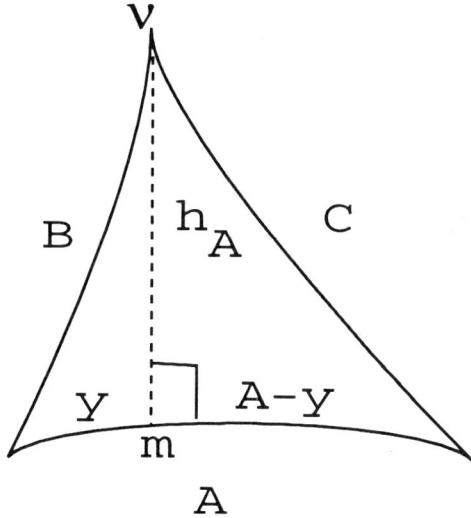

Figure 6.4: Acute triangle T with smallest side A and height h_A.

Lemma: 6.3.9 If $\triangle(A, B, C)$ is an acute triangle and $A \leq B \leq C$, then $h_A \geq A/2$.

Lemma: 6.3.10 $\cosh h_{teq} = \frac{\cosh t}{\cosh t/2}$.

Lemma: 6.3.11 If $A \geq t$, then $h_{Aeq} \geq h_{teq}$.

Lemma: 6.3.12 $h_{teq} \geq t/2$.

Lemma: 6.3.13 If $\triangle(A, B, C)$ is an acute triangle and $A \leq B \leq C$, then $h_A \geq B - (A/2)$.

Proof: Let T be any triangle whose base is chosen to be its smallest side and denoted A. Let v be the vertex opposite side A. We drop a perpendicular from v to A and let m be the point where this perpendicular, h_A hits A. Since A is the smallest side, m is interior to side A and m divides the triangle into two right triangles, one with base of length y and the other with base of length $A - y$. (See figure 6.4.) We may assume that $y \leq A/2$. The third sides of these two triangles are B and C so that since $B \leq C$, the triangle with y contains B and that with $A - y$ contains C. Compute that

$$\cosh h_A = \frac{\cosh C}{\cosh(A-y)} = \frac{\cosh B}{\cosh y} \qquad (6.17)$$

Since A is the shortest side of the triangle, $\cosh B \geq \cosh A$. Also, since $y \leq A/2$, $\cosh y \leq \cosh(A/2)$ whence $\frac{\cosh B}{\cosh y} \geq \frac{\cosh A}{\cosh(A/2)}$ with equality holding precisely when the triangle is equilateral. This proves lemmas 6.3.8 and 6.3.10.

Next use the formula for the double cosine (6.3) to notice that

$$\cosh h_{teq} = \frac{\cosh t}{\cosh(t/2)} = \frac{\cosh^2(t/2) + \sinh^2(t/2)}{\cosh(t/2)} \geq \cosh(t/2). \quad (6.18)$$

This gives lemmas 6.3.12 and lemma 6.3.9 follows from this and lemma 6.3.8. To obtain lemma 6.3.11 from lemma 6.3.10, just write $\cosh h_{teq}$ in exponential form to see that it is a decreasing function of t. To obtain lemma 6.3.13 note that

$$\cosh h_A \geq \frac{\cosh B}{\cosh(A/2)}.$$

Apply the addition formula for hyperbolic cosines to conclude

$$\cosh h_A \geq \frac{\cosh(B - (A/2))\cosh(A/2) + \sinh(B - (A/2))\sinh(A/2)}{\cosh(A/2)}$$

$$\geq \cosh(B - (A/2)).$$

$\square$

Chapter 7

The Poincaré Polygon Theorem and its partial converse; Knapp's theorem and its extension

Usually when one can determine discreteness directly it is because one can apply the Poincaré polygon theorem. The Poincaré polygon theorem says that if one has a finite sided polygon and certain side pairing transformations that satisfy a number of conditions, then one can conclude that the group generated by the side pairings is discrete and that the polygon is a fundamental domain for the group so that its images tile the plane. In the indeterminate case that we will be concerned with one has a polygon, P, with side pairings, but the side pairings do not satisfy all of the hypotheses of the Poincaré polygon theorem. In particular, they fail to satisfy the cycle condition at the vertices. In the neighborhood of a vertex the images of the polygon not just fill up the neighborhoods, but may overlap. In this case there is a theorem due to Knapp [20] which can be thought of as a partial converse to the Poincaré polygon theorem. It says that if the group is discrete there is an integer t, called **the covering number**, such that every point that is not the image of a boundary point is equivalent under the group to exactly t interior points of the polygon and that

$$\text{Area of } P = t \cdot \text{area of a fundamental domain.} \quad (7.1)$$

This can be interpreted as saying that the polygon forms not a *tiling* of the plane, but a *shingling*. *Shingles* are tiles that overlap, and t being finite means that the shingles overlap in a controlled (and understandable) manner. It is often stated that the Knapp count t can be extended to the boundary of the polygon. In our proof that our algorithm actually does what we say it does we will need the full extension of Knapp's theorem. Therefore, we begin this chapter by establishing an extension and end by using our extension to count images of vertices in certain cases that will be of concern.

7.1 Extending the Knapp Count

Let P be a polygon with side pairings and let D be the group generated by the side pairings. Let ∂P denote the boundary of P and assume that $\bar{P}$, the closure of P in $\mathbf{U}$, the upper half-plane, is compact. For $x \in \mathbf{U} - D\partial P$, recall that

$$t(x) = \text{ the number of distinct elements of } G \text{ that map } x \text{ into } P.$$

Definition: 7.1.1 *A point x on the boundary of P has a* **good neighborhood** *if it has a neighborhood whose intersection with $D\partial P$, the image under D of the boundary of P, consists of merely an arc of a side of P. The set of* **good** *points of ∂P is the set of points which have good neighborhoods and is denoted by $\mathcal{G}$.*

Definition: 7.1.2 *The set of* **bad** *points of ∂P is the set of points which do not have good neighborhoods and is denoted by $\mathcal{B}$.*

In [20] it was shown that

Theorem: 7.1.3 *Let P be a finite sided polygon with side pairings.*
Assume that the group generated by the side pairings, D, is discrete. Then

7.2. FACTS AND NOTATION

1. t is constant on $\mathbf{U} - D\partial P$.

2. Area $P = t \cdot$ Area $(\mathbf{U}/D)$ and in fact

3. t is constant $\forall x \in \partial P$ which have **good** neighborhoods.

Here *Area* denotes the non-euclidean area.

We want to extend the definition of the function t to all points on ∂P, particularly to the fixed points of elliptic elements on the boundary of P. These are all contained in the set $\mathcal{B}$. It will turn out that it is easy to obtain a well defined extension of t. However, there is a difference between counting the number of elements of the group that map a given point into a specific set and the number of images of the point in the given set. The difficult part of our task is to relate this extended function to a count of the number of distinct images in $\bar{P}$ of points in ∂P, especially vertices and fixed points of elliptic elements.

Definition: 7.1.4 *If x is a point of the boundary of P, we define $\underline{t}(x) = t(y)$ where y is any point in a neighborhood of x which is not equivalent under D to a boundary point of P.*

Since $t(y)$ is constant for such y, $\underline{t}(x)$ is a well defined extension of t. Our goal in the rest of this chapter is to establish a formula (7.4.2) relating $\underline{t}(x)$ to the number of images of x both interior to P and on the boundary of P when $x \in \partial P$.

7.2 Facts and Notation

Before we count images, we recall the some facts and fix some notation.

Fact: 7.2.1 *By definition (see p. 289 of [20]) if P is a polygon with side pairing, then for every point x within a side S_x there is a sufficiently small disc centered at x, N_x, such that*

$$N_x \subset S_x \cup P \cup L_x^{-1}(P)$$

where L_x is the side pairing transformation that pairs S_x.

When we refer to a **finite sided polygon** P **with sides** $\{S_i\}$, we mean the following. Each side S_i lies on a geodesic $\tilde{S}_i$ which divides **U** into two disjoint half-planes. If we orient S_i, then we can refer to the two half-planes as the **left** and the **right** half-plane of S_i. The polygon, P, is then the intersection of right half-planes determined by its sides.

With this understanding of what is meant by a finite sided polygon, we can see that fact 7.2.1 tells us that

Lemma: 7.2.2 *If P is a polygon with side pairing, then for every point x within a side S_x there is a sufficiently small disc centered at x, N_x, such that S_x separates N_x into two disjoint half-discs, one contained in P and the other contained in $L_x^{-1}(P)$.*

We also recall that D is discrete if and only if it is discontinuous and that

Fact: 7.2.3 *by definition (see p. 94 of [2]), D acts discontinuously on **U** if and only if for every compact subset K of **U**, $g(K) \cap K = \emptyset$ except for a finite number of $g \in D$.*

In particular, take $K = \bar{P}$.

Fact: 7.2.4 *If D is discrete, we have*

- *$\{g \in D | g(\bar{P}) \cap \bar{P} \neq \emptyset\}$ is finite.*

- *for any $x \in \partial P$, $\{g \in D | g(x) \in \bar{P}\}$ is finite.*

- *for any $x \in \partial P$, $\{g \in D | g(x) \in \partial P\}$ is finite.*

- *for any $x \in \partial P$, $\{g \in D | g(x) \in (\bar{P} - \partial P)\}$ is finite.*

Finally set $IntP = \bar{P} - \partial P$. It is also shown in [20] page 291 that

Fact: 7.2.5 *If D is discrete, the number of points in $\bar{P} \cap D(\partial P)$ that are equivalent to bad points is finite.*

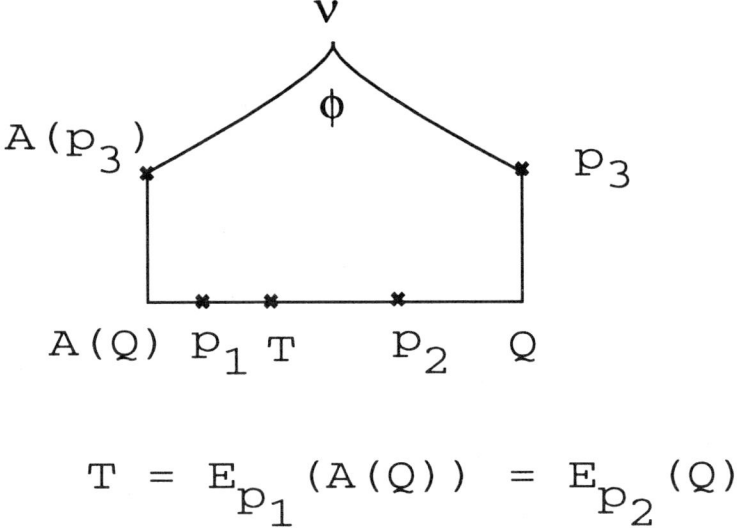

$$T = E_{p_1}(A(Q)) = E_{p_2}(Q)$$

Figure 7.1: The Pentagon $P_{A,B}$ and its eight sides

7.3 Restrict to the case of $P = P_{A,B}$, the pentagon determined by (A, B), $G = \langle A, B \rangle$ discrete

In what follows we want to extend the Knapp count in the case where P is the pentagon $P_{A,B}$ determined by a pair of hyperbolics with intersecting but distinct axes and D the group of side-pairings is the group $G^* = \langle E_{p_1}, E_{p_2}, E_{p_3} \rangle$.

We must be careful because strictly speaking *the pentagon, $P_{A,B}$, is not a pentagon at all*. Geometrically it is a pentagon, but (assuming $P \neq Q$) as a polygon with side pairings it is an eight sided figure with vertices, p_3, $A(p_3)$, v, Q, $A(Q)$ **and** p_1, p_2, and $T = E_{p_2}(Q)$. (See figure 7.1.) We adopt the convention that by a point lying on a side of the polygon, we mean a point on ∂P other than v, p_3, $A(p_3)$, p_1, p_2, Q, T or $A(Q)$. Further, after replacing (A, B) by a Nielsen equivalent pair if necessary, we may assume that p_1 and p_2 actually lie on the segment of the axis of A between Q and $A(Q)$. We assume that p_1 lies between $A(Q)$ and p_2. The argument for the other ordering is the same.

A fixed point of an elliptic element which lies on ∂P may or may not be an element of $\mathcal{B}$ (i.e. a point of order two need not be in $\mathcal{B}$.) Because G (and thus G^*) is discrete, the number of elliptic fixed points on ∂P is finite. All vertices of P are in $\mathcal{B}$ except p_1 and p_2. Thus the set consisting of the bad points of ∂P together with the elliptic fixed points that lie on ∂P is finite and contains all of the vertices. We let $\tilde{\mathcal{B}}$ be the set of all such points. We want to describe the neighborhoods of points in $\tilde{\mathcal{B}}$ in order to produce neighborhoods where we can easily identify the images of other points under the action of G^*.

To this end our first goal is to show that points in this set have neighborhoods whose intersection with $G^*\partial P$ resembles a *spoke*, that is all arcs of $G^*\partial P$ in this neighborhood pass through the fixed point.

We examine neighborhoods of all points of ∂P. If x is any point on a side of P, we can choose N_x, the disc of (7.2.1) small enough so that it contains no points of $\tilde{\mathcal{B}}$ other than possibly x itself and so that $S_x \cap N_x$ disconnects N_x. If x is a vertex where sides $S_{1,x}$ and $S_{2,x}$ intersect, we can choose as a neighborhood a disc centered at x small enough so that it contains no points of $\tilde{\mathcal{B}}$ other than x and so that the union of these two sides disconnects N_x into two components, one contained in P the other disjoint from P.

Definition: 7.3.1 *A disc N centered at a point $x \in \partial P$ is* **spoke-like** *or a* **spoke** *neighborhood if the intersection of $D\partial P$ with N is the union of a finite number of geodesic arcs each passing through x, each of which either intersects the boundary of N at two distinct points or intersects the boundary of N at one point and has x as an end-point. The set of all such geodesic arcs is called the set of* **spokes**.

Note that these geodesic arcs are all disjoint except for their one common point x. The *idea* of what follows is that if x has a spoke-like neighborhood and if y is interior to the neighborhood, but not the image of a boundary point, then *roughly speaking* an element of the group maps y to the interior of P if and only if it maps x to $\bar{P}$ and thus the behavior of x under G^* can be described by the behavior of y under G^*. To be correct we need to modify the statement slightly.

7.3. RESTRICT TO $P = P_{A,B}$.

Proposition: 7.3.2 *Assume that x has a spoke-like neighborhood and that $y \in P$ is in the neighborhood, but not the image of a boundary point. Then*

- *If an element of the group maps y to the interior of P, then it maps x to $\bar{P}$.*

- *If an element of the group maps x interior to $\bar{P}$, then it maps y to the interior of P.*

- *If an element of the group maps y to the complement of $\bar{P}$, then it maps x to the complement of $\bar{P}$ or to ∂P.*

- *If an element of the group fixes x or maps it to any other boundary point, it may or may not map y to the interior of P.*

Proof: Let N_x be a spoke neighborhood of X. The spokes divide N_x in sectors which contain no points of ∂P. Let $\gamma_{x,y}$ be a path connecting x and y lying entirely in the sector of N_x containing y. For $g \in D$, $g(\gamma_{x,y})$ is a path connecting $g(x)$ and $g(y)$. Assume first that $g(y)$ is interior to P, but $g(x)$ is exterior to P. Then $g(\gamma_{x,y})$ must intersect ∂P in a point z other than $g(x)$ or $g(y)$, whence $\gamma_{x,y}$ must intersect ∂P in $g^{-1}(z)$. But $\gamma_{x,y}$ contains no points of ∂P other than x. Thus $g(x) \in \bar{P}$. If $g(x)$ is in $\bar{P}$ with $g(y)$ exterior to $\bar{P}$, then again conclude that γ_{xy} must intersect ∂P in a point other than x to obtain a contradiction unless $g(x) \in \partial P$. If $g(x)$ is interior to $\bar{P}$, then conclude that $g(y)$ must be interior to $\bar{P}$ or on the boundary of $\bar{P}$. Since y in not in the image of the boundary, conclude that $g(y)$ must be interior to $\bar{P}$. $\square$

Thus if a point x has a spoke-like neighborhood, N_x, we can study the images of x under elements of the group and their relationship to P by studying the same thing for any $y \in N_x, y \notin D\partial P$.

We will show

Theorem: 7.3.3 *When $P = P_{A,B}$ and $D = G^*$, every element of the boundary of P has a spoke-like neighborhood.*

Proof: It is easy to see that if x is a good point of ∂P, then the N_x described in 7.2.1 is a spoke neighborhood of x with only one spoke, $arc_x = S_x \cap N_x$.

We want to describe what the intersection of $G^*\partial P$ with the neighborhood of bad point looks like. We treat the two cases separately.

- **Case 1:** x is an element of $\tilde{\mathcal{B}}$, but not a vertex of P.

Assume that x lies on S_x and that L_x is the side pairing transformation. Let N_x be any neighborhood of x chosen to lie in a small enough disc so that $arc_x = S_x \cap N_x$ separates N_x into two disjoint pieces, one contained in P and the other disjoint from P. Then $L_x(N_x)$ is a similar neighborhood of $L_x(x)$ with respect to $S'_x = L_x(S_x)$. We let $I_x = \{g \in G^* \mid g(\partial P) \cap N_x \neq \emptyset\}$.

We show first that I_x is a finite set. Suppose to the contrary that I_x is infinite. Then either there are an infinite number of elements that map ∂P into $\bar{P}$ or an infinite number map into the other component of $N_x - arc_x$. In the latter case, replace each such element g by $(L_x \cdot g)$ to produce an infinite number of elements of G that map ∂P into $L_x(N_x) \cap \bar{P}$. In either case, we have an infinite number of elements of G^* mapping ∂P into $\bar{P}$. This contradicts the fact that G^* is discrete (and thus discontinuous).

Next we show that after replacing N_x by a smaller neighborhood if necessary, we have $g \in I_x$ if and only if $x \in g(\partial P)$. First if $x \in g(\partial P)$, then $g \in I_x$. To prove the converse, recall that P has a finite number of sides. If $g \in I_x$, but $x \notin g(\partial P)$, then the distance from x to the image under g of each side of P is positive and we can replace N_x by a smaller neighborhood of x so that $g(\partial P) \cap N_x = \emptyset$. (I.e. if S is a side of P, then $d(x, \widetilde{g(S)}) > 0$ unless x lies on $\widetilde{g(S)}$. If x lies on $\widetilde{g(S)}$ but not on $g(S)$, then $d(x, g(S)) > 0$.)

If $g \in I_x$, pick z such that $g(z) = x$. Then z has a neighborhood N_z such that either arc_z or the intersection of $S_{1,z} \cup S_{2,z}$ with N_z disconnects N_z. Replacing N_x by the intersection of $g(N_z)$ over all $g \in I_x$, we may assume that $g(arc_z)$ or $g(S_{1,z} \cup S_{2,z}) \cap N_x$ disconnects N_x.

This shows that $G^*(\partial P) \cap N_x$ is a set of spokes going out from x. We have thus shown that N_x is a spoke neighborhood.

- **Case 2:** x is a vertex of P.

We consider the vertices Q, T, $A(Q)$, p_3, $A(p_3)$, p_1, p_2 and v. We let N_Q be a disc centered about Q. We choose N_Q small enough so that

7.3. RESTRICT TO $P = P_{A,B}$.

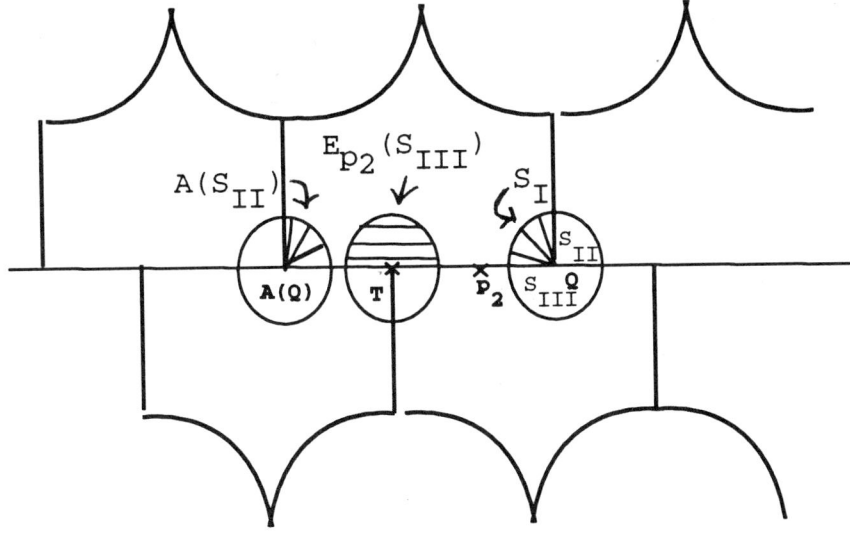

Figure 7.2: Neighborhoods of the vertices, Q, T, and $A(Q)$.

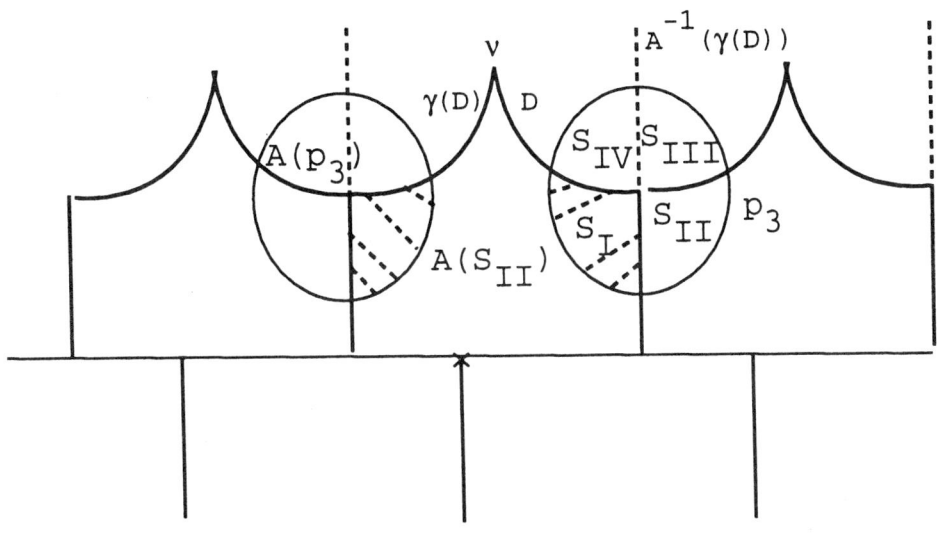

Figure 7.3: Neighborhoods of p_3 and $A(p_3)$.

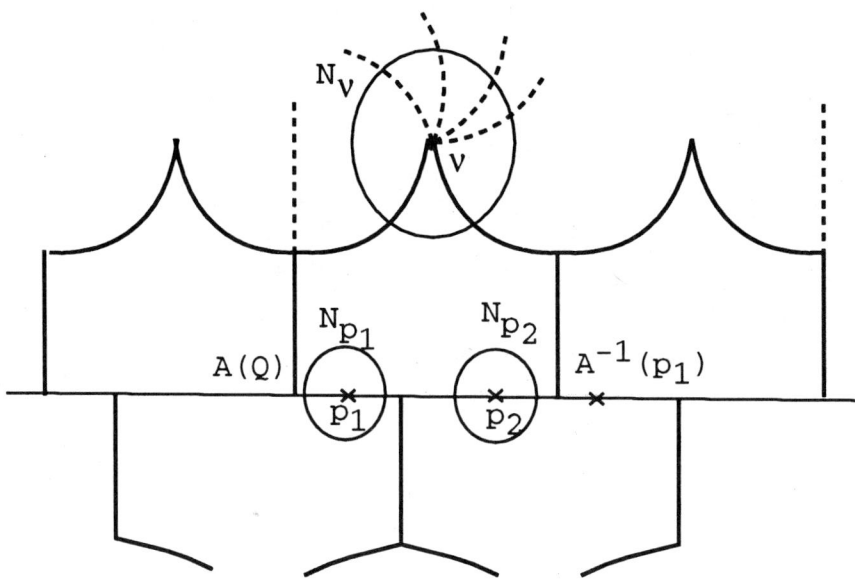

Figure 7.4: Neighborhoods of v and p_1.

h and Ax_A divide N_Q into three sectors. We name sectors as we move counterclockwise about Q so the three sectors are S_I the sector bounded by h and Ax_A moving counterclockwise from h to Ax_A, S_{II} bounded by Ax_A and h, and S_{III} bounded by Ax_A and Ax_A. (See figure7.2.) Further S_I is contained in P as is $A(S_{II})$ and $E_{p_2}(S_{III})$.

We let N_{p_3} be a disc centered at p_3 and notice that $D \cup A^{-1}\gamma(D)$ together with $h \cup E_{p_3}(h)$ divides the disc into four sectors. Naming sectors counterclockwise again, we have S_I the sector bounded by D and h, S_{II}, the sector bounded by h and $A^{-1}(\gamma(D))$, S_{III} the sector bounded by $A^{-1}(\gamma(D))$ and $E_{p_3}(h)$, and S_{IV}, the sector bounded by $E_{p_3}(h)$ and D. (See figure 7.3.) Note that S_I is in P as are $A(S_{II})$, $E_{p_3}(S_{III})$ and $A(E_{p_3}(S_{IV}))$. Finally, v has a neighborhood N_v such that $\{\gamma^q(D)\}$ divides N_v into sectors each one of which is mapped into P by an appropriate power of γ. Pick a neighborhood N_{p_1} of p_1 small enough so that it does not contain T, $A(Q)$ or Q and with $E_{p_1}(N_{p_1}) = N_{p_1}$ and a similar neighborhood of p_2. (See figure 7.4.)

Using these neighborhoods, argue as before that I_v, I_Q and I_{p_3} are all finite sets. Proceed as in the case of non-vertex points of $\tilde{\mathcal{B}}$ to produce a spoke neighborhood. Since A maps Q to $A(Q)$ and p_3 to

$A(p_3)$ it maps spoke neighborhoods to Q and p_3 to spoke neighborhoods of $A(Q)$ and $A(p_3)$. Also, E_{p_1} maps a spoke neighborhood of Q to a spoke neighborhood of T.

Note that for each x the spoke neighborhood constructed is invariant under $(G^*)_x$. Finally, note that it may happen that $Q = p_2$ or p_1. In that case, first of all, after replacing (A, B) by $A' = E_{p_1} E_{p_2} E_{p_1}$ and $B' = E_{p_3} E_{p_1}$ if necessary, we may assume that $Q = p_2$. In that case, N_Q consists of the region between Ax_A and h, which lies in P, the counterclockwise region between h and Ax_A whose image under A lies in P, and E_{p_2} of each of these regions. $\square$

Remark: 7.3.4 *The neighborhoods pictured in figures 7.2, 7.3, and 7.4 are spoke neighborhoods, but the full set of spokes does not necessarily appear in the figures. The full set of spokes depends upon what other boundary points are mapped into the given vertex and the order of the vertex.*

7.4 Counting the images of vertices

We can now use the spoke neighborhoods to count the images of bad points. First we set some more notation.

Definition: 7.4.1 We define δ_{ab}: *If a and b are any two distinct points on ∂P, let $\delta_{ab} = 1$ if there is an element of the group G^* identifying a with b and let $\delta_{ab} = 0$ otherwise.*

Note that if a is a fixed point of order n and b is a fixed point whose order is divisible two, then $\delta_{ab} = 0$ when n is odd because the stabilizers of a and b must have the same order. If x is any point in **U**, let $o(x)$ denote its order if x is fixed by an elliptic element and let $o(x) = 1$ otherwise.

Theorem: 7.4.2 *Let x be any point on ∂P. Let $o(v) = n$ and let γ rotate by $k2\pi/n$. Then*

$$\underline{t}(x) = k \cdot \delta_{xv} + o(x) \cdot \frac{\text{\# of images of } x \text{ on a side of } \partial P}{2} +$$

$o(x) \cdot \#$ of images of x interior to $P + o(x) \cdot (\delta_{xQ}) +$

$$o(x)/2 \cdot (\delta_{xp_1} + \delta_{xp_2} + \delta_{xp_3}).$$

Proof: Let N_x be a spoke neighborhood of x. After replacing N_x by a smaller neighborhood if necessary, since the number of elements of G^* that map x into $\bar{P}$ is finite, we may assume that if $g(x)$ is in the interior of $\bar{P}$, then so is $g(N_x)$. Let y be any point interior to P not lying on any spoke in a spoke neighborhood of x and assume that $m = o(x)$. We want to count the number of elements $g \in G^*$ that map y into P. Because y is not fixed by any element of G^* this is the same as counting the number of distinct images of y interior to P. We know that an element that maps y interior to P either maps x interior to P or x to a point on ∂P. We let h_x be a primitive rotation in the stabilizer of x. If g maps both x and y to the interior of P, then $g \circ h_x^q$ also maps x to the interior of P for $q = 1,...,m$ and no other elements of G^* send x to the same image. Since by construction the spoke neighborhood satisfies $h_x(N_x) = N_x$, y has m distinct images interior to P for each distinct interior image of x.

Next we want to understand the images of x on the boundary of P and the images of y under elements of I_x. Note that not every element of I_x maps y interior to P.

The images of x on sides of P fall into pairs for if z is an image of x that is not a vertex, then $L_z(z) = z'$ is also. Thus if there are $2r$ images of x on sides of P, we label them $z_1,...,z_r; z'_1,...,z'_r$ where $L_{z_i}(z_i) = z'_i$. Pick $g_1,...,g_r$ elements of G^* with $g_i(x) = z_i$. For y in N_x we want to count the number of elements of I_x that map y into P. First by our construction of the spoke neighborhoods, $N_{g(x)} = g(N_x)$ and each $N_{g(x)}$ is a neighborhood of $g(x)$ satisfying 7.2.2.

We claim that the number of g mapping y into P and x into one of the z_i is equal to $o(x) \cdot r$. If $g(y) \in (N_{z_i} \cap P)$ then $L_{z_i}(g(y)) \notin (L_{z_i}(N_{z_i}) \cap P)$. Conversely, if $g'(y) \in (L_{z_i}(N_{z_i}) \cap P)$, then $L_{z_i}^{-1}(g'(y)) \in N_{z_i}$ but not in P. Thus for each z, $\#g$ mapping x into z or x into z' and y into $(N_z \cap P) \cup (N_{z'} \cap P)$ equals $\#g$ mapping x to z and y to N_z. This number is merely $o(x)$.

If x is not equivalent to any vertex, we have our entire count. If x is equivalent to a vertex or actually is a vertex, we count as follows:

7.4. COUNTING THE IMAGES OF VERTICES

Assume that $\delta_{xv} = 1$. Let $g(x) = v$ and $g(N_x) = N_v$ (g may be the identity). If h_x is the primitive rotation for x, then $gh_xg^{-1} = h_v$ is the primitive rotation for v so that if γ rotates by $k2\pi/n$, $\gamma = h_v^k$ and for any point w in N_v, there are precisely k images of w in $N_v \cap P$. Now if g' sends x to v, then g' sends y to N_v, so that for some q, $h_v^q g'$ sends x to v and y into $P \cap N_v$ and there are precisely $k-1$ other elements of G^* that do this. Thus if v is in the image of x the number of elements of the group that map x to v and y to the interior of P is k.

Assume that $\delta_{xQ} = 1$. We claim that the number of elements that map x to Q and y into N_Q is equal to the number of elements that map x to Q and y into P plus the number of elements that map x to T and y into P plus the number of elements that map x to $A(Q)$ and y into P. To see this note that $N_Q = S_I \cup S_{II} \cup S_{III}$ and that if $g(x) = A(Q)$ and $g(y) \in P$, then $g(y) \in A(S_{II})$, so that $A^{-1}g(y) \in S_{II}$ and $A^{-1}g(x) = Q$. A similar statement holds for S_{III} and E_{p_1}. Argue as before that the number of images of y in N_Q is precisely $o(x)$. Thus the contribution here to $\underline{t}(x)$ here is $\delta_{xQ} \cdot o(x)$. Note that usually one expects $o(Q)$ to be one so that in these cases $o(x) = 1$.

If $\delta_{xp_i} = 1$ for $i = 1$ or $i = 2$, we count as follows: An element $g \in G^*$ that maps x to p_i maps N_x to N_{p_i}. If it maps y to $N_{p_i} \cap P$, then $E_{p_i}g(y) \notin P$ but $E_{p_i}g(x) = p_i$. Conversely, if it maps y to N_{p_i} but not in P, then $E_{p_i}g(y) \in P$ and $E_{p_i}g(x) = p_i$. Again, if $y \in N_x$ the number of images of y in $N_{p_i} = N_{g(x)}$ is $o(x)$. Half of these lie in P and half outside of P. Thus the contribution to the count here will be $o(x)/2$.

Finally, if $g(x) = p_3$, then $g(y)$ is in one of the four sectors. It is in S_{II} if and only if $A(g(y))$ is in P and $A(g(x)) = A(p_3)$. Also if $g(x) = p_3$, then $g(y) \in S_{III}$ if and only if $E_{p_3}(g(y)) \in P$ and $g(y) \in S_{IV}$ if and only if $A(E_{p_3}(g(y))) \in P$. Thus we again obtain a contribution of $o(x)/2$ to the count. □

We obtain several immediate corollaries.

Corollary: 7.4.3 *Let v be* **the vertex** *of the pentagon.*

- *If $o(v)$ is odd, $\underline{t}(v) - k$ is congruent to 0 modulo $o(v)$.*

- *If $o(v)$ is even, $\underline{t}(v) - k$ is congruent to 0 modulo $o(v)/2$.*

Another corollary is

Corollary: 7.4.4 *If $(t,k) = (2,2)$ or $(3,3)$, then the only image of v in $\bar{P}$ is v itself.*

For reasons which will become clear later, we will be interested in the case where G is a $(2,3,7)$ triangle group. In this case, if v is a point of order 7, it cannot be equivalent to p_3 since that would force it to be a point of order 14 at least. We can conclude that

Corollary: 7.4.5 *If $t = 9$ and $k = 2$ and v is a point of order 7, then either v has one image interior to P and no images on the boundary other than v itself or v has two images on sides of P and no images either interior to P or at other vertices of P or the points in the image of v are precisely Q, T and $A(Q)$.*

Part III

Geometric Equivalence and the Discreteness Theorem

Chapter 8

Constructing the standard acute triangles and standard generators

We have seen (chapter 7 and appendix A) that there are three different possibilities for a pair of hyperbolics with intersecting but distinct axis and non-primitive elliptic commutator that generate a discrete group. Namely if the group is discrete it is either a $(2,3,n)$ triangle group with $t = k = 3$, a $(2,4,n)$ triangle group with $t = k = 2$ or a $(2,3,7)$ triangle group with $t = 9, k = 3$. For each of these three cases we construct an acute triangle which we call the **standard acute triangle**. The standard acute triangle also is associated to a fixed pair of **standard generators**. We will want to keep track of the relationship between the pair of generators and the standard acute triangle. Again our aim will be to clarify and codify the relationship between the algebraic notation and the geometric picture.

The constructions basically follow a construction due to Purzitsky (see [31]), but they extend his construction to more cases and clarify it. Also we tie the geometry of this standard acute triangle to that of the corresponding standard pentagon and establish some distance lemmas which will be essential in proving the Nielsen equivalence theorems (chapters 9, 10 and 12).

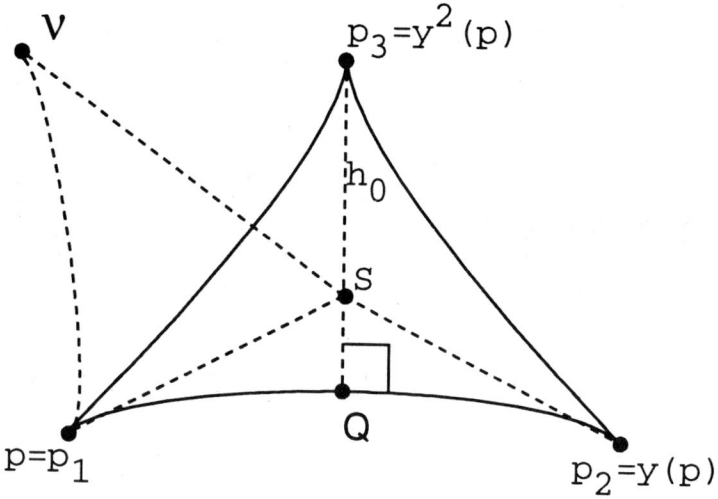

Figure 8.1: Standard equilateral triangle for $(2, 3, n)$, $t = 3$, $k = 3$.

8.1 The standard acute triangle for the $(2, 3, n)$ triangle group with $t = 3$ and $k = 3$

Let G be a $(2, 3, n)$-triangle group and assume that n is relatively prime to 3. Then G has the presentation

$$\langle\, x, y, z \mid x^2 = y^3 = z^n = xyz = 1 \,\rangle.$$

Let p, S and v be the respective fixed points of x, y and z.

Define p_1, p_2, and p_3 by $p_1 = p$, $p_2 = y(p)$ and $p_3 = y^2(p)$ Also set $\bar{p}_2 = E_p(p_2)$ and $\bar{p}_3 = E_p(p_3)$. Compute that $E_{p_1} E_{p_2} E_{p_3} = (xy)^3 = E_{\bar{p}_2} E_{p_1} E_{p_3}$. Let $\gamma = E_{p_1} E_{p_2} E_{p_3}$. Then $\gamma(v) = v$. Since z is a counterclockwise rotation about its fixed points, $xy = z^{-1}$ is a clockwise rotation about v.

Definition: 8.1.1 *We define Stact, the* **standard acute triangle**

8.1. STACT: $(2, 3, N) T = 3, K = 3$

determined by x and y, to be the equilateral triangle $\triangle(p, y(p), y^2(p))$ (figure 8.1).

It is easy to see that

Lemma: 8.1.2 $\triangle(p, y(p), y^2(p))$ *is an equilateral triangle whose height passes through S. If T denotes the side of this triangle, then $T_d = D_0(2, 2)$.*

Proof: In the notation of chapter 4, since p, S and v are the vertices of a $(2, 3, n)$ triangle, we have $d(p, S) = D_0(2, 3)$, $d(p, v) = D_0(2, n)$ and $d(S, v) = D_0(3, 7)$ (Lemma 4.2.1). In other words, the tile at v, T_v, is precisely $\triangle(p, S, v) \cup R_{Sv}(\triangle(p, S, v))$ and $T = d(p, R_{Sv}(p))$. Use the hyperbolic law of cosines to conclude that $\cosh T = \cosh^2 D_0(2, 3) - \sinh^2 D_0(2, 3) \cdot \cos(2\pi/3)$. Use proposition 4.4.1 to conclude that T is precisely $D_0(2, 2)$. Since y rotates the sides of $\triangle(p, y(p), y^2(p))$ into each other, this is clearly an equilateral triangle and the height from each vertex to the opposite side passes through S. (Namely, if Q is the point where the height intersects the opposite side, the height divides the triangle into two right triangles with the same hypotenuse and one common leg. Using the hyperbolic law of cosine for right triangles, the third sides must be equal so that the point Q bisects the base. S must be on the height for otherwise it could not be equidistant from the vertices of the base.) $\square$

Set $T_0 = D_0(2, 2)$. Since we will need this fact later, let h_0 denote the length of the height of $\triangle(p, y(p), y^2(p))$ to any of its sides. Then we know by lemma 6.3.9 that $h_0 \geq T_0/2$. We can compute h_0 more precisely.

Lemma: 8.1.3 *Let L be a hyperbolic segment whose length satisfies $\cosh L = \cosh D_0(2, 3)/\cosh((T/2))$. Then $h_0 = D_0(3, n) + L$.*

Proof: Since Q is the point where h intersects the side $[p, y(p)]$, then $\triangle(p, Q, S)$ is a right triangle so that $\cosh[Q, S] = \cosh[S, p]/\cosh[p, Q]$. But $[p, S]_d = D_0(2, 3)$, $2[p, Q] = T$, and $h_d = [y^2(p), S]_d + [S, Q]_d$. (See figure 8.1.) $\square$

Recall that $R_v^{-1} = xy$.

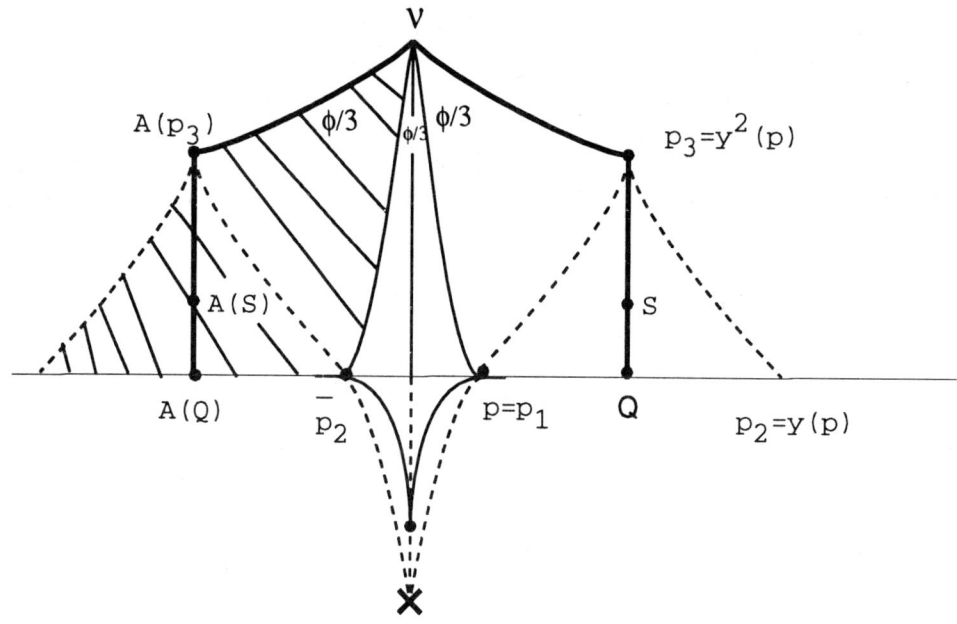

Figure 8.2: The extended tiles containing $P_{A,B}$

Let $A = E_{p_1}E_{p_2} = E_p E_{y(p)}$ and $B = E_{p_3}E_{p_2} = E_{y^2(p)}E_{y(p)}$. Then we will show that the figure with vertices $v, p_3, Q, A(Q)$, and $A(p_3)$ is precisely the pentagon determined by A and B.

Theorem: 8.1.4
- The pentagon with vertices v, p_3, Q, $A(Q)$, and $A(p_3) = R_v^{-3}(p_3)$ is the pentagon $P_{A,B}$.

- $P_{A,B}$ contains no fixed points of the group in its interior.

- The fixed points on the boundary are p_3, $R_v^{-1}(p_3) = p$, $R_v^{-2}(p_3) = \bar{p}_2$, $R_v^{-3}(p_3) = A(p_3)$, S and $A(S) = R_v^{-2}(S)$ and v.

Proof: By construction $P_{A,B}$ has vertex v and fixed points p_3, $p = p_1$, $\bar{p}_2 = E_{p_1}(y(p))$ and $A(p_3)$ on its boundary.

8.1. STACT: $(2,3,N)T=3, K=3$

Extending definition 4.6.1 to an arbitrary $(2,3,n)$ triangle group, we consider the extended tile at v, $ET_v = T_v \cup \triangle(p,S,y(p)) \cup \triangle(y(p),S,y^2(p))$ and its two images under R_v^{-1} (figure 8.2).
Let $\bar{S} = R_v^{-1}(S)$. We compute the following:

- $R_v^{-1}(p_3) = xy(p_3) = xy(y^2(p)) = x(p) = p = p_1$.

- $R_v^{-1}(p) = xy(p) = x(y(p)) = E_p(y(p)) = \bar{p}_2$.

- $A(p_3) = R_v^{-1}(\bar{p}_2)$ because $(xy)^3(p_3) = A(p_3) = E_{p_1}E_{p_2}(p_3)$, but $(xy)^3(p_3) = R_v^{-3}(p_3) = R_v^{-2}(R_v^{-1}(p_3)) = R_v^{-2}(p) = R_v^{-1}(R_v^{-1}(p)) = R_v^{-1}(\bar{p}_2)$.

- $R_v^{-1}(\bar{S}) = xyx(S) = xyxy^{-1}(S) = A(S)$ since $A = E_{p_1}E_{p_2} = E_{\bar{p}_2}E_{\bar{p}_1} = (xyxy^{-1}x) \cdot (x)$.

We want to claim that $R_v^{-1}(ET_v)$ has vertices v, p, $\bar{p}_3$ and $\bar{p}_2$ and contains $\bar{S}$, that $R_v^{-2}(ET_v)$ has vertices v, $\bar{p}_2$, $E_{\bar{p}_2}(p)$, $A(p_3)$ and contains $A(S)$ and that $A(Q) \in R_v^{-2}(ET_v)$. We verify these claims shortly. From them one can conclude that $P_{A,B}$ is contained in $ET_v \cup R_v^{-1}(ET_v) \cup R_v^{-2}(ET_v)$.

There are no fixed points of the group interior to T_v (4.1.6), and thus since $\triangle(p,S,y(p))$ is the image of $\triangle(p,S,y^2(p))$ which is contained in T_v, there are no fixed points interior to ET_v other than S and thus no fixed points interior to $ET_v \cup R_v^{-1}(ET_v) \cup R_v^{-2}(ET_v)$ other than S, $R_v^{-1}(S)$ and $R_v^{-2}(S)$.

The other fixed points of the group that lie on the boundary of the union of these three extended tiles are v, p_3, p, $y(p)$, $\bar{p}_2$, $\bar{p}_3$, $E_{\bar{p}_2}(p)$ and $R_v^{-3}(p_3)$. Both $R_v^{-1}(S)$ and $R_v^{-1}(p_3)$ lie below Ax_A and thus exterior to $P_{A,B}$. $E_{\bar{p}_2}(p)$ lies to the left of $[A(p_3), A(Q)]$ and $y(p)$ lies to the right of $[p_3, Q]$. All of the other points lie on the boundary of $P_{A,B}$. This proves the theorem once we verify the claims.

Since $R_v^{-1} = xy$, $E_p(S) = R_v^{-1}(S) = \bar{S}$. Now E_p maps the three points of order two closest to S to the three of order two points closest to $\bar{S}$ and points above the axis of A to points below the axis of A. Also R_v^{-1} maps the three points of order two closest to S to the three points of order two closest to $\bar{S}$. Thus is must be that $R_v^{-1}(\{p_3, y(p), p\}) = \{p, E_p(p_3), E_p(y(p))\}$. Since $R_v^{-1}(p_3) = p$ and $R_v^{-1}(p) = \bar{p}_2$, we have

$R_v^{-1}(y(p)) = \bar{p}_3$. Now $E_{\bar{p}_2}$ maps $\bar{S}$ to $A(S)$ since $\bar{S} = E_{p_1}(S)$ and thus it maps the three fixed points of order two closest to $\bar{S}$ to the three fixed points of order two closet to $A(S)$. Since $R_v^{-1}(\bar{S}) = A(S)$, the set of three fixed points of order two closest to $\bar{S}$ has the same image under R_v^{-1} as under $E_{\bar{p}_2}$. Since $R_v^{-1}(p) = \bar{p}_2$ and $R_v^{-1}(\bar{p}_2) = A(p_3)$, we must have $R_v^{-1}(\bar{p}_3) = E_{\bar{p}_2}(p)$. Since the segment $[E_{\bar{p}_2}(p), \bar{p}_2]$ is in $R_v^{-2}(ET_v)$ and $A(Q)$ lies on this segment, it lies in $R_v^{-2}(ET_v)$. $\square$

8.2 The standard acute triangle for the $(2, 4, n)$ triangle group with $t = 2$ and $k = 2$

Let G be a $(2, 4, n)$-triangle group. Then we may assume that

$$G = \langle\, x, y, z \mid x^2 = y^4 = z^n = xyz = 1 \,\rangle.$$

Recall that triangles are named **counterclockwise** so that as we move counterclockwise around $\triangle(p, S, v)$ we encounter p S and v in that order. Also x and y are counterclockwise rotations about their fixed points so that $z^{-1} = xy$ is a clockwise rotation about v.

Let p, S and v be the respective fixed points of x, y and z. Define p_1, p_2 and p_3 by $p_1 = p$, $p_2 = S$, and $p_3 = y^3(p)$. Note that $y^2 = E_{p_2}$ and $E_{p_3} = E_{y^3(p)} = y^3 E_p y^{-3} = y^3 x y^{-3}$. Compute that $E_{p_1} E_{p_2} E_{p_3} = xy^2 y^3 xy^{-3} = xyxy = (xy)^2 = z^{-2}$. Let $\gamma = E_{p_1} E_{p_2} E_{p_3}$. Then $\gamma(v) = v$ and γ is a clockwise rotation about v through an angle of $2 \cdot 2\pi/n$.

Definition: 8.2.1 *We define Stact, the standard acute triangle determined by x and y, to be the right isosceles triangle $\triangle(p, S, y^3(p))$ (figure 8.3).*

Note that $p_3 = y^3(p) = R_v(p)$. Here R_v is the *counterclockwise* rotation. Since $\triangle(v, p, S)$ contains no fixed points of the group other than v, p and S, the quadrilateral with vertices p, S, p_3 and v contains no fixed points of the group in its interior and only those four fixed points on its boundary.

8.3. STACT: $(2,3,7)T = 9; K = 2$

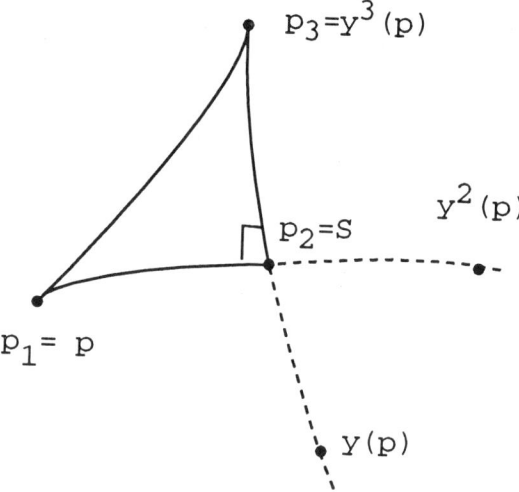

Figure 8.3: Standard right triangle for $(2,4,n)$, $t = 2$, $k = 2$.

Note that $R_v^{-1}([v, p_3]) = [v, p]$. Since $R_v^{-1}(S) = E_p(S) = E_p E_S(S)$, $[E_p(S), p, S]$ is a geodesic and $[p_3, S]$ is perpendicular to this geodesic. If $p' = R_v^{-1}(p)$, then $[p', E_p(S)]$ is also perpendicular to this geodesic. Thus the figure with vertices v, p_3, S, $E_p(S)$ and p' is a pentagon and is precisely the pentagon determined by A, B if $A = E_p E_S$ and $B = E_{p_3} E_S$ (figure 8.4). We have seen

Theorem: 8.2.2

- *The pentagon with vertices v, p_3, S, $E_p(S) = A(S)$, and p' is the pentagon $P_{A,B}$.*

- *$P_{A,B}$ contains no fixed points of the group in its interior.*

- *The fixed points on the boundary are v, p_3, S, p, $A(S)$, and p'.*

8.3 The standard acute triangle for the $(2, 3, 7)$ triangle group with $t = 9$ and $k = 2$

If G is a $(2, 3, 7)$ triangle group, then roughly speaking, the three fixed points of order two that generate G are obtained by taking any fixed

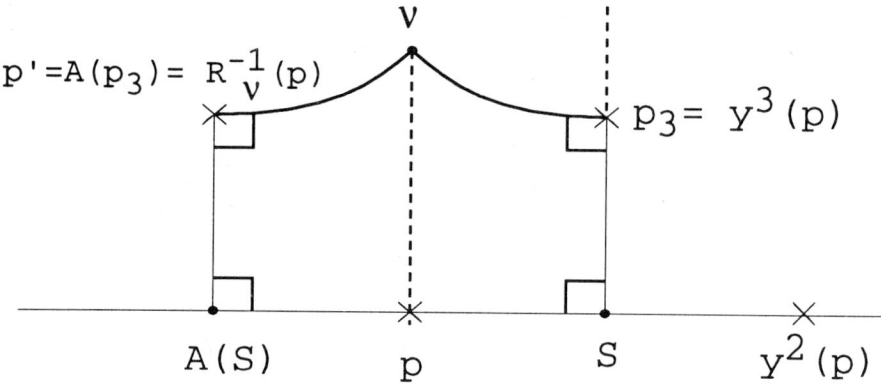

Figure 8.4: The standard pentagon, $(2, 4, n)$

point, $\underline{v}$ of order seven, any point of order two that is *closest* to $\underline{v}$ along with its image under the rotation of order seven and the fourth power of its image under the rotation. To be more precise:

Let G be a $(2, 3, 7)$-triangle group. Then G has the presentation

$$\langle\, x, y, z \mid x^2 = y^3 = z^7 = xyz = 1 \,\rangle.$$

Let p, S and v be the respective fixed points of x, y and z. Let $\delta = yx$. Let p_1, p_2, and p_3 be the vertices of the equilateral standard triangle constructed in 8.1 so that $\gamma = E_{p_1} E_{p_2} E_{p_3} = (xy)^3$.

Since $x \cdot \delta \cdot x = (xy)$, δ is a clockwise rotation about its fixed point, which is $x(v) = \underline{v}$. Define q_1, q_2, and q_3 by

$$q_1 = \delta^{-2}(p_2),\, q_2 = \delta^{-3}(p_2),\, \text{ and } q_3 = \delta(p_2).$$

Calculate that

$$E_{q_1} = \delta^{-2} x \delta^2,\, E_{q_2} = \delta^{-3} x \delta^3,\, \text{ and } E_{q_3} = \delta x \delta^{-1}.$$

Compute that

$$E_{p_3} E_{p_2} E_{p_1} = \delta x \delta^{-1} \delta^{-3} x \delta^3 \delta^{-2} x \delta^2.$$

8.3. STACT: $(2,3,7)T = 9; K = 2$

Compute that

$$E_{q_1}E_{q_2}E_{q_3} = (yx)^{-2}\cdot x\cdot (yx)^2\cdot (yx)^{-3}\cdot x\cdot (yx)^3\cdot yxy^{-1}$$

$$= xy^{-1}xy^{-1}x\cdot yxyxxy^{-1}\cdot xyxyxyxyxy^{-1}$$

$$= xy^{-1}(xy)(xy)(xy)(xy)(xy)xy^{-1} = xy^{-1}(xy)^6\cdot y^{-1}x\cdot xy^{-1}$$

$$= xy^{-1}(xy)^6 y^{-2} = xy^{-1}y^{-1}xy = (xy)^2.$$

But this is a rotation by $2\cdot 2\pi/7$ which fixes v. We define the following transformations

$$C = E_{q_1}E_{q_2},\ D = E_{q_3}E_{q_2},\ C' = E_{\tilde{q}_1}E_{\tilde{q}_2},\ \text{and}\ D' = E_{\tilde{q}_3}E_{\tilde{q}_2}$$

where $\tilde{q}_2 = q_1$, $\tilde{q}_1 = \tilde{E}_{q_1}(\tilde{q}_2)$, and $\tilde{q}_3 = q_3$.

Then (C, D) and (C', D') both give generators for the case $(2, 3, 7)$, $t = 9, k = 2$ with (C', D') corresponding to the triangle before the acute triangle.

Lemma: 8.3.1 Let $A = xyxy^2$, $B = y^2xy^2y^2$, $C = xyxy^2xy^2$ and $D = y^2xyxy^2xyxyx$. Then $\operatorname{tr} A = \operatorname{tr} B = \operatorname{tr} C$.

Proof: $A = E_{p_1}E_{p_2}$ and $B = E_{p_3}E_{p_2}$ Since A and B are the sides of an equilateral triangle, their traces are equal. We compute that $\delta^{-3}A^{-1}\delta^3 = C$. Namely $(yx)^{-3}yxy^2x(yx)^3 = xy^{-1}(xy)^4x = xy^2(xy)^{-3}x = xy^2y^{-1}xy^{-1}xy^{-1}xx = xyxy^2xy^2 = C$. □

We could define the standard acute triangle to be the triangle with vertices q_1, q_2 and q_3. However, this is cumbersome. We will instead take the image of this triangle under x and replace R_v by $R_v = xR_vx$. Namely if $t_1 = x(q_1)$, $t_2 = x(q_2)$, and $t_3 = x(q_3)$, then compute that $R_v(t_1) = t_2$ and $R_v^4(t_1) = t_3$. Finally, recall that $R_v = z$ and set $p = t_1$ and define $Stact_9$ as follows:

Definition: 8.3.2 *We define the* **standard acute geometric triangle determined by** x, *and* z *to be the isosceles triangle* $\triangle(p, z(p), z^3(p))$.

CHAPTER 8. THE STANDARD ACUTE TRIANGLES

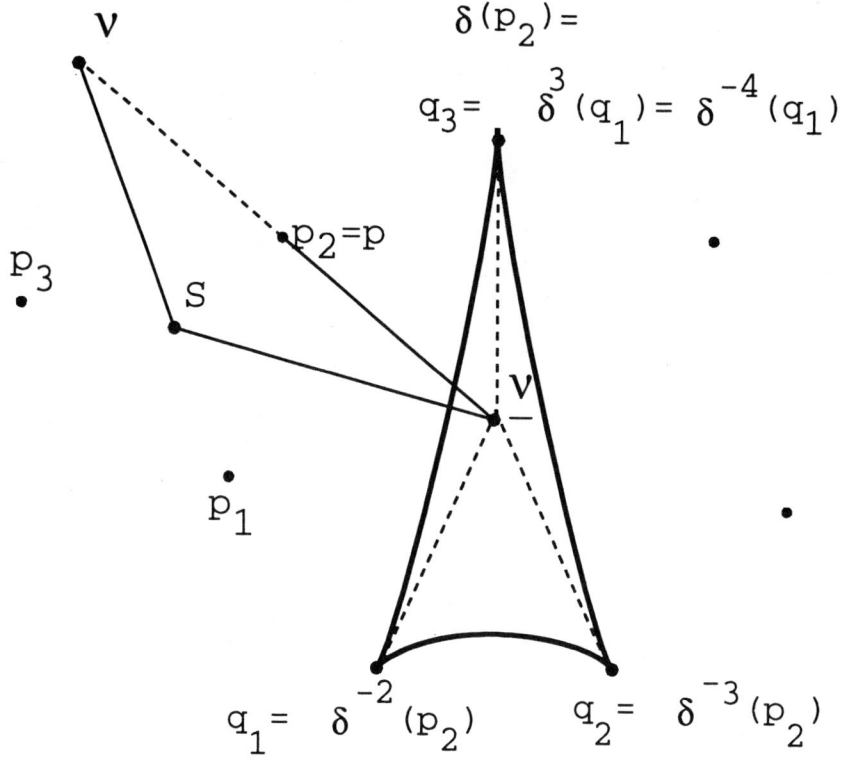

Figure 8.5: (An image of) the standard isosceles triangle for $(2, 3, 7)$, $t = 9$, $k = 2$.

While the construction of the pentagon corresponding to this triangle is straightforward, the location of interior and boundary fixed points of the group is much more complicated in this case because of the difference in the extended Knapp count (7.4.4). Therefore, it merits an entire chapter of its own (chapter 11).

8.4 Distances in the standard $(2, 3, n)$ $k = 3$, $t = 3$ pentagon

We compute distances in the standard pentagon for the $(2, 3, n)$ $t = 3$, $k = 3$. The other two cases are handled in subsequent chapters.

We let P be the pentagon constructed for the standard acute $(2, 3, n)$ triangle when $k = 3$ and $t = 3$. We consider $P_3 = P \cup A(P) \cup A^{-1}(P)$.

Lemma: 8.4.1 *Let x be any point not in P_3 above $\mathcal{D}$. Assume that q is a fixed point of the group of order two lying below $\mathcal{D}$ and that τ is a geodesic connecting q to x crossing either D or $D' = \gamma(D)$. Then $\tau_d \geq$ the minimum of $\{h_0, D_0(2, n), T_0\}$.*

Proof: We assume that τ crosses D, the proof for D' is essentially the same. If τ exits P, it either crosses $A(h)$, H, D' or β.

If it crosses β, $\tau_d \geq h_0$ because h is a common perpendicular to D and Ax_A. If it crosses $A(h)$, it also crosses H so that then $\tau_d \geq T_0$ because Ax_A is perpendicular to H and h and $d(H, h) = T_0$. If τ crosses h, then either it goes to $A^{-1}(p_1)$, $A^{-1}(p_2)$ or $A^{-1}(p_3)$ or it exits $A^{-1}(P)$. In the first three cases its length is either at least h_0 or at least T_0. In the latter case, it can exit $A^{-1}(P)$ across β in which case $\tau_d \geq h_0$ or across $A^{-1}(h)$ in which case $\tau_d \geq 2T_0$ or across $A^{-1}(D)$ in which case $\tau_d \geq T_0$ or across $A^{-1}(D')$. However, D and $A^{-1}(D')$ both lie on one geodesic since $A^{-1}(D') = E_{p_3}(D)$. Since τ cannot cross the same geodesic twice, this cannot happen. If τ exists P at D', since it eventually must return below $\mathcal{D}$, it must enter some image of P say $g(P)$ for some $g \in G$ and must exit $g(P)$ along a side other than $g(D')$, whence $(\tau \cap d(P))_d$ has the possible lengths already discussed for τ_d when τ does not cross D'. □

Corollary: 8.4.2 *Let q be any fixed point of order two. Then $d(p_1, q) > T_0$ unless $q = y(p), y^2(p), \bar{p}_2 = E_p(y(p))$, or $E_p(p_3)$.*

Proof: Recall $p = p_1$. Since $\triangle(p, y(p), y^2(p))$ is an equilateral triangle $d(y(p), p) = d(p, y^2(p))$ and we have seen that this distance is T_0. Since $E_p(p) = p$, the two other distances are also T_0.

Suppose now that q lies above the fundamental tiling strip. Let τ be a geodesic connecting q to p_1 and let x be the point where it crosses $\mathcal{D}$. Then $d(q, p_1) \geq d(x, p_1) + d(x, q)$. Now if x is not in P but in some image of P, the distance from x to p_1 is at least the distance from x to the image of p_1 in that image of P where x lies (proposition 5.6.3). Therefore, we may assume that x lies on D or D'. We want to estimate $d(x, q)$. For simplicity we assume x lies on a D' side. The argument if x is on a D side is essentially the same. If τ stays inside $R_v^{-2}(P)$ or exits $R_v^{-2}(P)$ on an image of an h or β side, apply the lemma to see that $d(x, q) \geq \min\{h_0, D_0(2, n), T_0\}$. Thus we only need to worry about the case that τ exists $R_v^{-2}(P)$ on the image of the D' side. However, if this happens, we again apply the procedure to $R_v^{-4}(P)$. We cannot be stuck in a D' loop more than a finite number of times.

Whence
$$\tau_d \geq h_0 + \min\{T_0, h_0, D_0\}.$$

Since $h_0 > T_0/2$ and $D_0 > T_0$, $d(q, p_1) > T_0$. The case that q lies below the fundamental tiling strip is handled similarly.

If q lies in the fundamental tiling strip, but on or to the left of $A(h)$ or to the right of $A^{-1}(H)$, then $d(q, p_1) > 3T_0/2$.

We have covered all of the possibilities. □

These distance formulae will be used in chapter 9 to prove the Nielsen equivalence theorem for the $(2, 3, n)$ $t = 3$ $k = 3$ case.

The distances in the $(2, 4, n)$ pentagon are much easier to compute and these computations are done in chapter 10 where the $(2, 4, n)$ Nielsen equivalence is proved.

Chapter 9

Generators and Nielsen equivalence for the $(2,3,n)$ $t=3$ $k=3$ case.

9.1 Introduction

We have constructed a standard set of generators for the $(2,3,n)$ triangle group when $k=3$, namely those coming from $E_p, E_{y(p)}$, and $E_{y^2(p)}$.

The purpose of this section is to show

Theorem: 9.1.1 *If (t_1, t_2, t_3) is any other triple of points that generate a $(2,3,n)$ triangle group with $k=3$ and $t=3$ and determine an acute triangle, then there is an element of the group that maps the triple to $(p, y(p), y^2(p))$.*

As an immediate corollary we obtain

Theorem: 9.1.2 *If (A, B) and (C, D) are two pairs of hyperbolic generators for the $(2,3,n)$ triangle group with elliptic commutator where $k=3$, then $tr[A,B] = tr[C,D]$ if and only if (A,B) is Nielsen equivalent to (C,D).*

The proof proceeds by considering all possible triples of fixed points of order two and ruling out almost all of them. We build upon the notation of chapters 4 and 8.

9.2 Types of triples: distances

Let t_1, t_2, and t_3 be any three other points of order two in the tiling that generate G with $E_{t_1} E_{t_2} E_{t_3}$ a rotation by an angle of $3 \cdot 2\pi/n$. There are two ways that t_i can be a fixed point of order two. It could be an image of p or n could be even and it could be an image of v and fixed by a conjugate of $z^{n/2}$. However, we can rule out the possibility that there is a v_n, a fixed point of order n, among the t_i as that would contradict the Knapp count for the pentagon P determined by this triple (corollary 7.4.4). After conjugation by an element of the group, we may assume that $t_1 = p$ and we consider the possibilities for t_2 and t_3.

Proposition: 9.2.1 *It must be that* $d(p, t_2) = T_0$ *and* $d(p, t_3) = d(t_2, t_3) = T_0$.

Proof: Suppose that $T = d(p, t_2)$. By lemma 8.1.2, $T \geq T_0$. Since we may assume that the triangle $\triangle(p, t_2, t_3)$ is an acute triangle with smallest side $[p, t_2]$, we know that $h_T \geq T/2$ (lemma 6.3.9). Applying lemmas 6.3.8 and 6.3.11 we have $h_T \geq h_{eqT} \geq h_{eqT_0} = h_{T_0}$ since $T \geq T_0$. The variation equation for the pentagon tells us that

$$\sinh T \cdot \sinh h_T = \sinh T_0 \cdot \sinh h_{T_0} = \cos(3 \cdot 2\pi/n). \quad (9.1)$$

Since sinh is an increasing function and since $T \geq T_0$ and $h_T \geq h_{T_0}$, equation 9.1 tells us that $T = T_0$ and $h_T = h_{T_0}$. In fact it must be that $\triangle(t_1, t_2, t_3)$ is an equilateral triangle so that $T = T_0$ and $d(p, t_3) = d(t_2, t_3) = T_0$. □

9.3 Locating t_2 and t_3

We are now able to locate t_2 and t_3 and prove theorem 9.1.1. Namely, corollary 8.4.2 tells us what the possibilities for t_2 and t_3 are.

Namely, if $p_1 = p$, $p_2 = y(p)$ and $p_3 = y^2(p)$ with $t_1 = p_1$, then $t_2, t_3 \in \{y(p), y^2(p), E_p(y(p)), E_p(y^2(p))\}$. There are twelve possibilities, but those that give equilateral triangles with side T_0 are

- $t_2 = y(p), t_3 = y^2(p)$ or vice-versa.

9.3. LOCATING T_2 AND T_3

- $t_2 = E_p(y(p)), t_3 = E_p(y^2(p))$ or vice-versa.

In the first case the two triples of fixed points are equal and in the second case $E_p(\{p_1, p_2, p_3\}) = \{t_1, t_2, t_3\}$.

This completes the proof of theorem 9.1.1. The corollary follows.

Chapter 10

Generators and Nielsen equivalence for the $(2,4,n)$ $t=2$ $k=2$ case.

10.1 Introduction

We have constructed standard set of generators for the $(2,4,n)$ triangle group, namely those coming from E_p, E_S, and $E_{y^3(p)}$.

The purpose of this section is to show

Theorem: 10.1.1 *If (t_1, t_2, t_3) is any other triple of points that generate a $(2,4,n)$ triangle group with $k=2$ and $t=2$ and determine an acute triangle, then there is an element of the group that maps this triple to $(p, S, R_v(p))$.*

As a corollary we obtain

Theorem: 10.1.2 *If (A, B) and (C, D) are two pairs of hyperbolic generators for the $(2,4,n)$ triangle group with elliptic commutator where $k=2$, then $tr[A,B] = tr[C,D]$ if and only if (A,B) is Nielsen equivalent to (C,D).*

The proof proceeds by considering all possible triples of fixed points of order two and ruling out almost all of them. First we set some notation building upon the notation of chapters 4 and 8. We may assume that $A = E_p E_S$ and $B = E_{y^2(p)} E_S$ are the generators corresponding to the standard acute triangle and $P_{A,B}$ the corresponding pentagon with height h_0 and base b_0. By construction $h_0 = b_0 = D_0(2,4)$.

10.2 Types of triples

Let t_1, t_2, and t_3 be any three other points of order two in the tiling that generate G with $E_{t_1} E_{t_2} E_{t_3}$ a rotation by an angle of $2 \cdot 2\pi/n$. We let P be the pentagon corresponding to this triple and b and h its base and height. There are any number of ways that t_i can be a fixed point of order two. It could be conjugate to p. It could be conjugate to S and thus fixed by a conjugate of y^2, or finally n could be even and it could be conjugate to v and fixed by a conjugate of $z^{n/2}$. We denote these possibilities by v_2, v_4 and v_n. We will show

Lemma: 10.2.1 *There must be either*

- *two v_2's and one v_4 or*

- *three v_2's with $d(t_1, t_2) \geq D_0(2,2)$ and $D_0(2,2) \leq d(t_1, t_3) \leq 2D_0(2,4)$.*

Remark: 10.2.2 *We will eventually rule out the second possibility. We let b and h be the base and height of the pentagon determined by the triple (t_1, t_2, t_3). In what follows we assume that $b = d(t_1, t_2)$ is the shortest side of $\Delta(t_1, t_2, t_3)$ and that the triangle contains no obtuse angle. From the facts that $h_0 = b_0 = D_0(2,4)$, that heights and bases vary inversely and that $h \geq b/2$ (lemma 6.3.9), we conclude that $b < 2D_0(2,4)$.*

Proof: We rule out the possibility that there is a v_n among the t_i as that would contradict the Knapp count (corollary 7.4.4). We consider the other possibilities. First of all, there is either a v_4 interior to P or on the boundary. If it were interior, we could choose a small enough neighborhood, N_4, such that N_4 were completely contained in P, but so that v_4 were the only fixed point of the group in N_4. Then if x were any other point of N_4, four images of x, namely x, $R_4(x)$, $R_4^2(x)$,

10.2. TYPES OF TRIPLES

and $R_4^3(x)$, would also be in P contradicting the covering number of 2. If two of the t_i's were v_4's and if Q is not a t_i, then one of the v_4's must be inside β so that it would have a neighborhood, N_4 with x and $R_4^3(x)$ inside P. If $g(v_4)$ is the other t_i of order four, then at least one, possibly two, of $\{g(R_4^t(x))|t=0,1,2, \text{ or } 3\}$ is also in P. Thus we either contradict the covering number of 2 or conclude that g is a power of R_4, contradicting that the t_i are distinct points. If Q is a t_i and two of the t_i's are v_4's, argue again that there is a v_4 interior to the β side unless $t_2 = Q$ and t_2 and t_3 are v_4's. In this case $b \geq D_0(2,4) = b_0$ and $h \geq D_0(4,4) = 2D_0(2,4) > h_0 = D_0(2,4)$. This contradicts the inverse variation of h and b. Thus, at most one t_i is a v_4, forcing two t_i's to be v_2's. Thus one possibility is one v_4 and two v_2's. If all three t_i's were v_2's, both b and L, the length of the next longest side, would be at least $D_0(2,2)$. We see that $L < 2D_0(2,4)$ as follows. Assume to the contrary that $L \geq 2D_0(2,4)$. Since $b < 2D_0(2,4)$ and $D_0(2,4) < D_0(2,2) < 2D_0(2,4)$, apply 6.3.13 to conclude that $h \geq D_0(2,4) = h_0$. We have $b > b_0$ and $h \geq h_0$. This contradicts the inverse variation of the heights and bases. □

10.2.1 Distances in the standard pentagon

We now assume that P is the standard $(2,4,n)$ pentagon, that is the pentagon constructed from the standard generators of chapter 8.

Remark: 10.2.3 *Note that we* **do not** *follow all of the notation of chapter 8. In particular, we no longer use p_3 as another name for $y^3(p)$. The term p_3 takes on a new meaning below.*

We consider P, $A(P)$, $A^{-1}(P)$ along with $W(n)$.
(See figures 10.1 and 10.2.)
If we label the vertices of P, v, p, and S and set $p_1 = p$, $z_1 = S$, then the images of p and S on $W(n)$ are $\{p_i = R_n^{i-1}(p)\}$ and $\{z_i = R_n^{i-1}(S)\}$. (Subscripts are taken modulo n, of course.) Let $P_k = R_v^k(P)$. Further P has vertices v, $R_v(p_1) = p_2$, z_1, $R_v^{-1}(z_1) = z_{n-1}$ and $R_v^{-1}(p_1) = p_{n-1}$ so that $R_v^k(P)$ has vertices v, p_{k+2}, z_{k+1}, z_k, and p_k with p_{k+1} lying on the boundary between z_k and z_{k+1}.

We note that $[z_{n-1}, p_1]$ lies on the β side of P, but on the h side of $R_v^{-1}(P)$. Similarly, $[p_1, z_1]$ lies on the β-side of P but on the $A(h)$ side

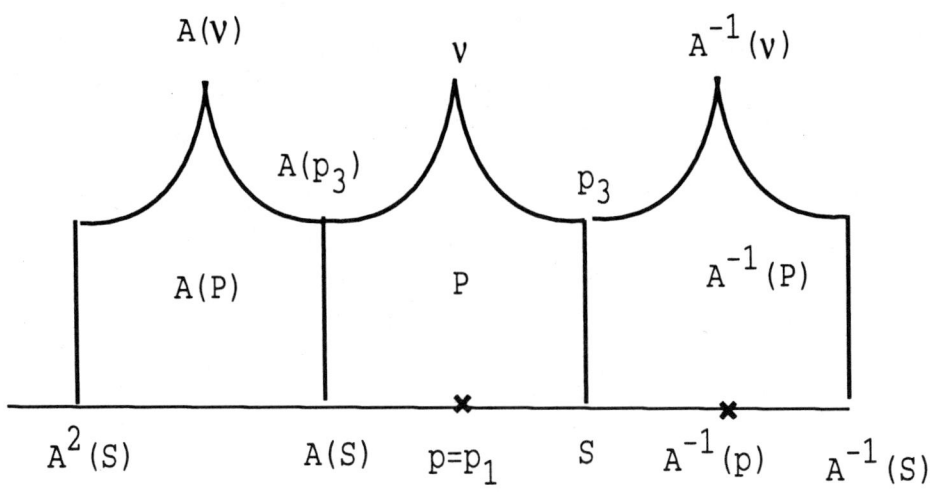

Figure 10.1: P, $A(P)$ and $A^{-1}(P)$

of $R_v(P)$. Thus the h side of $R_v^k(P)$ lies on the β side of $R_v^{k+1}(P)$ and the $A(h)$ side lies on the β side of $R_v^{k-1}(P)$.

Lemma: 10.2.4

- $d(p, z_2) \geq 2D_0(2,4)$.
- $d(p, p_3) \geq 2D_0(2,4)$.

Proof: The segment $[p, z_2]$ is the hypotenuse of a right triangle with one side $[z_2, z_1]$. Further, p_2 lies on this segment midway between z_1 and z_2. Thus $d(p, z_2) \geq 2d(p_2, z_1) = 2D_0(2,4)$. Since the triangle with vertices v, p_3 and z_2 has an angle of $\pi/4$ at the vertex z_2, the perpendicular from p_3 to the axis of A intersects the segment $[v, z_2]$. Since $[z_2, z_1]$ is a common perpendicular to the axis of A and $[v, z_2]$, we have
$$d(p_3, p) \geq d(p_3, Ax_A) \geq d(z_2, z_1) = 2D_0(2,4).$$
□

We will show:

Proposition: 10.2.5 *If x is any fixed point of order two in the tiling, then $d(x, p_1) \geq 2D_0(2,4)$ unless $x = p_2, p_{n-1}, E_{p_1}(p_2)$, or $E_{p_1}(p_{n-1})$.*

10.2. TYPES OF TRIPLES

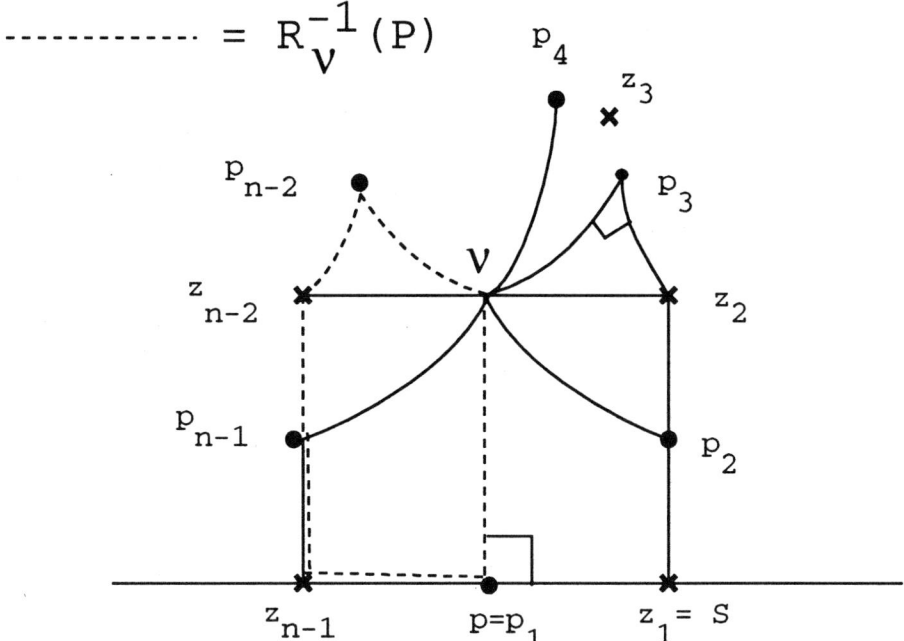

Figure 10.2: The Wedge at n and the rotational images of P

If x is any fixed point of order four in the tiling, then $d(x,p_1) \geq 2D_0(2,4)$ unless $x = z_1$ or z_{n-1}.

Proof: In what follows we assume that x is either of order two or of order four. If x lies in the fundamental tiling strip and above the axis of A, but not in P, $A(P)$, or $A^{-1}(P)$, then $d(x,p) > 3D_0(2,4)$. Assume next that x lies above the fundamental tiling strip. We let τ be the geodesic connecting x to p, τ_P its intersection with P and x_D the point where it crosses $\mathcal{D}$. We know that $(\tau_P)_d \geq h_0 = D_0(2,4)$. By proposition 5.6.3, we may assume that $x_D \in D$ or D' and that τ does not cross $\widetilde{h}$ or $\widetilde{A(h)}$.

Suppose first that x actually lies in $W(n)$ so that $x = p_i$ or z_i for some i. Then since every h-side is also a β-side, we may assume that x is on the β side of P_k for some k. Further τ must exit P_k along a D or D' side so that $(\tau_{P_k})_d \geq D_0(2,4)$. If P and P_k are disjoint or intersect at most along a D or D' side, then $d(x,p) \geq (\tau_{P_k})_d + (\tau_P)_d = 2D_0(2,4)$. If P_k and P have some interior intersection, then either $P_k = R_v(P)$ or $R_v^{-1}(P)$. In these cases, since x is not in P, x must be one of z_2, p_3, z_{n-1} and p_{n-2}. For all of these by lemma 10.2.4 $d(x,p) > 2D_0(2,4)$. Assume next that x lies across D or D', but not in $W(n)$. Then τ must enter $W(n)$ along D or D' and then exit $W(n)$ passing through some P_k. Again since every h-side is a β-side, the exit must be along a β side so again the intersection of τ with $W(n)$ has length at least $D_0(2,4)$ as long as P and P_k have no interior intersection. Then $d(x,p) = d(x,W(n)) + (\tau \cap W(n))_d + (\tau_P)_d > 2D_0(2,4)$. If P and P_k do have some interior intersection, then either τ exits across $\widetilde{h}$ or $\widetilde{A(h)}$, which has been ruled out, or τ enters P_{k+1} on a D or D' side and exits on a true β side giving a sufficient minimal distance. If $x \in A(P)$ or $A^{-1}(P)$, then $x \in \{A^2(p_3), A^2(S), A(p), A(p_3), A(S), S, p_3, A^{-1}(p), A^{-1}(S), A^{-1}(p_3)\}$ and the distances between p and these points are at least $2D_0(2,4)$ except for S, $A(S)$, $y^3(p)$ and $A(y^3(p))$. If the point x is below the axis of A either in the fundamental tiling strip or below it, replace x by $E_p(x)$ and repeat the arguments. □

10.3 Location of t_1, t_2 and t_3

We are now able to locate t_1, t_2 and t_3 and to prove theorem 10.1.1 and its corollary. Each of the distances $d(t_i, t_j)$ is either $D_0(2,2)$, $D_0(2,4)$ or greater than or equal to $2D_0(2,4)$. If the smallest such distance were greater than or equal to $2D_0(2,4)$, then we saw that the height would be too big. Thus we may assume that at least one distance is $D_0(2,2)$ or $D_0(2,4)$.

We first show that some t_i must be a fixed point of order four. Assume to the contrary that all three t_i's are fixed points of order two. Conjugate so that $t_1 = p$. Then both t_2 and t_3 must be at a distance $D_0(2,2)$ from p. Using proposition 10.2.5 consider all possibilities for t_1 and t_2 and verify that one either obtains a straight line instead of a triangle or an equilateral right triangle with legs $D_0(2,2)$ and hypotenuse $2D_0(2,4)$. This gives values for h and b that are too big.

Thus we may assume that some t_i is a fixed point of order four. If the smallest distance between fixed points is $D_0(2,4)$, we may assume that after conjugation by an element of the group $t_1 = p$ and $t_2 = S$. Arguing again that the length of the next smallest side cannot exceed $2D_0(2,4)$, we must have $d(t_3, p) = D_0(2,2)$. Proposition 10.2.5 tells us that t_3 is either p_1, p_{n-1}, $E_p(p_1)$ or $E_p(p_{n-1})$. If $t_3 = E_p(p_{n-1})$, then $R_v \cdot E_p$ maps the triple $\{p, S, t_3\}$ to the triple $\{p, S, p_2\}$ sending t_3 to p, S to S and p to p_2. The other two possibilities for t_3 give obtuse triangles. If the smallest distance between the t_i is $D_0(2,2) = b$, conjugate so that $t_1 = p$. We may assume that t_2 is the other point of order two and that t_3 is the point of order four. Then proposition 10.2.5 tells us that $d(t_3, p)$ and $d(t_3, t_2)$ are both at least $2D_0(2,4)$. Lemma 6.3.13 then implies that $h > D_0(2,4)$ giving a contradiction.

This proves theorem 10.1.1 and its corollary.

Chapter 11

Constructing the standard $(2,3,7)k=2; t=9$ Pentagon: calculating the 2 – 2 spectrum

In this section we carefully construct the standard pentagon for the $(2,3,7)$ pentagon when $t=9$ and $k=2$. The main purpose of this construction is to locate all of the fixed points of the group which are either interior to the pentagon or on its boundary and to understand where these are mapped under various elements of the group. We also prove some lemmas about the distances in the $(2,3,7)$ tiling. Namely, we can consider the 2-2 **spectrum**, that is, the set of all distances between fixed points of order two in the tiling. As a result of our construction we are able to give a complete list of the elements of the 2-2 spectrum which are less than $2D_0(2,2)$. This will play an important role in showing that there are up to conjugation and Nielsen transformations only one set of generators for the $(2,3,7)$ $t=9$ $k=2$ case. In particular, we are able to establish a short list (up to conjugation) of the possible pairs $\{t_1, t_2\}$ corresponding to the two first elements of the triple(t_1, t_2, t_3) (theorem 11.7.1). In the next chapter we prove the Nielsen equivalence by ruling out almost all members of this list. We build upon the notation of earlier chapters, in particular chapters 4 and 5.

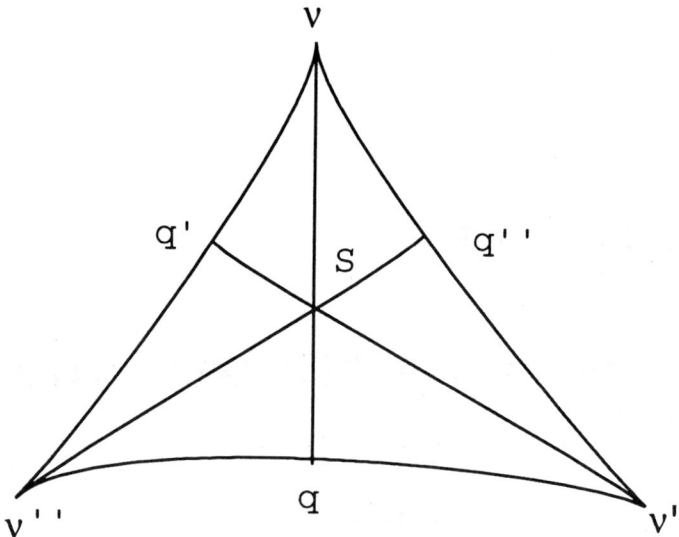

Figure 11.1: Labeling the wedge about three, $W(S)$.

11.1 Step 1: Label the wedge about the three

Following the notation of chapter 4, let $\Delta = \Delta(2, 3, 7)$. If the vertices of Δ are v, S and p where v is fixed by the rotation of order seven, S by the rotation of order three and p by that of order two, Δ can also be written as $\Delta(a, b, c)$. We construct the wedge at S, $W(S)$. (See figure 11.1.) The vertices are v, $v'' = R_3(v)$ and $v' = R_3^2(v)$ and $q' = p$, $R_3(p) = q$ and $R_3^2(p) = q''$. Note that both the reflection through side $[p, S]$ and the rotation about p of order two both carry v into v''. That is, $E_p(v) = v''$ and $R_{23}(v) = v''$. We have $[q', S]$ is a (segment of a) perpendicular to $[v, v'']$ through q'. Since $W(S)$ is in fact an equilateral triangle with the three sevens as its vertices, its height, the perpendicular from v' to $[v, v'']$, must bisect the base and intersect the base at q'. Thus $[q', S]$ is a subsegment of the geodesic segment $[v', q']$. Similarly, the points q and v lie on another geodesic passing through S.

11.2. STEP 2: DOUBLE AND EXTEND

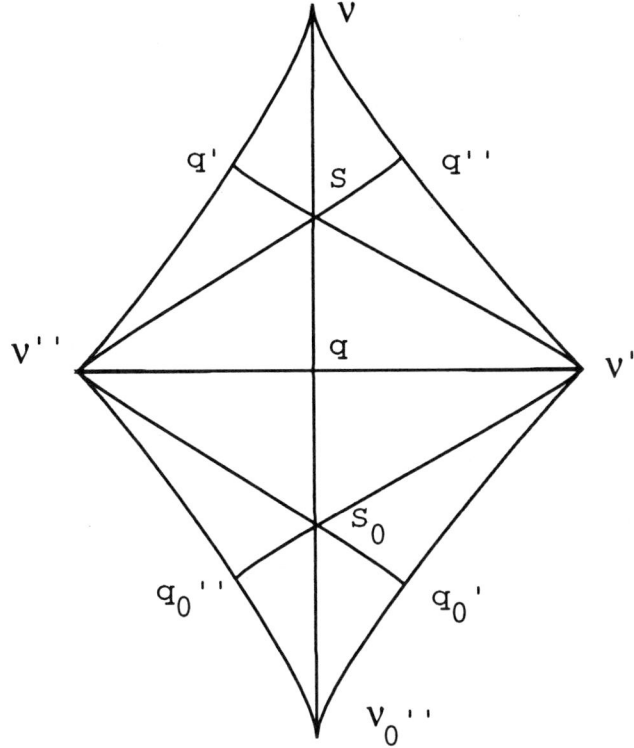

Figure 11.2: The double wedge three.

11.2 Step 2: Doubling and extend the wedge about three

We apply E_q to $W(S)$ and obtain a figure with four more fixed points of the group, namely $E_q(q') = q'_0$, $E_q(q'') = q''_0$, $E_q(S) = S_0$, and $E_q(v) = v''_0$. Next we apply R_v to the segments $\widetilde{[v, S]}$ and $\widetilde{[v, q'']}$. (See 11.2 and 11.3.) We know by construction that $[v', S, q']$ is a geodesic as is $[v'', S, q'']$. Since rotating by an element of order three about S_0 permutes the three points in the set $\{q'_0, q, q''_0\}$, we see that $[v', S_0, q''_0]$ is a geodesic as is $[v'', S_0, q'_0]$.

We set
$$S''' = R_v(S),$$

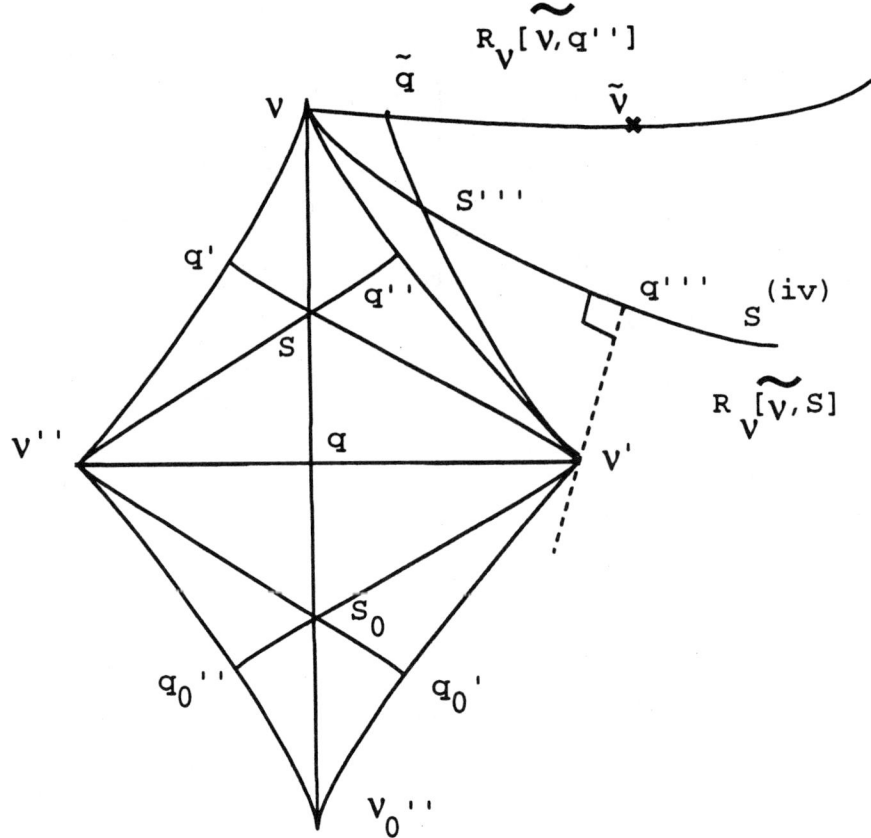

Figure 11.3: Extending the double wedge to include $R_v([\widetilde{v,S}])$ and $R_v([\widetilde{v,q''}])$.

11.2. STEP 2: DOUBLE AND EXTEND

$$q''' = R_v(q),$$
$$S^{(iv)} = R_v(E_q(S)) = R_v(S_0),$$
$$\tilde{q} = R_v(q''),$$
$$\tilde{v} = R_v(v').$$

One of our difficulties is that points in the tiling are often the images of a given point under a number of different words or elements of the group. In order to recognize what is happening in the tiling one needs to keep track of all of the different names for the same point. In particular we see that

Lemma: 11.2.1

$$R_v(S) = E_{q''}(S) = R_{vq''}(S) = S'''.$$

$$R_v(q') = q'' \text{ and } R_v(v'') = v'.$$

Proof: We know that $R_v = R_{vq''}R_{vS}$. Thus $R_v(S) = R_{vq''}R_{vS}(S)$. Since $R_v(S) = S$, $R_v(S) = R_{vq''}(S)$. But it is also true that $R_{vq''}(S) = E_{q''}(S)$. Next $R_v(q') = R_{vq''}R_{vS}(q') = R_{vq''}(q'') = q''$. Finally $R_v = R_{q''}R_S^{-1}$. Calculate that $R_v(v'') = R_{q''}R_S^{-1}(v'') = R_{q''}(v) = v'$. □

Lemma: 11.2.2 $E_{q''}(q') = q'''$ and $E_{q''}(q) = \tilde{q}$.

Proof: If $R_v(S) = S'''$, then R_v maps the wedge at S to the wedge at S''' and thus the three points of order two closest to S, namely, $\{q, q', q''\}$, to the three points of order two closest to S''', namely $\{q'', \tilde{q}, q'''\}$. Since $E_{q''}(S) = S'''$, $E_{q''}$ must also map the three points closest to S to the three points closest to S'''. Since $E_{q''}(q'') = q''$, either $E_{q''}(q') = \tilde{q}$ and $E_{q''}(q) = q'''$ or vice-versa. We need to determine which occurs. A similar argument lets us conclude that $E_{q''}$ must map the three points of order seven closest to S, namely $\{v, v', v''\}$ to the three points of oder seven closets to S''', namely $\{v, v', \tilde{v}\}$. Since $E_{q''}$ interchanges v and v', we have $E_{q''}(v'') = \tilde{v} = R_v(v')$. Since $E_{q''}(v') = v$, $E_{q''}$ either maps $[q', v']$ to $[q''', v]$ or $[\tilde{q}, v]$. But the latter segment does not pass through S''' which the image of the geodesic $[q', S, v']$ must do. □

Lemma: 11.2.3 *The angle between $[v, S''', q''']$ and $[q''', v']$ is a right angle.*

Proof: This follows from the fact that $\triangle(q''', v', S''') = E_{q''}(\triangle(q', v, S))$.
□

11.3 Step 3: Drop the perpendiculars to $[q_0'', q_0']$

We drop a perpendicular from q''' to the line $\mathcal{A} = [\widetilde{q_0'', q_0'}]$. We also drop a perpendicular from $R_v^{-2}(q''')$ to this line.

We let Q and Q' be the points where these perpendiculars hit $\mathcal{A}$. Set $A = E_{q_0''} E_{q_0'}$ and $B = E_{q'''} E_{q_0'}$. Let $P = P_{A,B}$ be the pentagon determined by the pair (A, B). (See figure 11.4.)

Theorem: 11.3.1 *The polygon with sides $[Q, q''']$, $[Q', R_v^{-2}(q''')]$, $[R_v^{-2}(q'''), v]$, $[v, q''']$ and $[Q, Q']$ is precisely P, the pentagon determined by A and B. It is the standard pentagon determined by the standard acute triangle for $t = 9$.*

To see that P is precisely the pentagon determined by (A, B), it suffices to show that $E_{q_0''} E_{q_0'} E_{q'''}(v) = v$. This and the rest of the theorem are an immediate consequence of the following:

Theorem: 11.3.2 *The triangle $\triangle(E_{q_0'}(q_0''), q_0', q''')$ is the standard geometric triangle for the $(2, 3, 7), t = 9, k = 2$ group.*

Proof: We begin with $\triangle(v, S, q'')$ which is $\triangle(v, S, p)$ of section 8.3. Since $E_p(v) = \underline{v}$, and $E_{q''}(v) = v'$ and since p corresponds to q'', $\underline{v}$ corresponds to v'. Thus $R_{v'}$ corresponds to $R_{\underline{v}}^{-1}$. We use $=$ to mean equal under this correspondence. Affirmative answers to the following questions will prove the theorem.

- Is $q_1 = R_{\underline{v}}^{-2}(p)$ equal to $R_{v'}^2(q'')$?

- Is $q_2 = R_{\underline{v}}^{-3}(p)$ equal to $R_{v'}^3(q'')$?

- Is $q_3 = R_{\underline{v}}(p)$ equal to $R_{v'}^{-1}(q'')$? or

11.3. STEP 3: DROP PERPENDICULARS

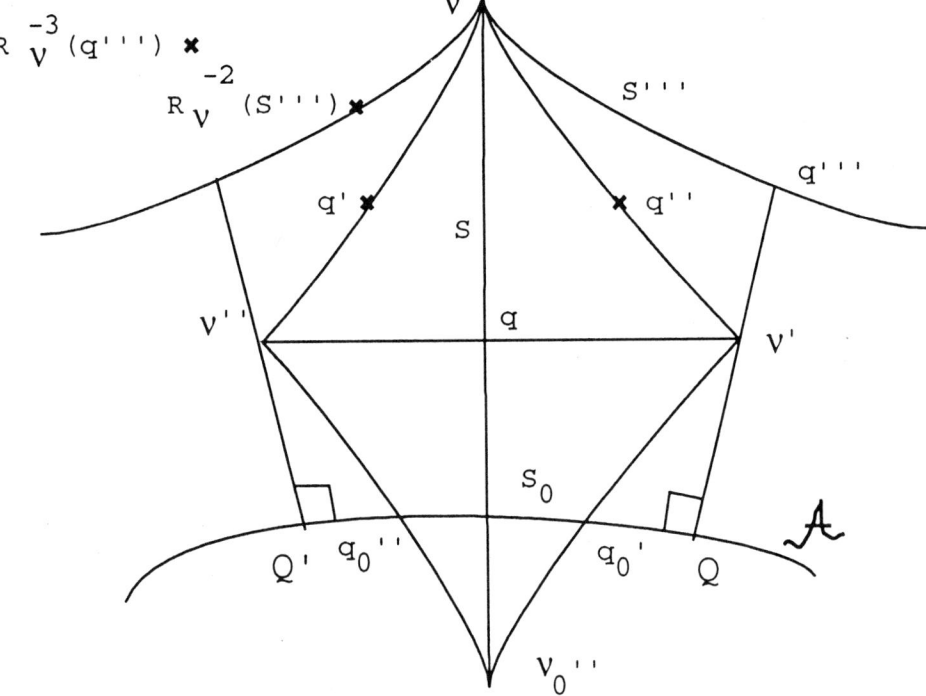

Figure 11.4: Dropping the perpendiculars to form the pentagon.

- Is $\tilde{q}_1 = E_{q_1}(q_2)$, $\tilde{q}_2 = q_1$, and $\tilde{q}_3 = q_3$?

We calculate that since $v' = E_{q''}(v)$, $R_{v'} = E_{q''} R_v E_{q''}$. Using the results of the previous lemmas, verify that

$$R_{v'}(q'') = E_{q''} R_v E_{q''}(q'') = E_{q''}(R_v(q'')) = E_{q''}(\tilde{q}) = q.$$

We want to claim that $R^2_{v'}(q'') = q'_0$ or that $R_{v'}(q) = q'_0$.

By construction all of the six subtriangles in the wedge at S are $(2,3,7)$-triangles so that all of those in $E_q(W(S))$ are also. This allows us to conclude that distances and angles in the wedges are what we think they should be. Therefore, we can conclude that $\prec (S, v', S_0)$ is $2\pi/7$ as is $\prec (q, v', q'_0)$ and that $[S, v']_d = [S_0, v']_d = D_0(3,7)$ and $[q, v']_d = [q'_0, v']_d = D_0(2,7)$. This says that $R_{v'}(q) = q'_0$ and $R_{v'}(S) = S_0$. (See theorem 4.2.5.) In a similar manner we can conclude that $R_v^{-1}(S) = S'''$. Now $ET(v) = \{v, q', q, q''\}$ and contains S. Thus $E_{q''}(ET(v)) = ET(v') = \{v', q''', \tilde{q}, q''\}$ and contains S'''. Thus $R^2_{v'}(ET(v'))$ is also a fundamental extended tile and $= \{v', q, q''_0, q'_0\}$ and contains S_0. In particular, identifying the labeling of chapter 4 in the extended wedge, with our current labeling in $EW(v')$, we have $p_1 = q$, $p_2 = q'_0$, $z_1 = S_0$, $v' = v$, and $q_1 = q''$. Since $E_{p_2}(q_1) = p_3 = R_v(p_2)$, the image of p_2 under R_v, we can infer that $E_{q'_0}(q''_0) = R_{v'}(q'_0)$ which is the next image of q'_0 under the rotation. □

Proof: (of theorem 11.3.1). To complete the proof of the theorem, we need only notice the fact that $E_{q_1} E_{q_2} E_{q_3}(v) = v$ under the correspondence translates to $E_{q''_0} E_{q'_0} E_{q'''}(v) = v$. □

Remark: 11.3.3 *We can see that v' lies on the h-side $[q''', Q]$ of this pentagon and that v'' lies on the h-side $[A(q'''), Q']$ as follows. Lemma 11.2.3 says that v' lies on the perpendicular to $[v, q''']$ at q'''. But by construction $[Q, q''']$ is a perpendicular to $[v, q''']$ at q'''. A similar argument shows that the second perpendicular $[Q', A(q''')]$ passes through v''.*

Remark: 11.3.4 $R_{v'}(S''') = S$, *whence* $R^2_{v'}(S''') = S_0$. *Since* $[v', S''', \tilde{q}]$ *is a geodesic so is* $[v', S_0]$ *and* $R_{v'}(\tilde{q})$ *must lie on this geodesic. Whence we must have* $R_{v'}(\tilde{q}) = q''_0$.

11.4 Distances to D and the two-two spectrum

Recall that $D = [v, q''']$, $D' = [v, A(q''')]$, and $D_0 = D_0(2, 7)$. We recall the definitions of the five T or 2-2 distances:

Definition: 11.4.1
$$T_0 = D_0(2,2),$$
$$T_1 = 2T_0,$$

Define T_2, T_3 and T_4 so as to satisfy

$$\cosh T_2 = \cosh^2 D_0 - \sinh^2 D_0 \cdot \cos(2 \cdot 2\pi/7), \text{ and}$$

$$\cosh T_3 = \cosh^2 D_0 - \sinh^2 D_0 \cdot \cos(3 \cdot 2\pi/7).$$

$$\cosh T_4 = \cosh D_0 \cdot \cosh Z_1 - \sinh D_0 \cdot \sinh Z_1 \cdot \cos(5 \cdot \pi/7).$$

We call $\{T_0, T_1, T_2, T_3, T_4\}$ the **two-two distances**.

Note that since $\cos 4\pi/7$ is negative, $\cosh T_2 > \cosh^2 D_0 > \cosh D_0$ whence $T_2 > D_0$. Similarly $T_3 > D_0$ and $T_4 > Z_1 > D_0(2, 7)$. We will show

Lemma: 11.4.2
$$d(q'', D) = T_0/2.$$
$$d(q'_0, D) > 2T_0.$$
$$d(q''_0, D) = d(q'_0, D') = 5T_0/2.$$
$$d(q, D) = 3T_0/2.$$
$$d(q', D) > D_0/2.$$

Proof: Since $E_{q''}(q) = \tilde{q}$ and $E_q(q''_0) = q''$, $[q''_0, q, q'', \tilde{q}]$ is a geodesic. Let m be the point where it intersects $[v, S''', q''']$. Since S''' permutes $\{q'', q''', \tilde{q}\}$, we know that $[\widetilde{q'', \tilde{q}}]$ is perpendicular to $[v, S''', q''']$ and m bisects $[q'', \tilde{q}]$ so that $d(q'', m) = T_0/2$. Similarly, since S_0 permutes $\{q, q'_0, q''_0\}$, the line $[q'_0, S_0, v'']$ is perpendicular to $[q''_0, q]$ and if it intersects it at m_0, then $d(m_0, q) = T_0/2 = d(q'', D)$. (See figure 11.5.) Thus $\triangle(m_0, q'_0, m)$ is a right triangle with hypotenuse $[q'_0, m]$.

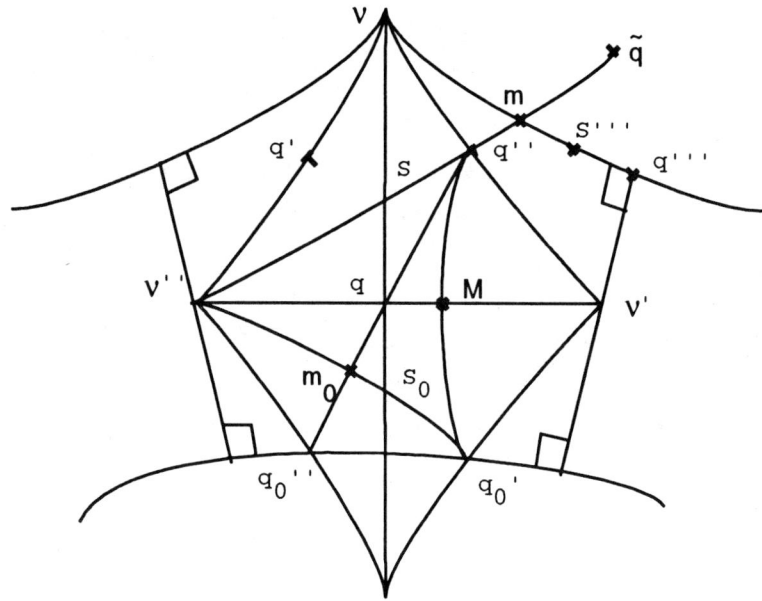

Figure 11.5: m and m_0

Thus $[q_0', m]_d > d(m_0, q) + d(q, q'') + d(q'', m) = 2T_0$ and $d(q_0'', m) = d(q_0'', q'') + d(q'', m) = 2T_0 + T_0/2 = 5T_0/2$. Since $[q, q'', m]$ is a geodesic perpendicular to $[v, S''', q''']$, $d(q, D) = d(q, q'') + d(q'', m) = 3T_0/2$. Now the segment $[m, m_0]$ is a common perpendicular between the two geodesics $[\widetilde{v, q'''}]$ and $[\widetilde{q_0', S_0}, m_0]$. If L is the perpendicular from q_0' to D, then $L_d \geq [m, m_0]_d$. Thus $d(q_0', D) \geq 2T_0$. Both q' and $\tilde{q}$ lies at a distance $D_0(2, 7)$ from v and at an angle $4\pi/7$ apart. Thus $d(q', \tilde{q}) = T_2$. The perpendicular from q' to D must pass across $[v, v']$. Thus $d(q', D) > d(q', [v, v'])$. But $[v, v']$ is perpendicular to $[q', \tilde{q}]$, whence $d(q', [v, v']) = T_2/2$. Since $T_2 > D_0(2, 7)$, $d(q', D) > D_0(2, 7)/2$. □

11.5 More distance computations

We consider the quadrilateral v, q'', S, q'. We know that $d(q', q'') = T_0$, $d(v, q') = d(q'', v) = D_0(2, 7)$ and that $d(q', S) = d(S, q'') = D_0(2, 3)$. Thus $\triangle(q', v, q'')$ is an isosceles triangle as is $\triangle(q', S, q'')$. Thus if the

11.5. MORE DISTANCE COMPUTATIONS

segment $[v, S]$ intersects the segment $[q', q'']$ at N, then N is the midpoint of $[q', q'']$. We let h_7 denotes the length of the segment $[v, N]$ and h_3 denote the length of the segment $[N, S]$. We note that $T_0 < 2D_0(2,3)$ and $h_7 < D_0(2,7)$ and that if h_0 denotes the height of the pentagon $P_{A,B}$ that we constructed, then $h_0 = D_0(2,7) + h_7$.

Lemma: 11.5.1
$$D_0(2,7) < h_7 + T_0/2.$$
$$D_0(2,7) > T_0.$$
$$D_0(2,7) < D_0(3,7) + D_0(2,3) < 2T_0.$$
$$T_3 < 3T_0.$$
$$T_2 < 2T_0.$$

Proof: Since $\triangle(v, N, q')$ has sides of length $D_0(2,7), T_0/2$ and h_7, the first inequality follows from the triangle inequality. Let $\alpha = \prec (v, q', N) = \prec (v, q'', N)$ and $\beta = \prec (S, q', N) = \prec (S, q'', N)$. Then $\alpha + \pi/7 < \pi/2$ and $\beta + \pi/3 < \pi/2$ so that $\beta < \pi/6$. Since $\alpha + \beta = \pi/2$, this says that $\alpha > \pi/3$. In any triangle, the largest side is opposite the largest angle. Thus we consider $\triangle(q', v, q'')$ and ask whether α is greater than $2\pi/7$ to decide whether $D_0(2,7)$ is greater than T_0. Since $\alpha > \pi/3 > 2\pi/7$, we conclude that $D_0(2,7) > T_0$. Next we look at the extended wedge at v and in particular at the polygon with vertices v, p_1, z_1, p_2, q_2, and z_2. Then the segment $[v, z_1, q_1]$ intersects the segment $[p_1, p_2]$ at some point, call it N. Since $E_{p_2}(p_1) = q_2$, $[p_1, p_2, q_2]$ is a geodesic as is $[q_2, z_2, v]$. Thus v, p_1, q_2 determines a triangle. Note the following lengths: $[v, p_1]_d = [v, p_2]_d = D_0(2,7)$, $[p_1, p_2]_d = [p_2, q_2]_d = T_0$, $[p_1, q_2]_d = 2T_0$, $[v, q_2]_d = [v, z_2]_d + [z_2, q_2]_d = D_0(7,3) + D_0(3,2) = Z_1$. The angle $\prec (v, p_1, p_2)$ is the angle α above and $\prec (p_2, p_1, z_1)$ is the angle β above. Since $\prec (p_1, v, q_2) = 3\pi/7$, $2T_0 > Z_1$ if and only if $\alpha < 3\pi/7$. But $\prec (p_1, v, z_1) = \pi/7$, since $\triangle(p_1, v, N)$ must have positive area and since $\prec (v, N, p_1)$ is a right angle, $\alpha < \pi/2 - \pi/7 = 5\pi/14$. Thus $Z_1 < 2T_0$. Finally, consider the points p_1, p_2, p_3, p_4 in the wedge about 7 and the triangles $\triangle(p_1, p_2, p_3)$ and $\triangle(p_1, p_3, p_4)$. By the triangle inequality, $T_2 = d(p_1, p_3) < d(p_1, p_2) + d(p_2, p_3) = 2T_0$ and $T_3 = d(p_1, p_4) < d(p_1, p_3) + d(p_3, p_4) \leq 2T_0 + T_0 = 3T_0$. □

Lemma: 11.5.2 $2D_0(2,7) > h_0 = h_7 + D_0(2,7) > 2T_0$

Proof: The polygon with vertices $m_0, q'_0, Q, q''',$ and m is a pentagon with four right angles. The length of the sides are $[m, m_0] = 2T_0$, $[m_0, q'_0]_d = h_3 + D_0(2,3)$, $[q'_0, Q]_d = T_0/2$, $[Q, q''']_d = h_7 + D_0(2,7)$, and $[q''', m]_d = D_0(2,3) + h_3$. By page 87 of [7] we have

$$\frac{\cosh[m_0, q'_0]}{\sinh[Q, q''']} = \frac{\cosh[q'_0, Q]}{\sinh[m_0, m]}.$$

Thus $[m_0, q'_0] > [q'_0, Q]$ implies $[Q, q'''] \geq [m_0, m]$. Since $h_3 + D_0(2,3) > T_0/2$, $h_7 + D_0(2,7) > 2T_0$. (Note: $h_3 + D_0(2,3) > T_0/2$ because $\triangle(p_1, z_1, N)$ is a triangle with sides $T_0/2$, $D_0(2,3)$ and h_3.) □

11.6 Distances to q'_0

Eventually we want to determine which triple of points of order two are possible generators for the $(2,3,7) t = 9, k = 2$ group. We need to understand more about distances. Exactly why we choose to prove the specific results we do will become apparent in the next section when we begin to narrow down the list of possible triples. The purpose of this section is to prove two theorems:

Theorem: 11.6.1 *The distance between q'_0 and any point of order two in the tiling is either greater than $2D_0(2,7)$ or between $2D_0(2,7)$ and $2T_0$ but greater than h_0 or is in the set $\{T_0, T_1, T_2, T_3, T_4\}$.*

and

Theorem: 11.6.2 *If y is a point of order two with*

$$d(q'_0, y) = T_0, T_1, T_2, T_3 \text{ or } T_4,$$

then $\exists g \in G$, with

$$g\{q'_0, y\} = \{q'_0, q''_0\}, \{q'_0, A(q'_0)\}, \{q'_0, q''\}, \{q'_0, q'''\} \text{ or } \{q'_0, A(q''')\}.$$

Note that the order of the pairs of points may be reversed by g.

11.6. DISTANCES TO Q'_0

We begin by proving

Lemma: 11.6.3
- Every fixed point interior to the pentagon is in $EW(v')$ or $EW(v'')$ and q'_0 is in both extended wedges.
- The point $\tilde{q}$ lies in $EW(v')$.
- The point q'_0 lies in $EW(v'')$.

Proof: By construction every point of order two in the pentagon is at a distance $D_0(2,7)$ from either v' or v'' and thus lies in $W(v')$ or $W(v'')$. We saw that $[\tilde{q}, S''', v']$ is a geodesic. Since S''' is a closest three to v', $[\tilde{q}, S''', v']$ lies in $EW(v')$. Thus $\tilde{q} \in EW(v')$. The last fact follows from the fact that $[v'', S_0, q'_0]$ is a geodesic. □

As a corollary we see that the distances between points of order two in the pentagon are the distances that one finds in extended wedges.

Proposition: 11.6.4 The distance from q'_0 to any of the points of order two in $R_v^2(P_{A,B})$ that are not in P is greater than $2D_0(2,7)$.

Proof: Let x be any point of order two in $R_v^2(P)$. $P \cup R_v^2(P)$ is a convex set and P and $R_v^2(P)$ share the common boundary D. (See figure 11.6.) Thus $d(x, q'_0) \geq d(x, D) + d(D, q'_0)$. But $d(q'_0, D) \geq h_d = D_0(2,7) + h_7$ and $d(x, D) > T_0/2$. Since $D_0(2,7) < h_7 + T_0/2$, conclude that $d(x, q'_0) \geq h_7 + D_0(2,7) + T_0/2 > 2D_0(2,7)$. □

Proposition: 11.6.5

- The distance between any point of order two in $R_v^{-2}(P)$ which is not in P and q'_0 is greater than $2D_0(2,7)$).
- The distance between any point of order two in $R_v^{-4}(P)$ or $R_v^4(P)$ and q'_0 is greater than $2D_0(2,7)$.

Proof: Using the same proof for q''_0 and $R_v^{-2}(P)$ as for q'_0 and $R_v^2(P)$, we see that the distance between any point x of order two in $R_v^{-2}(P)$ and q''_0 is greater than $2D_0(2,7)$.

The line segment $[R^{-2}(A(q''')), v]$ makes an angle of $6\pi/7$ with H. Thus if $x \in R_v^{-2}(P)$, the perpendicular from x to the axis of A crosses

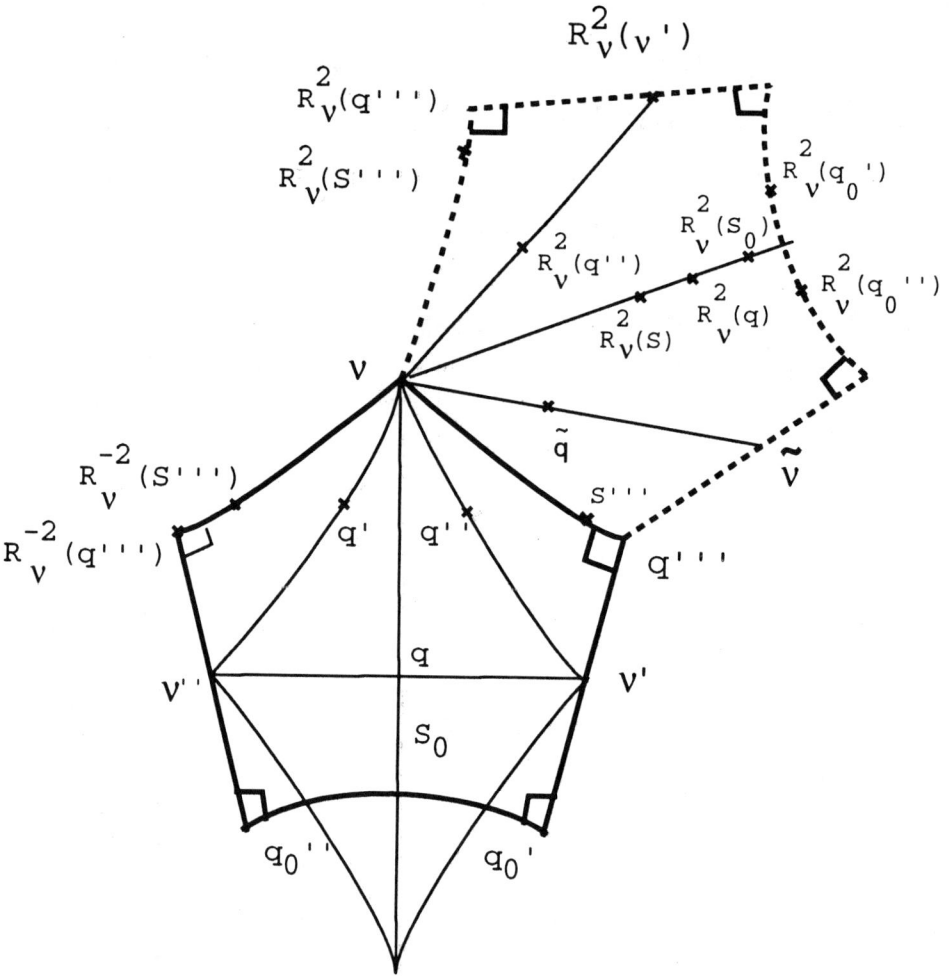

Figure 11.6: $P \cup R_v^2(P)$

11.6. DISTANCES TO Q'_0

the axis of A in $[A(Q), T]$ and is thus closer to q''_0 than to q'_0. Thus $d(x, q'_0) \geq d(x, q''_0) > 2D_0(2,7)$. Since the images of P under the fourth power of the rotation or its inverse are each disjoint from the original pentagon, the same arguments can be applied to these cases. □

Notice that since we computed distance to q''_0 when x was closer to q''_0, we have actually shown:

Theorem: 11.6.6 *Let y be any point of order two in $\cup_{n=1}^{7}(R^n_v(P))$. Then either $d(y, q'_0) > 2D_0(2,7)$ and $d(y, q''_0) > 2D_0(2,7)$ or $y \in P$.*

Lemma: 11.6.7 *If x is any point of order two above the axis of A between $\widetilde{A(h)}$ and $\tilde{h}$ but not in the image of P under any power of R_v, then $d(x, q'_0) > 2D_0(2,7)$ and $d(x, q''_0) > 2D_0(2,7)$.*

Proof: (See figure 11.7.) It suffices to consider the case where x is between $\tilde{H}$ and $\tilde{h}$ so that $[x, q'_0]$ crosses D. In this case $d(x, q''_0) \geq d(x, q'_0)$. If x is between $\widetilde{A(h)}$ and $\tilde{H}$, then it is easy to modify the argument given below to show that $d(x, q'_0) \geq d(x, q''_0) > 2D_0(2,7)$.

If x is not any image of P under a power of R_v, then $[x, q'_0]$ must cross either $R_v^2(h)$ or $R_v^2(R_v^2(A(h)))$. However, $E_{q'''}(h) = R_v^2(A(h))$ and $h \cup E_{q'''}(h)$ is one geodesic. Thus $E_{R_v^2(q''')}(R_v^2(h))$ and $R_v^2(h)$ lie on one geodesic. But

$$E_{R_v^2(q''')}(R_v^2(h)) = R_v^2(E_{q'''}(h)) = R_v^4(A(h))$$

since $E_{R_v^2(q''')} = R_v^{-2} E_{q'''} R_v^2$. Thus $[x, q'_0]$ crosses $\widetilde{R_v^2(h)}$. It must also cross $R_v^2(H)$ as well as D. Thus $d(x, q'_0) \geq d(\widetilde{R_v^2(h)}, R_v^2(H)) + d(D, q'_0)$. Since $d(\widetilde{R_v^2(h)}, R_v^2(H)) = d(\tilde{h}, H) \geq T_0$, $d(x, q'_0) > 2D_0$. □

If we combine theorem 11.6.6 with lemma 11.6.7, we obtain immediately

Corollary: 11.6.8 *If x is any point of order two above the axis of A lying between $\widetilde{A(h)}$ and $\tilde{h}$ but not in P, then $d(x, q'_0) > 2D_0(2,7)$ and $d(x, q''_0) > 2D_0(2.7)$.*

From this we can prove

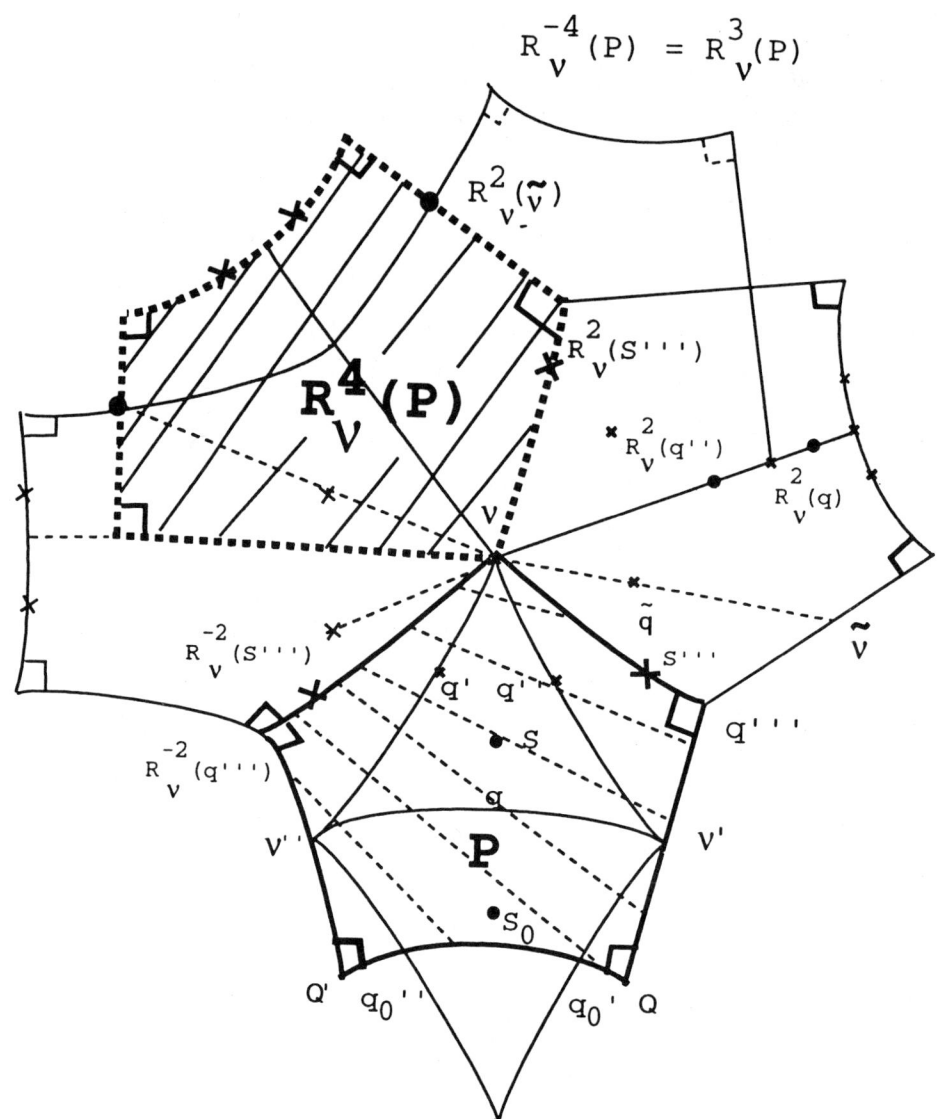

Figure 11.7: $R_v^4(P)$

11.6. DISTANCES TO Q'_0

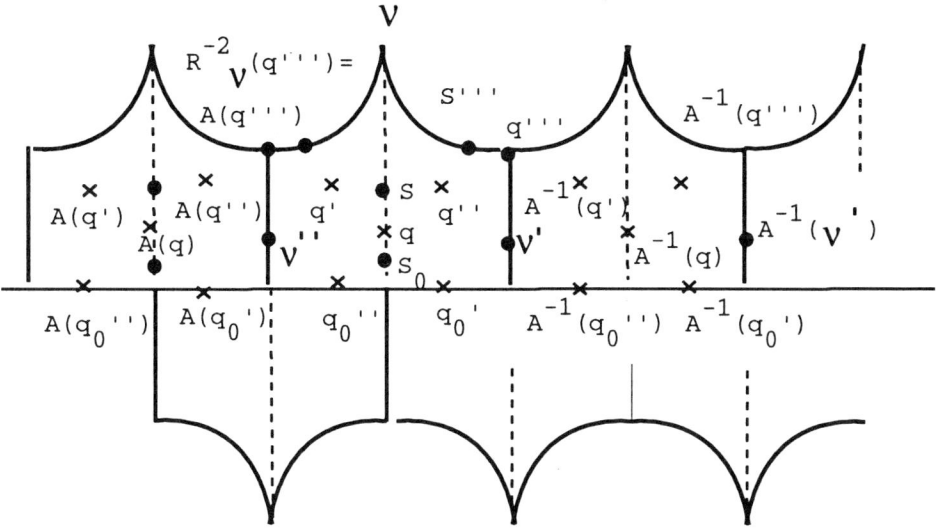

Figure 11.8: Distances in P and adjacent P's

Theorem: 11.6.9 *Let y be a point of order two above the fundamental tile strip, then $d(y, q'_0) > 2D_0(2, 7)$*

Proof: Following the notation of chapter 5 we may assume that i_y is chosen so that $\tilde{y} = A^{i_y}(y)$ satisfies the hypothesis of corollary 11.6.8 so that $m_0 > 2D_0(2, 7)$ and conclude by proposition 5.5.3 that $d(y, q'_0) \geq_m 0 > 2D_0(2, 7)$. □

This theorem allows us to narrow down our concern to distances between points of order two in the fundamental tiling strip and q'_0. Thus we compute 17 distances (See figure 11.8). These are all of the distances between q'_0 and a point of order two in $P \cup A(P) \cup A^{-1}(P)$. Recall that $h_0 = D_0(2, 7) + h_7$.

Lemma: 11.6.10   • $d(q'_0, q''_0) = T_0$.

- $d(q'_0, q) = T_0$.
- $d(q'_0, q''') = T_3$.
- $d(q'_0, q') = 2T_0$.

- $d(q'_0, q'') = T_2$
- $d(q'_0, A(q'_0)) = 2T_0$.
- $d(q'_0, A(q')) > d(q''_0, A(q')) = T_4$.
- $d(q'_0, A(q''')) = T_4$.
- $d(q'_0, A(q'')) = D_0(2,3) + D_0(3,7) + D_0(2,7)$.
- $d(q'_0, A(q)) = T_4$.
- $d(q'_0, A(q''_0)) = 3T_0$.
- $d(q'_0, A^{-1}(q'_0)) = 2T_0$.
- $d(q'_0, A^{-1}(q)) = d(q'_0, q'') = T_2$.
- $d(q'_0, A^{-1}(q''')) > d(A^{-1}(q''_0), A^{-1}(q''')) = T_4$.
- $d(q'_0, A^{-1}(q')) = T_3$.
- $d(q'_0, A^{-1}(q''_0)) = T_0$.
- $d(q'_0, A^{-1}(q'') = T_4$.

Proof: By construction $d(q', q'') = d(q', q) = d(q'', q) = T_0$. Since $E_q\{q', q'', q\} = \{q''_0, q'_0, q\}$, $d(q''_0, q'_0) = d(q, q'_0) = d(q, q''_0) = T_0$. Since $E_q(q'_0) = q'$, $d(q'_0, q') = 2T_0$. Since $E_{q''}(q'_0) = A(q'_0)$, $d(q'_0, A(q'_0)) = 2T_0$. Further $d(q'_0, A(q'_0)) = d(q'_0, A^{-1}(q'_0))$. We need to show that $R_{v'}^{-1}$ permutes the points $q'_0, q, q', q'', q''', A^{-1}(q'), A^{-1}(q)$ cyclically in that order. Each of the seven points is at a distance $D_0(2,7)$ from v' either by construction or as the image under A^{-1} of a point at that distance from $A^{-1}(v') = v''$. Further, A^{-1} maps points to the right of $A(h)$ to points to the right of h, so that moving clockwise about v' to the right of h we encounter $A^{-1}(q')$, $A^{-1}(q)$ and $A^{-1}(q''_0)$ in that order. Now by corollary 4.2.3 there are precisely seven fixed points of order two at a distance $D_0(2,7)$ from v'. Combine corollary 4.2.3 with theorem 4.2.5 to conclude that $R_{v'}^{-1}$ permutes these points in the cyclical order described. Similarly conclude that the clockwise rotation at v'' cyclically permutes the points $q, q''_0, A(q'_0), A(q), A(q''), A(q'''), q'$. This shows that with the

11.6. DISTANCES TO Q'_0

exception of $A(q')$, $A^{-1}(q''')$, and $A(q''_0)$ any point of order two lies either in a wedge about v' or v'' and thus in a common extended wedge with q'_0. In all cases we have already computed the distances. For example, both q' and q'_0 are on $EW(v'')$ with an angle of $k = 5$. Both q'_0 and $A(q''')$ are on $EW(v'')$ at an angle with $k = 5$. $d(q'_0, A(q'')) = D_0(2,3) + D_0(3,7) + D_0(2,7) > 2D_0(2,7)$ since both points lie on $EW(v'')$ at a wedge angle of π.

We can compute directly that $d(q'_0, A(q''_0)) = 3T_0$. In triangle $\triangle(A(q'), q''_0, q'_0)$ the angle at q''_0 is greater than $\pi/2$ whence $[A(q'), q'_0]$ is the longest side. Thus $d(q'_0, A(q')) > d(q''_0, A(q')) = T_4$. Since the triangles $\triangle(q'_0, A^{-1}(q'''), A^{-1}(Q))$ and $\triangle(A^{-1}(q''_0), A^{-1}(q'''), A^{-1}(Q))$ are both right triangles with one side $A^{-1}(Q), A^{-1}q''']$, we must have $[q'_0, A^{-1}(q''_0)]_d > [A^{-1}(q''_0), A^{-1}(q''')]_d = T_4$. □

Lemma: 11.6.11 $T_3 > D_0(2,7) + h_7 = h_0$ and $T_4 > D_0(2,7) + h_7 = h_0$.

Proof: $T_4 = d(A(q'''), q'_0)$, but $[A(q'''), q'_0]$ is the hypotenuse of the right triangle $\triangle(A(Q), A(q'''), q'_0)$ and the side $[A(Q), A(q''')]$ has length $h_0 = h_7 + D_0(2,7)$. Also $[q'_0, q''']$ is the hypotenuse of the right triangle $\triangle(q'_0, Q, q''')$ with side h_0. □

We are now able to prove theorem 11.6.1

Proof: (of theorem 11.6.1) If x lies above the axis of A and above the fundamental tile strip, apply theorem 11.6.9. It is easy to see that if x is a point of order two in $A^2(P)$ or in $A^{-2}(P)$, but on or to the right of $A^{-2}(H)$, then $d(x, q'_0) \geq 3T_0$. (See figure 11.8.) Recall that $3T_0 > T_3 > h_0$.

Further if x is a point of order two in $A^n(P)$ where $|n| \geq 3$, x is at least $3T_0$ from q'_0. Further compute that $d(q'_0, A^{-2}(q')) > d(A^{-1}(q''_0), A^{-2}(q')) = d(q''_0, A^{-1}(q')) > h_0$ since the latter two points lie on $EW(v')$ at an angle with $k = 5$. Combine this with the above lemma to obtain the theorem in the case that x lies above the axis of A. If x lies below the axis of A, then $E_{q'_0}(x)$ lies above the axis of A and is at the same distance from q'_0 as x. □

We can also prove theorem 11.6.2

Proof: (of theorem 11.6.2) All of the instances when $d(q'_0, y)$ is in the set $\{T_0, T_1, T_2, T_3, T_4\}$ are when y is either one of the seventeen points of lemma 11.6.10 or $E_{q'_0}(y)$ is. For each such y, we could either look at the picture and write down the exact element of the group that maps each pair into the corresponding pair or notice that in all cases the pair $\{q'_0, y\}$ was shown to lie in some extended wedge and then invoke the remarks at the end of chapter 4. □

11.7 Locating the three points of order two

We let (t_1, t_2, t_3) be any triple of points of order two that give a pentagon with angle $4\pi/7$. We want to locate these three points on the tiling. First of all after conjugating by an element of the group, we may assume that $t_1 = q'_0$. We want to show:

Theorem: 11.7.1 *If $d(q'_0, t_2) \leq 2D_0$, then $d(q'_0, t_2)$ is either T_0, T_1 or T_2.*

Proof: Apply theorem 11.6.1. Lemma 11.7.2 below rules out points with the distance greater than h_0. Note that $T_3 > h_0$ and $T_4 > h_0$. □

Lemma: 11.7.2 *It cannot be that $d(x, q'_0) > h_0$.*

Proof: Note that we have $h_0 > 2T_0$. If $b = d(x, q'_0) > h_0$, recall that we may assume by lemma 6.3.9 $h \geq b/2$ so that $h > T_0$. Our initial value for b_0 is T_0. Since $h > b_0$ and $\sinh h \sinh b = \sinh h_0 \sinh b_0$, it must be that $b < h_0$. But $b = d(x, q'_0) > h_0$. This gives a contradiction. □

Chapter 12

Finding the other seven and proving geometric equivalence

12.1 Introduction

In what follows we assume that G is a $(2,3,7)$ triangle group and that $t = 9$ with $k = 2$. We let $P = P_{A,B}$ be the pentagon corresponding to an arbitrary pair of generators (A, B) whose commutator is the square of a rotation by $2 \cdot 2\pi/7$. Recall that following the notation of section 5.2 the h side of P is the segment $[p_3, Q]$, the D side of is the segment $[v, p_3]$, and the β side is the segment $[Q, A(Q)]$. We saw in chapter 7 that either there is an image of $v = v_7$ interior to P or two images of v_7 on the boundary of P, one on a side and the other on its paired side, or the image of v_7 consists of Q, $A(Q)$, and T (corollary 7.4.5). In this chapter we consider the possibility that Q is an image of v_7 to be one of the ways in which v_7 can have an image on the β side of P.

The purpose of this chapter is to use all of the geometric lemmas about distances in $(2,3,7)$ triangle group and distances in the pentagon shingling to show

Theorem: 12.1.1 *There is a seven on the h side.*

As a consequence of this, we will see that

Theorem: 12.1.2 *If (C, D) generates a $(2, 3, 7)$ triangle group with $k = 2$ and $t = 9$, then there is an element of the group G that maps $Act_{C,D}$ onto $Stact_9$, the standard triangle defined in section 8.3.*

Notation: 12.1.3 *Recall that in general we use Stact to denote any of the three standard acute triangles. When it may not be clear from the context what the value of t is, we write $Stact_t$.*

The corollary of this theorem is, of course,

Theorem: 12.1.4 *If (A, B) and (C, D) are two pairs of hyperbolic generators for the $(2, 3, 7)$ triangle group with elliptic commutator where $k = 2$, then $tr\,[A, B] = tr\,[C, D]$ if and only if (A, B) is Nielsen equivalent to (C, D).*

12.2 The variation of h and b

In chapter 11 we constructed the pentagon corresponding to *Stact* and we obtained for the height h_0 and base b_0, the values $h_0 = D_0(2, 7) + h_7$ and $b_0 = T_0$. The height h and base b of any other pair of generators with $k = 2$ must satisfy

$$\sinh h \sinh b = \sinh h_0 \sinh b_0. \tag{12.1}$$

Here h_7 denotes the height of the triangle with sides D_0, D_0 and T_0 where the angle between the D_0 sides is $2\pi/7$ and $D_0 = D_0(2, 7)$. Similarly h_3 is the height of the triangle with two sides of length $D_0(2, 3)$ and angle $2\pi/3$. Our aim is to show

Theorem: 12.2.1 $b < 2D_0$.

The idea of the proof is the following. We show first that when the length doubles, its hyperbolic sine more than doubles. Thus since h and b vary inversely and the product of their hyperbolic sines is constant, if b doubles h must be half the initial value. But we also know that $h \geq b/2$. We have $h < h_0 < 2D_0(2,7)$. (This is lemma 11.5.2.) Thus $h_0/2 < D_0$. But if $b \geq 2D_0 > 2T_0$, we have $h \leq h_0/2 < D_0$. But since $h \geq b/2$, $h \geq D_0$ which gives a contradiction. We begin with

12.2. THE VARIATION OF H AND B

Lemma: 12.2.2 *If $h \neq 0$, $\sinh 2h > 2\sinh h$.*

Proof: If $h \neq 0$, then $\sinh 2h = 2\sinh h \cosh h > 2\sinh h$. □

Corollary: 12.2.3 *For any $K \neq 0$, $\sinh K/2 < \frac{\sinh K}{2}$.*

Corollary: 12.2.4 *If $b \geq 2b_0 = 2T_0$, then $h < h_0/2$.*

Proof: We know $\sinh(h/2) < (\sinh h)/2$. Combining equation 12.1 with $b \geq 2b_0$ and the double angle formula for hyperbolic sines (6.4), gives

$$\sinh h_0 \cdot \sinh b_0 = \sinh h \sinh b \geq \sinh h \cdot \sin 2b_0 = \sinh h \cdot 2 \cdot \sinh b_0 \cosh b_0.$$

Thus $(\sinh h_0)/2 \geq \sinh h$. By 12.2.2 $(\sinh h_0)/2 < \sinh(h_0/2)$. Thus $\sinh h < \sinh(h_0/2)$ or $h < (h_0/2)$. □

This proves the theorem.

Corollary: 12.2.5 *If h and b are the height and base of a $(2,3,7)$ pentagon with $t = 9$ and $k = 2$, then $b = T_0, T_1,$ or T_2 and $h > D_0(2,7)/2$.*

Proof: Theorem 11.7.1 from chapter 11, tells us that if $b < 2D_0$, the only possibilities for b are $T_0, 2T_0 = T_1$ and T_2. Now if $b = T_0$, $h = h_0 > D_0(2,7)$. Also $T_1 > D_0$ and $T_2 > D_0$ (11.4) so that $h > D_0(2,7)/2$. □

If we let $\{p_1, p_2, p_3\}$ be the vertices of the triangle determining the pentagon P, we may assume that the sides of the triangle follow our labeling convention so that $b = d(p_1, p_2)$ is the length of its smallest side. We use the following notation.

Notation: 12.2.6 *The triangle $\triangle(p_1, p_2, p_3)$ is the next to the last triangle along the axis of $A = E_{p_1} E_{p_2}$ so that $\triangle(p_2, E_{p_2}(p_1), p_3) = \triangle(p_2, \bar{p}_1, p_3)$ is the acute triangle where $\bar{p}_1 = E_{p_2}(p_1)$. Thus if $\{t_1, t_2, t_3\}$ denotes the vertices of $Act_{A,B}$, then $t_1 = p_2$, $t_2 = \bar{p}_1$ and $t_3 = p_3$.*

12.3 Rule out a seven on the β side

Lemma: 12.3.1 *There is no seven on β.*

Proof: Assume that v' is a seven lying on β. Note that we allow for the possibility that $v' = Q$. Then v' lies in the interval $[A(Q), p_1]$, $[p_1, T]$, $[T, p_2]$ or $[p_2, Q]$. Note that E_{p_1} identifies the first two intervals and E_{p_2} identifies the second two intervals. We want to show that $\beta_d \geq 4D_0(2, 7)$. Assume first that v' lies in $[A(Q), p_1]$. The length of β is the same as the length of the interval $[v, A(v)]$. However,

$$[v', A(v')] = [v', p_1] \cup [p_1, E_{p_1}(v')] \cup [E_{p_1}(v'), p_2] \cup [p_2, E_{p_2}(E_{p_1}(v'))].$$

Each of these subintervals has a two and a seven as an end point. Thus each has length greater at least $D_0(2, 7)$. This proves the assertion. If v' lies in any of the other four subintervals argue in a similar manner. In all cases $\beta_d \geq 4D_0(2, 7)$ whence $b_d \geq 2D_0(2, 7)$ which we already ruled out. $\square$

12.4 Rule out a seven on the D side

Next we want to rule out the possibility that there is a seven on the D side. The idea of the argument is that if there is a seven on the D side, then $D \geq 3D_0(2, 7)$. The formula 6.16 $\cosh D \cdot \sin 2\pi/7 = \cosh b$, then forces b to also be large.

We begin with

Lemma: 12.4.1 *If $D \geq 3D_0(2, 7)$, then $b \geq 2D_0(2, 7)$.*

This has as a corollary

Theorem: 12.4.2 *There can be no seven on a D side.*

Proof: If there is a seven on the D side, then the length of the side is at least $D_0(7, 7) + D_0(7, 2)$ since the end points are points of order seven and two. But we saw (proposition 4.4.1) that $D_0(7, 7) = 2D_0(2, 7)$. $\square$

12.4. RULE OUT A SEVEN ON THE D SIDE

We now prove lemma 12.4.1: We let $D_0 = D_0(2,7)$ and recall that $\cosh D_0(2,7) = \frac{1}{2\sin \pi/7}$. We assume that $b \leq 2D_0$ and obtain a contradiction. We know (via 6.16) that

$$\cosh 3D_0 \cdot \sin 2\pi/7 \leq \cosh D \cdot \sin 2\pi/7 = \cosh b \leq \cosh 2D_0.$$

Using the formulae for cosh and sinh of a sum (6.1 and 6.2), $\cosh 3D_0$ simplifies to

$$\cosh 3D_0 = \cosh 2D_0 \cosh D_0 + \sinh 2D_0 \sinh D_0$$

$$= \cosh 2D_0 \cosh D_0 + 2\cosh D_0 \sinh D_0 \sinh D_0$$

$$= \cosh D_0 \cdot (\cosh 2D_0 + 2\sinh^2 D_0)$$

$$= \cosh D_0 \cdot (\cosh^2 D_0 + \sinh^2 D_0 + 2\sinh^2 D_0)$$

$$= \cosh D_0 \cdot (\cosh^2 D_0 + 3\sinh^2 D_0).$$

We have

$$\cosh D_0 \cdot (\cosh 2D_0 + 2\sinh^2 D_0) \cdot \sin 2\pi/7 \leq \cosh 2D_0.$$

Since $\cosh D_0 \cdot \sin 2\pi/7 = \cos \pi/7$, we obtain

$$(\cos \pi/7)(1 + 2\frac{\sinh^2 D_0}{\cosh 2D_0}) \leq 1.$$

We set

$$\mathcal{Q} = 2\frac{\sinh^2 D_0}{\cosh 2D_0}.$$

Our inequality becomes

$$\cos \pi/7 \leq 1/(1+\mathcal{Q}).$$

Now $\cos \pi/7 > \cos \pi/6 > 1.732/2 > .85 > 4/5$. Suppose $\mathcal{Q} > 1/4$. Calculate that $\frac{1}{1+\mathcal{Q}} < 4/5$. This would give a contradiction proving the lemma. Therefore, we show

Lemma: 12.4.3 $\mathcal{Q} > 1/4$.

Proof:

$$Q = 2\frac{\sinh^2 D_0}{\cosh 2D_0} = \frac{2\sinh^2 D_0}{\cosh^2 D_0 + \sinh^2 D_0}.$$

Let $x = \cosh D_0$ so that $\sinh^2 D_0 = x^2 - 1$. Then $Q = \frac{2x^2-2}{x^2+x^2-1}$. Suppose to the contrary that $Q < 1/4$. Compute that $x^2 < 7/6$. Recall that $x = \frac{1}{2\sin\pi/7}$. Conclude that $3/14 < \sin^2 \pi/7$.

Estimate that $(2.2)/5 < \sin\pi/7$ since $1/5 = 3/15 < 3/14$. Using trig tables, compute that $\pi/7$ radians is less than 26 degrees and $\sin 26 < .4386$. This contradicts $Q < \frac{1}{4}$. □

12.5 Interior sevens

We have now ruled out sevens on D or on β. We now want to rule out an interior seven. Our assumptions are that $d(p_1, p_2) = T_0, T_2$ or T_3 and that $2h \geq D_0(2,7)$.

Now there are two seven's closest to p_3, one on each side of $\widetilde{[v, p_3]}$. Let w be the seven on the tile side of $[v, p_3]$. If w were simultaneously above the fundamental tiling strip, then $d(w, A(p_3)) < d(w, p_3)$ or $d(w, A^{-1}(p_3)) < d(w, p_3)$ so that either $A(w)$ or $A^{-1}(w)$ would be closer to p_3 than w. Thus we may assume that w is either in the fundamental tiling strip or below it. If w were to lie below the fundamental tiling strip, then $d(p_3, w)$ would b greater than $2h$ thus greater than D_0, which cannot happen. Thus w lies in the fundamental strip. In what follows our goal is to locate w and to show that w must actually lie on h. This will force b to equal T_0.

We first show

Lemma: 12.5.1
- If $b = T_0$, w must lie in P or $A^{-1}(P)$.

- If $b = T_1$ or T_2, w $\underline{\text{must lie inside}}$ $P \cup A^{-1}(P) \cup E_{p_1}(P) \cup E_{p_2}(P)$ between $\tilde{H}$ and $\overline{A^{-1}(H)}$.

Remark: 12.5.2 *In all cases there is an element of order seven inside $P \cup A^{-1}(P)$ for if w is not in P or $A^{-1}(P)$, then $E_{p_1}(w)$ or $E_{p_2}(w)$ is.*

We first prove

12.5. INTERIOR SEVENS

Lemma: 12.5.3 *If x is any point lying in $\mathcal{P}$ or below the fundamental tiling strip and τ a geodesic connecting x to p_3, then either x lies in $P \cup A^{-1}(P)$, or τ crosses the axis of A so that $\tau_d \geq h_d$ or τ crosses $A(h)$ or $A^{-1}(h)$ in which case $\tau_d \geq 2b_d$. If τ crosses $\widetilde{H}$ or $\widetilde{A^{-1}(H)}$, then $\tau_d \geq b_d$.*

Proof: There are only three routes by which τ can exit $P \cup A^{-1}(P)$. Let τ_q be the point where τ crosses either the axis of A or $A(h)$ or $A^{-1}(h)$. If τ_q lies on Ax_A, then p_3, Q, τ_q determines a right triangle with one side h. The hypotenuse, which is the segment $[p_3, \tau_q]$, is the same as the intersection of τ with P and, therefore, has length at most τ_d. If τ_q lies on $A(h)$ or $A^{-1}(h)$, then $[p_3, \tau_q]$ is a transversal between h and $A(h)$ or $A^{-1}(h)$. But Ax_A is a common perpendicular to any two out of these three lines and, therefore, $\tau_d \geq [p_3, \tau_q]_d \geq 2b_d$. Similarly, since H and $A^{-1}(H)$ are perpendicular to Ax_A, if τ crosses $\widetilde{H}$ or its inverse image under A, then $\tau_d \geq [h, H]_d = b_d$. □

Proof: (of lemma 12.5.1). We have $d(w, p_3) = D_0(2, 7)$. Let τ be a geodesic connecting w and p_3.

- If $b = T_0$, $h_d = h_0 < D_0(2,7)$ and $2b_d = 2T_0 > D_0(2,7)$. Thus $h_d > \tau_d$ and $2b_d > \tau_d$.

- If $b = T_1$ or T_2, then $b_d > D_0(2,7)$ and $2h \geq D_0(2,7)$. Thus $b_d > \tau_d$ and $2h \geq D_0(2,7)$.

Thus τ cannot cross $\widetilde{H}$ or $\widetilde{A^{-1}(H)}$.

If τ crosses the axis of A, then it must enter either $E_{p_1}(P)$ or $E_{p_2}(P)$. If it exits either of these, it must exit across the image of a D or D' side so that its intersection with $E_{p_1}(P)$ or $E_{p_2}(P)$ must have length at least h_d.

Thus if it were to exit either of these, the total length of τ would be at least $2h_d$. Since this is at least $D_0(2,7)$, it cannot exit either one. □

12.6 Notation

We need to refer to the standard pentagon constructed in chapter 11. In order to use the notation of that chapter, we make a few modifications. When referring to the standard sides and points of the standard pentagon constructed in that chapter we replace a label by the corresponding boldface label. That is, we replace A by $\mathbf{A}$, Q by $\mathbf{Q}$ and v by $\mathbf{v}$. We use $\mathbf{St(P)}$ to denote this standard pentagon. Its h-side, D-side and β-side are denoted by $\mathbf{h}$, $\mathbf{D}$ and $\boldsymbol{\beta}$. Similarly, we let $\mathbf{H}$ denote the perpendicular from $\mathbf{v}$ to the axis of $\mathbf{A}$. $\mathbf{B} = E_{\mathbf{q}_0} E_{\mathbf{q}'''}$. Other notation remains the same unless noted. For example, $R_{\mathbf{v}}$ is the rotation with fixed point $\mathbf{v}$.

Let $\mathcal{A}$ be the axis of $\mathbf{A} = E_{\mathbf{q}'_0} E_{\mathbf{q}_0''}$.

Lemma: 12.6.1
- $d(\mathbf{q}, \mathcal{A}) = h_3 + D_0(2,3)$.
- $d(\mathbf{q}''', \mathcal{A}) = d(\mathbf{A}(\mathbf{q}'''), \mathcal{A}) = h_7 + D_0(2,7) = h_0$.
- $d(\mathbf{q}', \mathcal{A}) = d(\mathbf{q}'', \mathcal{A}) > 2(h_3 + D_0(2,3))$.

Proof: We refer to figure 11.5 and section 11.5. Recall that $\mathbf{N}$ is the point where $[\mathbf{q}', \mathbf{q}'']$ intersects $[\mathbf{v}, \mathbf{S}]$. Let $\mathbf{N}_0 = E_{\mathbf{q}}(\mathbf{N})$. Since $E_{\mathbf{q}}([\mathbf{N}, \mathbf{S}, \mathbf{q}]) = [\mathbf{N}_0, \mathbf{S}_0, \mathbf{q}]$ and $E_{\mathbf{q}}(\triangle(\mathbf{q}', \mathbf{q}'', \mathbf{q})) = \triangle(\mathbf{q}'_0, \mathbf{q}''_0, \mathbf{q})$, $[\mathbf{N}, \mathbf{S}, \mathbf{q}, \mathbf{S}_0, \mathbf{N}_0]$ is a geodesic of length $2h_3 + 2D_0(2,3)$ and is a common perpendicular to $[\mathbf{q}', \mathbf{q}'']$ and $\mathcal{A}$. Also $[\mathbf{q}, \mathbf{S}_0, \mathbf{N}_0]$ is perpendicular to $\mathcal{A}$ and has length $h_3 + D_0(2,3)$. This says that $d(\mathbf{q}', \mathcal{A}) \geq [\mathbf{N}, \mathbf{N}_0])_d$ and that $d(\mathbf{q}, \mathcal{A}) = [\mathbf{q}, \mathbf{N}_0]_d$. The lemma for $\mathbf{q}$, $\mathbf{q}'$ and $\mathbf{q}''$ follows from this. We also note that $d(\mathbf{q}''', \mathcal{A}) = [\mathbf{q}''', \mathbf{Q}]_d = [\mathbf{q}''', \mathbf{v}']_d + [\mathbf{v}', \mathbf{Q}]_d$. By construction $[\mathbf{q}''', \mathbf{v}']_d = D_0(2,7)$. Also $[\mathbf{v}', \mathbf{Q}]$ is the height of the triangle $\triangle(\mathbf{v}', \mathbf{q}'_0, \mathbf{A}(\mathbf{q}_0''))$, which is precisely h_7. □

Remark: 12.6.2 *We note that $[\mathbf{q}, \mathbf{N}_0]$ is the height of an equilateral triangle with base T_0. Thus $T_0 > [\mathbf{q}, \mathbf{N}_0]_d > T_0/2$.*

12.6.1 $b = T_0$

If $b_d = T_0$, then by 12.1 we must have $h_d = h_0$. Thus w lies in P or $A^{-1}(P)$ between $\widetilde{H}$ and $\widetilde{A^{-1}(H)}$. There is also a fixed point of order 7,

12.6. NOTATION

V at a distance $D_0(2,7)$ from p_2 either on the perpendicular bisector of p_1 and p_2 or between p_2 and $\bar{p}_1$. Do a case by case analysis to see that if V and w are not equal, then we obtain two sevens interior to P, contradicting the extended Knapp count. Thus we must have $V = w$ whence p_2 and p_3 lie on the same $W(V)$. Either p_1 or $\bar{p}_1$ is also in this $W(V)$. Since $d(p_1, p_2) = T_0$, we can list the possibilities for p_3. If $p_2 = R_V(p_1)$, the possibilities for p_3 are $R_V^2(p_1)$, $R_V^3(p_1)$, $R_V^4(p_1)$, $R_v^5(p_1)$ and $R_V^6(p_1)$. If $\bar{p}_1 = R_V(p_2)$, the possibilities for p_3 are $R_V^2(p_2)$, $R_V^3(p_2)$, $R_V^4(p_2)$, $R_v^5(p_2)$ and $R_V^6(p_2)$.

We know that $d(p_3, \widetilde{[p_1, p_2]}) = h_0$.

We compute that $d(R_V^2(p_1), \widetilde{[p_1, p_2]}) = d(\mathbf{q}, \mathcal{A}) = h_3 + D_0(2,3) < h_7 + D_0(2,7) = h_0$. Further $d(R_V^3(p_1), \widetilde{[p_1, p_2]}) = d(\mathbf{q}'', \mathcal{A}) < d(\mathbf{q}_0', \mathbf{q}'') < 2T_0 < h_0$. But $d(R_V^4(p_1), \widetilde{[p_1, p_2]}) = h_0$. The possibility that $p_3 = R_V^{4+s}(p_1)$ gives the same height as $R_V^{4-s}(p_1)$. Thus we have ruled out all possibilities when $p_1 \in W(V)$ expect $p_3 = R_V^4(p_1)$. In this case, p_3 lies on the perpendicular bisector of p_1 and p_2 forcing $\triangle(p_1, p_2, p_3)$ to be an acute triangle. Since $\triangle(p_2, \bar{p}_1, p_3)$ is the acute triangle, this case is also ruled out. Similar height arguments rule out all possibilities when $\bar{p}_1 \in W(V)$ except $p_3 = R_V^4(p_2)$. Note that in this case, V actually lies on h and not interior to P. We have shown

Proposition: 12.6.3 *It cannot be that $b = T_0$ unless there is a seven on h and no interior sevens.*

12.6.2 Rule out $b = 2T_0 = T_1$.

If $b = 2T_0$, apply lemma 11.5.2 and theorems 11.6.2 and 11.6.9 to conclude that $t_1 = \mathbf{q}_0'$ and $t_2 = \mathbf{A}(\mathbf{q}_0')$ or that $t_1 = \mathbf{q}_0''$ and $t_2 = \mathbf{A}^{-1}(\mathbf{q}_0'')$. In both these cases the axis of $E_{t_1} E_{t_2}$ is $\mathcal{A}$. For both cases we want to consider what the possible t_3's are. If t_3 lies above the fundamental tiling strip, then $d(t_3, \mathcal{A}) \geq h_0$. Since $b = 2T_0$, we know that $h < h_0/2$. Thus t_3 cannot lie above the fundamental tiling strip. Thus t_3 must be an image under a power of $\mathbf{A}$ of $\mathbf{q}$, $\mathbf{q}'$, $\mathbf{q}''$, $\mathbf{q}'''$ or $\mathbf{A}(\mathbf{q}''')$.

If t_3 were equal to $\mathbf{q}'''$ or any of its images under $\mathbf{A}$ then $d(t_3, \mathcal{A}) = h_0$ which is too large.

If $b = 2T_0$, we must have $h < h_0/2$. We note that $h_0 < 2D_0(2,7)$ so that when $b = 2T_0$, we must have $h < D_0$. We will prove that

$d(\mathbf{q}'', \mathcal{A}) > D_0$. This will show that t_3 cannot be $\mathbf{q}'$ or $\mathbf{q}''$ or any of their images under A or its inverse. We consider the quadrilateral with vertices $\mathbf{S}, \mathbf{N}_0, \mathbf{Q}$ and $\mathbf{v}'$. It has two right angles, at $\mathbf{N}_0$ and $\mathbf{Q}$ and the angle at $\mathbf{v}'$ is $4\pi/7$. Thus the angle at $\mathbf{S}$ is at most $3\pi/7$. Lemma 6.3.7 tells us that in a quadrilateral with two right angles, the side opposite the larger non-right angle is larger than the side opposite the other non-right angle. Thus $d(\mathbf{S}, \mathbf{N}_0) > d(\mathbf{Q}, \mathbf{v}')$. But $d(\mathbf{Q}, \mathbf{v}') = D_0(2, 7)$. Since $d(\mathbf{q}'', \mathcal{A}) \geq d(\mathbf{N}_0, \mathbf{N}) > d(\mathbf{N}_0, \mathbf{S})$, $D(\mathbf{q}'', \mathcal{A}) > D_0(2, 7)$ giving the desired contradiction.

Thus we need only consider the case where t_3 is $\mathbf{q}$ or an image of $\mathbf{q}$. Assume first that $t_3 = \mathbf{q}$. Then $h = [\mathbf{q}, \mathbf{N}_0]_d < T_0$. But $h \geq b/2 = 2T_0/2 = T_0$ giving a contradiction. Since images of $\mathbf{q}$ under powers of $\mathbf{A}$ have the same distance from $ax_\mathbf{A}$ as $\mathbf{q}$ does, t_3 is not any image of $\mathbf{q}$.

Thus, it cannot occur that $b = 2T_0$.

12.6.3 Rule out $\{\mathbf{q}, \mathbf{A}^{-1}(\mathbf{q}), \mathbf{q}'''\}$.

We continue to assume that $d(p_1, p_2) \leq d(p_i, p_3)$ for $i = 1$ or 2. The fact that $h \geq b/2$ depends upon this assumption. However, the construction of the pentagon determined by $A = E_{p_1} E_{p_2}$ and $B = E_{p_3} E_{p_2}$ does not make use of this assumption. Whatever the relative lengths of the side of the triangle $\triangle(p_1, p_2, p_3)$, we still have the following:

- The axis of A is a common perpendicular to the h and H sides so that $d(p_1, p_2) = b = d(h, H)$.

- The D side lies on the perpendicular to h at p_3.

- The extended Knapp count holds.

Proposition: 12.6.4 *Assume that $p_1 = \mathbf{q}$, $p_2 = \mathbf{A}^{-1}(\mathbf{q})$ and $p_2 = \mathbf{q}'''$. Then $E_{p_1} E_{p_2} E_{p_3} = \gamma$ cannot be a rotation by $2 \cdot 2\pi/7$.*

As a corollary we have

Corollary: 12.6.5 *$E_{p_2} E_{p_3} E_{p_1}$ is not a rotation by $2 \cdot 2\pi/7$.*

12.6. NOTATION

Proof: (of 12.6.4). Since $d(\mathbf{q}, \mathbf{v}') = d(\mathbf{A}^{-1}(\mathbf{q}), \mathbf{v}')$, $[\mathbf{q}''', \widetilde{\mathbf{v}', \mathbf{Q}}]$ is perpendicular to $[\mathbf{q}, \mathbf{A}^{-1}(\mathbf{q})]$. Let K be the point of intersection of these two lines. Then $[\mathbf{q}''', K]$ is the h side of $P_{A,B}$ and $\mathbf{v}'$ lies on this h side. The D side of this pentagon lies on $[\mathbf{v}, \widetilde{\mathbf{S}'''}, \mathbf{q}''']$ because it lies on the perpendicular to h through $p_3 = \mathbf{q}'''$. If the vertex v of $P_{A,B}$ were to equal $\mathbf{v}$, the vertex of $P_{\mathbf{A},\mathbf{B}}$ of chapter 11, then the H side of $P_{A,B}$ would lie along the segment through $\mathbf{v}$ that makes an angle of $2 \cdot 2\pi/7$ with $\mathbf{D}$. Thus H would lie on $\mathbf{H}$. I.e. $d(H, h) = d(\mathbf{H}, \mathbf{h})$. But $d(\mathbf{H}, \mathbf{h}) = T_0$ by construction and $2T_0 = d(p_1, p_2) = d(H, h)$. Thus v must lie further along $\mathbf{D}$ than $\mathbf{v}$. Thus $P_{A,B}$ has sevens on both its D and its h sides, contradicting the extended Knapp count. □

Proof: (of 12.6.5). If $E_{p_1} E_{p_2} E_{p_3} = \gamma$ cannot be a rotation by $2 \cdot 2\pi/7$, then $E_{p_2} E_{p_3} E_{p_1}$ which is conjugate to it cannot be a rotation by $2 \cdot 2\pi/7$. □

In particular

Corollary: 12.6.6 If $t_1 = p$, $t_2 = R_7^2(p)$, and $t_3 = R_7^5(p)$ or $t_3 = R_7^4(p)$ where p is in $W(7)$, then $E_{t_1} E_{t_2} E_{t_3}$ cannot be a rotation of order 7 through an angle of $2 \cdot 2\pi/7$.

12.6.4 Rule out $b = T_2$.

In this case, we let w be the seven closest to p_3. Our naming convention assures that $p_3 = t_3$ is closer to $p_2 = t_1$ than $\bar{p}_1 = t_2$. (See figure 12.1.)

Further, we know that there is a seven either on the perpendicular bisector of p_1 and p_2 or p_2 and $\bar{p}_1$. Call it V. We return to the wedge at 7, $W(V)$, and let h_2 be the height of the triangle $\triangle(V, p, R_V^2(p))$.

Lemma: 12.6.7 $h_2 < T_2/2$.

Proof: The proof refers to figure 12.2. Let E be the point where $[V, R_V(p)]$ intersects $[p, R_V^2(p)]$ so that $[p, E]_d = T_2/2$. $\triangle(p, 7, E)$ is a right triangle and $h_2 = [7, E]_d$. Let $\alpha = \measuredangle (p, 7, R_V(p))$ and $\beta = \measuredangle (7, p, E)$. Then $\alpha = 2\pi/7$ and $[7, E]_d \leq [p, E]$ if and only if $\beta \leq 2\pi/7$. We know that $\beta < 2\pi/7$ because $\alpha + \beta + \pi/2 < \pi$. □

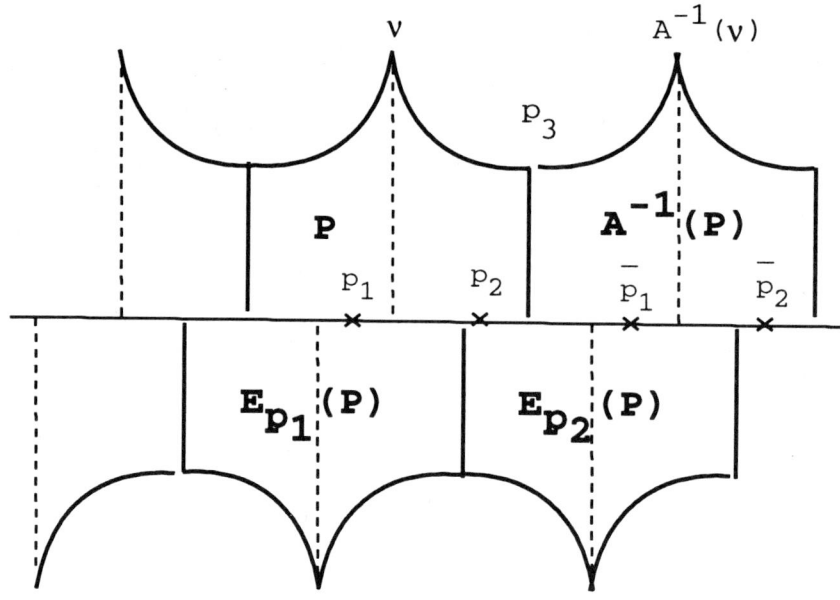

Figure 12.1: T_2

We want to locate V in the tiling. We know that the height from V to $\mathcal{A}$ is h_2. Now for a general pentagon constructed in this manner $h \geq b/2$. Thus in this case, $h \geq T_2/2 > d(V, \mathcal{A})$. Thus V lies in P or $A^{-1}(P)$. We will show

Lemma: 12.6.8 *Assume that V and w are not on $\tilde{h}$ or $\widetilde{A(h)}$. Then exactly one of the following occurs.*

1. *$w = V$ and both lie in P.*

2. *$w = V$ and both lie in $A^{-1}(P)$.*

3. *$E_{p_1}(w) = A(V)$ and both lie in P.*

4. *$E_{p_2}(w) = V$ and both lie in P to the right of H or $E_{p_2}(w) = A(V)$ and both lie in P to the left of H.*

Proof: We note that if $V \in P$, then V is to the right of H and if $V \in A^{-1}(H)$, then V is to the left of $A^{-1}(H)$. We consider the eight cases.

12.6. NOTATION

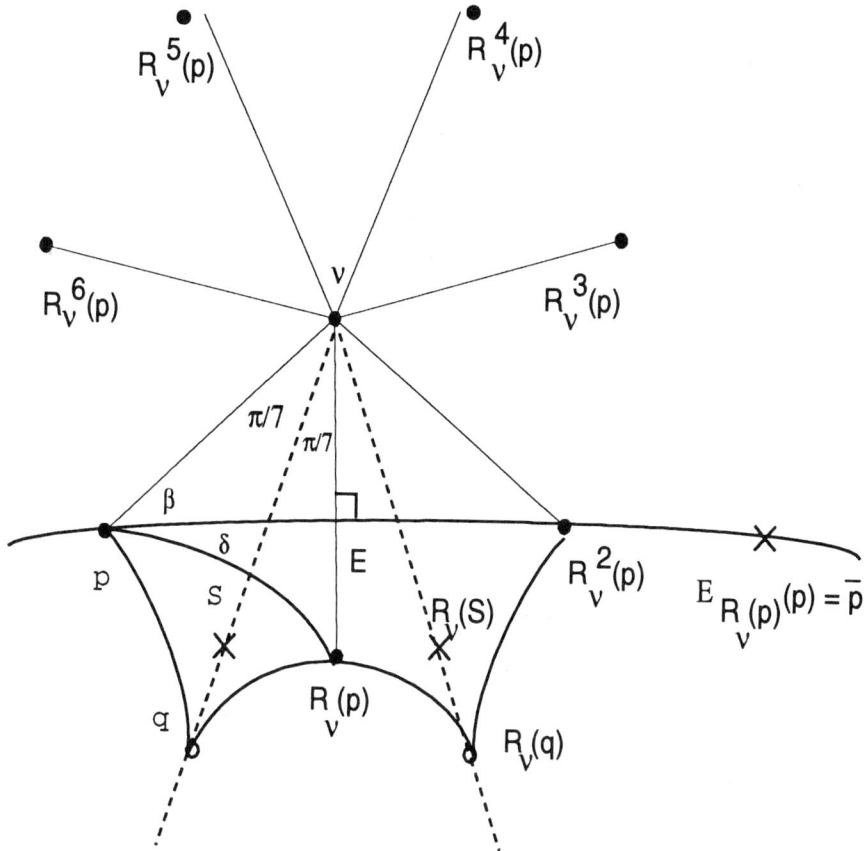

Figure 12.2: h_2

- $w \in P$ and
    $V \in P$ or
    $V \in A^{-1}(P)$.
- $w \in A^{-1}(P)$ and
    $V \in P$ or
    $V \in A^{-1}(P)$.
- $w \in E_{p_1}(P)$ and
    $V \in P$ or
    $V \in A^{-1}(P)$.
- $w \in E_{p_2}(P)$ and
    $V \in P$ or
    $V \in A^{-1}(P)$.

In all cases we obtain two sevens interior to P. However, by the extended Knapp count, we know that only one seven (if any) can lie interior to P. Thus any two interior seven's must be equal. We do a case by case analysis and rule out half of the possibilities:

- If $V \in A^{-1}(P)$, then $A(V)$ is to the left of H, but if $w \in P$, w is to the right of H. Thus is cannot be that $A(V) = w$.

- If $w \in A^{-1}(P)$, $A(w) \in P$ and to the left of H. If $V \in P$, it is to the right of H. Thus it cannot be that $A^{-1}(w) = V \in P$.

- If $w' = E_{p_1}(w)$ lies in P, then it lies to the left of H. If V simultaneously lies in P, it is to the right of H. Thus it cannot be that $w' = V$ and both are in P.

- If $w \in E_{p_2}(P)$, w either lies to the left or to the right of $E_{p_2}(\tilde{H})$, so that w' then either lies to the right or left of $\tilde{H}$. If $w' = E_{p_2}(w)$ lies in P and it lies to the left of H, then V which lies to the right of H cannot lie in P. If V lies in $A^{-1}(P)$, then $A(V)$ lies in P to the left of H and this is a possibility. Also if w' is to the right of H, then it can happen that V lies in P but not that V lies in $A^{-1}(P)$. Thus we either have $E_{p_2}(w) = V \in P$ or $E_{p_2}(w) = A(V) \in P$.

12.6. NOTATION

☐

In all cases the perpendicular from p_3 to $\widetilde{[p_1, p_2]}$ intersects this geodesic between p_2 and $\bar{p}_1$. The four cases to consider are the following.

1. $p_1, p_2, p_3 \in W(w) = W(V)$ and $V = w \in P$.

2. $p_2, p_3, \bar{p}_1 \in W(w) = W(V)$ and $V = w \in A^{-1}(P)$.

3. $\bar{p}_1, p_2 \in W(V)$, $p_3 \in W(w)$, $A(V) = E_{p_1}(w)$ and $V \in A^{-1}(P)$.

4. $p_1, p_2 \in W(V)$, $V \in P$, and $p_3 \in W(w)$ and $E_{p_2}(w) = V$ whence $E_{p_2}(p_3) \in W(E_{p_2}(w))$ or $V \in A^{-1}(P)$, $p_2, \bar{p}_1 \in W(V)$, $V = E_{\bar{p}_1}(w)$ and $p_3 \in W(w)$.

We want to rule out each of these cases. We first consider case 1 where we may assume that $p = p_1$ and $p_2 = R_V^2(p)$. We know that p_3 is one of $\{R_V(p), R_V^3(p), R_V^4(p), R_V^5(p), R_V^6(p)\}$. The treatment for the case that $p_3 = R_V^5(p)$ is the same as that for $p_3 = R_V^4(p)$, namely both possibilities are ruled out by 12.6.6. The treatment for the case that $p_3 = R_V^6(p)$ is the same as that for $p_3 = R_V^3(p)$. If $p_3 = R_V^3(p)$, then $d(t_2, t_3) = T_0 < T_2 = d(t_1, t_2)$. This contradicts our assumption that $[t_1, t_2]$ was the shortest side of the triangle. If $p_3 = R_V(p)$, then p_3 and V lie on opposite sides of $\widetilde{[p_1, p_2]}$ from each other, which is not the case.

For case 2 the argument is essentially the same as in case 1.

In case 3, again we may assume that $p_2 = p$, $\bar{p}_1 = R_V^2(p)$. Now $p_3 \in W(w)$ where $E_{p_1}(w) = A(V)$ or $E_{p_2}(w) = V$. Thus $E_{p_2}(p_3) \in W(E_{p_2}(w)) = W(V)$. Now p_3 and V lie on the same side of Ax_A so that $E_{p_2}(p_3)$ lies on the opposite side of the axis from V. The only point of order two in $W(V)$ and on the opposite side of the axis of A from V is $R_V(p)$. Conclude that $E_{p_2}(p_3) = R_V(p)$. Since $E_{p_2}(Ax_A) = Ax_A$, $d(p_3, Ax_A) = d(E_{p_2}(p_3), Ax_A) = d(R_V(p), Ax_A) = h_2 < T_2/2$ which is too small. Thus case 3 is ruled out. (See figure 12.3.)

We now turn to the first part of case 4 where $V = E_{p_2}(w) \in P$ to the right of H, $p_3 \in W(w)$, and $E_{p_2}(p_3) \in W(V)$. We may assume that $p_1 = p$ and $p_2 = R_V^2(p)$. Since p_3 lies above the axis of A, $E_{p_2}(p_3)$ must lie below the axis of A and must, therefore, equal $R_V(p)$. Again

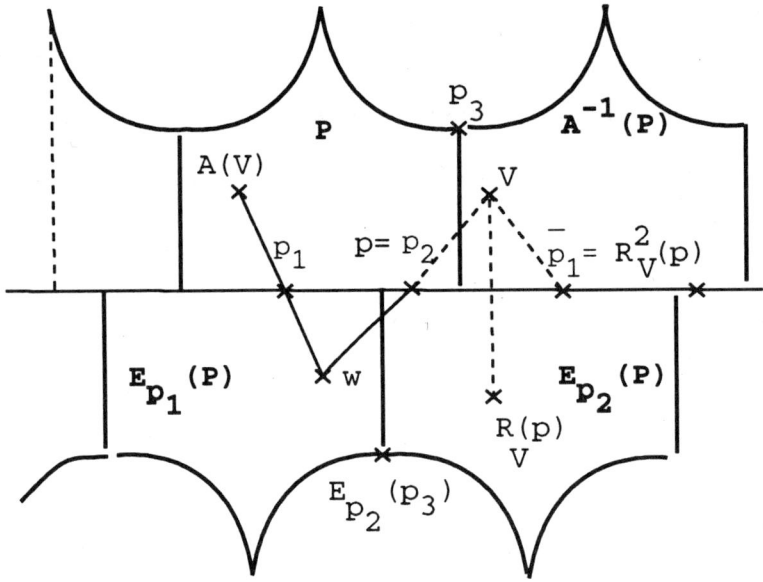

Figure 12.3: Case 3.

this gives a height that is too small. (See figure 12.4.) In the second part of case 4 we have $V \in A^{-1}(P)$, $p_2, \bar{p}_1 \in W(V)$, $V = E_{\bar{p}_1}(w)$, and $p_3 \in W(w)$. Thus $E_{\bar{p}_1}(p_3) \in W(V)$. Again p_3 and $E_{\bar{p}_1}(p_3)$ lie on opposite sides of Ax_A forcing $E_{\bar{p}_1}(p_3)$ to be $R_V(p)$ if $p_2 = p$ and $\bar{p}_1 = R_V^2(p)$. Again this gives a height that is too small.

We have proved

Theorem: 12.6.9 *It cannot be that $b = T_2$.*

In fact we have established a slightly stronger theorem:

Theorem: 12.6.10 *There are no interior sevens. If there is a seven on an h side, then $b = T_0$ and $h = h_0$ with $(t_1, t_2, t_3) = (p, R_v(p), R_v^4(p))$.*

12.7 Summary and proof of geometric and Nielsen equivalence

We have thus ruled out all of the possibilities except that $b = T_0$, $h = h_0$ and that after applying some element of the group the points

12.7. GEOMETRIC EQUIVALENCE $(2,3,7)T = 9; K = 2$

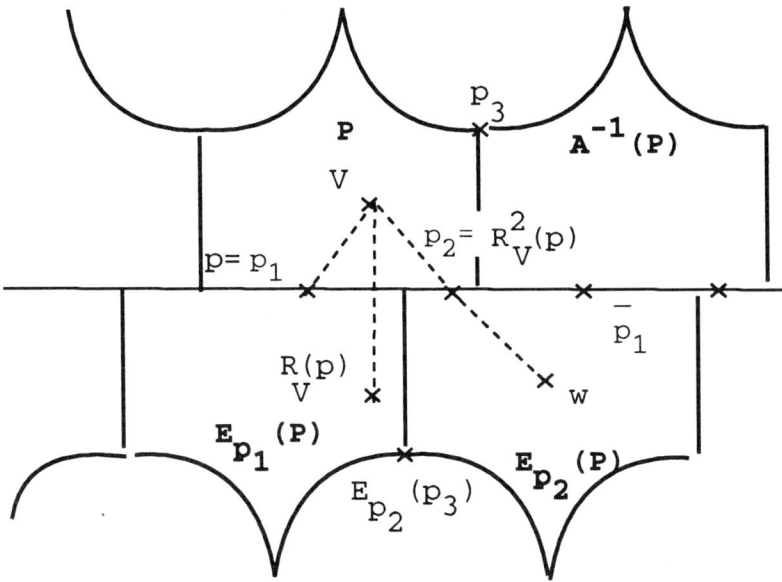

Figure 12.4: Case 4 part one.

t_1, t_2, and t_3 all lie on some wedge about a seven with $t_2 = R_7(t_1)$ and $t_3 = R_7^4(t_1)$. In short, we have not only proved theorem 12.1.1, we have actually proved theorem 12.1.2.

Chapter 13

The Proof of the Discreteness Theorem

We are now able to prove the discreteness theorem (theorem 3.1.1). First we note that the geometric equivalence theorem follows immediately when the outline of its proof in chapter 3 is taken together with theorems 9.1.1, 10.1.1, 12.1.2 and A.0.2.

13.1 The Proof of the Discreteness Theorem

We begin with A and B and construct the pentagon associated to A and B as in chapter 5. Apply lemma 5.3.1 to conclude that G is discrete if $[A, B]$ is either hyperbolic, parabolic, or elliptic with γ a primitive rotation. If $[A, B]$ is a rotation of infinite order, G is not discrete. Thus we may assume that $[A, B]$ is elliptic and rotates by an angle 2θ and that $\gamma = E_{p_1} E_{p_2} E_{p_3}$ rotates by an angle of $\theta = \pm k \cdot 2\pi/n$ where k and n are integers with $2 \leq k < n/2$.

Lemma: 13.1.1 $Tr\,[A, B] = -2\cos\theta$.

Proof: Let a, b, e_1, e_2, e_3, and g be matrices in $SL(2, R)$ whose images in $PSL(2, \mathbf{R})$ are respectively $A, B, E_{p_1}, E_{p_2}, E_{p_3}$, and γ with $g = e_1 e_2 e_3$. Recall that replacing a and/or b by its negative leaves $Tr\,[a, b]$ unchanged so that $Tr\,[A, B]$ is well defined. Also e_i is conjugate to the matrix $\pm \begin{pmatrix} 0 & -1 \\ 1 & 0 \end{pmatrix}$ so that $e_i^2 = -1$. We have $[A, B] = \gamma^2$ and $[a, b] = (e_1 e_2 e_3)(e_2 e_2)(e_1 e_2 e_3)$ so that $[a, b] = -g^2$. Thus $Tr\,[A, B] = Tr\,[a, b] = -Tr\,g^2$. Now $Tr\,g = \pm 2\cos\frac{\theta}{2}$. Since for any matrix X with determinant 1, $Tr\,(X^2) = (Tr\,X)^2 - 2$, we have $Tr\,(g^2) = (\pm 2\cos\frac{\theta}{2})^2 - 2 = 4\cos^2\frac{\theta}{2} - 2 = 2\cos\theta$. □

Thus we may assume that we are in case 4 of the discreteness theorem. Apply the Matelski-Beardon area count (theorem A.0.2) to conclude that either $k = 2$ or 3 or G is not discrete. Conclude further by the same theorem (theorem A.0.2) that if G is discrete, then either G^* is

- a $(2, 3, n)$ triangle group with $k = 3$ and $t = 3$,

- a $(2, 4, n)$ triangle group with $k = 2$ and $t = 2$, or

- a $(2, 3, 7)$ triangle group with $k = 2$ and $t = 9$.

Following chapter 8 construct a standard acute triangle, $Stact = Stact_t$, in each of these cases. The standard triangles are respectively the equilateral triangle, the right isosceles triangle, and the non-right isosceles triangle.

If $k = 3$ and $t = 3$, apply (the forward implication of part 1 of) the geometric equivalence theorem (9.1.1) to conclude that there is an isometry $h \in G^*$ with $h(Stact_3) = \Delta(t_1, t_2, t_3)$. Since $Stact_3$ is an equilateral triangle, so is $\Delta(t_1, t_2, t_3)$. If $k = 2$ and $t = 2$, apply (the forward implication of part 1 of) the geometric equivalence theorem (10.1.1) to conclude that there is an isometry $h \in G^*$ with $h(Stact_2) = \Delta(t_1, t_2, t_3)$. Since $Stact_2$ is a right isosceles triangle, so is $\Delta(t_1, t_2, t_3)$. If $k = 2$ and $t = 9$, apply (the forward implication of part 1 of) the geometric equivalence theorem (12.1.2) to conclude that there is an isometry $h \in G^*$ with $h(Stact_9) = \Delta(t_1, t_2, t_3)$. Since $Stact_9$ is the non-right isosceles triangle, so is $\Delta(t_1, t_2, t_3)$.

The discreteness theorem will be established if we can show that if $Act_{A,B}$ is any one of the three triangle types with $k = 2$ or $k = 3$, G is discrete. This is theorem 13.2.1 which is proved in the next section. Once this is done, theorem 3.1.2 has been established.

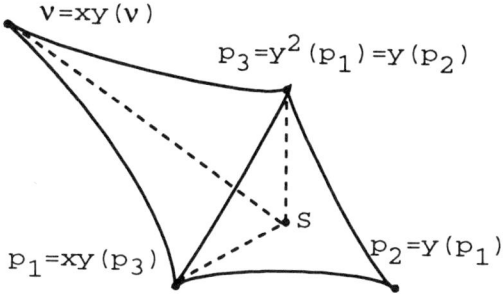

Figure 13.1: Equilateral triangle.

13.2 The proof of sufficiency

In what follows we assume that we have replaced A and B by a Nielsen equivalent pair if necessary and that $T = T_{A,B}$ is either a right isosceles triangle, an equilateral triangle, or the isosceles triangle with sides T_0, T_3 and T_3 as described in 3.1.1. We want to show that A and B generate a discrete group.

Theorem: 13.2.1 *Assume that $[A, B]$ is the square of a rotation by an angle of $k2\pi/n$ where k and n are integers and $1 < k < n/2$. If either*

1. *$T_{A,B}$ is an equilateral triangle and $k = 3$ or*

2. *$T_{A,B}$ is a right isosceles triangle and $k = 2$ or*

3. *$T_{A,B}$ is a non-right isosceles triangle with sides T_0, T_3 and T_3 and $k = 2$,*

then $G = \langle A, B \rangle$ is discrete.

Proof: We treat the three cases separately.

1. **Assume that $T = T_{A,B} = \triangle(p_1, p_2, p_3)$ is an equilateral triangle.**

   We let y be the counterclockwise rotation of order three permuting the p_i and S its fixed point interior to T so that $y(p_1) =$

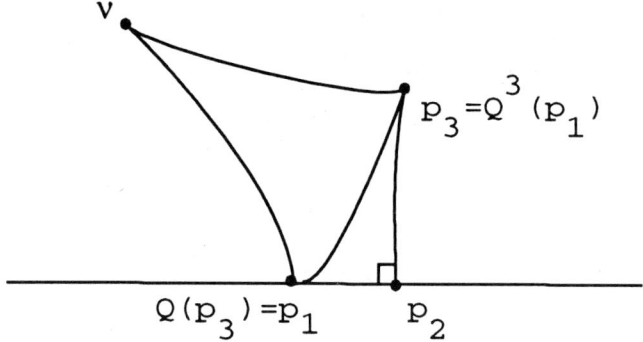

Figure 13.2: The right isosceles triangle.

p_2, $y(p_2) = p_3$, and $y(p_3) = p_1$. Then if $x = E_{p_1}$, $E_{p_2} = yxy^{-1}$ and $E_{p_3} = y^2 x y^{-2}$. Let $z = E_{p_1} E_{p_2} E_{p_3}$. Calculate that $z = (xy)^3$. Whence
$$\langle x, y \rangle \supset \langle E_{p_1}, E_{p_2}, E_{p_3} \rangle \supset \langle x, z \rangle.$$

Since $z^2 = [A, B]$, z is a rotation by $k2\pi/n$. Here, we may assume that $k = 3$, otherwise the group will not be discrete. Since n and 3 are relatively prime by assumption, there is an s such that z^s rotates by $2\pi/n$ as does $(xy)^{3s}$. We let v be the fixed point of z. Then xy is also elliptic, fixes v, and rotates by $2\pi/n$. Thus $xy = z^s$ so that $y = z^s x$. This implies that $\langle x, y \rangle = \langle E_{p_1}, E_{p_2}, E_{p_3} \rangle$.

We need to see that $\langle x, y \rangle$ is discrete. Since $xy(v) = v$ and $xy(y^2(p_1)) = p_1$, $xy[v, y^2(p_1)] = [v, p_1]$ (Figure 13.1). Further $y([S, y^2(p_1)]) = [S, p_1]$. Therefore, one can apply the Poincaré polygon theorem to the quadrilateral with vertices $v, y^2(p_1), S, p_1$ to conclude that $\langle xy, y \rangle$ is discrete.

2. **Assume that $T = T_{A,B} = \triangle(p_1, p_2, p_3)$ is a right isosceles triangle.**

    We let Q be the counterclockwise rotation of order four fixing p_2 and sending p_3 to p_1. Then if $x = E_{p_1}$, $E_{p_2} = Q^2$ and $E_{p_3} = Q^{-1} x Q$. Let $z = E_{p_1} E_{p_2} E_{p_3}$. Calculate that $z = xQxQ$. Whence $\langle x, Q \rangle \supset \langle E_{p_1}, E_{p_2}, E_{p_3} \rangle$. It suffices to show that $\langle x, Q \rangle$ is discrete. Since $z^2 = [A, B]$, z is a rotation by $k2\pi/n$. Here, we may assume

13.2. THE PROOF OF SUFFICIENCY

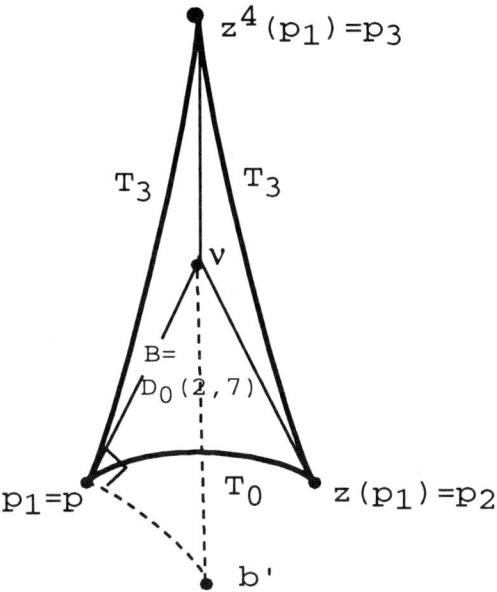

Figure 13.3: Non-right isosceles triangle.

that $k = 2$, otherwise the group will not be discrete. Since n and 2 are relatively prime by assumption, there is an s such that z^s rotates by $2\pi/n$ as does $(xQ)^{2s}$. We let v be the fixed point of z. Then xQ is also elliptic, fixes v, and rotates by $2\pi/n$. Thus $xQ = z^s$. Whence $Q = xz^s$ so that $\langle x, Q \rangle = \langle x, xQ \rangle$.

We need to see that $\langle x, xQ \rangle$ is discrete. Since $xQ(v) = v$ and $xQ(Q^{-1}(p_1)) = p_1$, $xQ[v, p_3] = [v, p_1]$ (Figure 13.2). Further $Q[p_2, Q^{-1}(p_1)] = [p_2, p_1]$. Therefore, one can apply the Poincaré polygon theorem to the quadrilateral with vertices $v, y^2(p_1), p_2, p_1$ to conclude that $\langle xQ, Q \rangle$ is discrete.

3. **Assume that $T = T_{A,B} = \triangle(p_1, p_2, p_3)$ is the non-right isosceles triangle.** We begin with a preliminary fact.

Fact: 13.2.2 *Let T be a triangle with sides A, B and C and opposite angles α, β and γ. Let T' be another triangles with sides A', B' and C' and angles α', β' and γ'. There is an isometry h with $h(T) = T'$ if any of the following conditions hold ([7] (p.99-100).):*

(SSS) $A = A', B = B'$, and $C = C'$.
(SAS) $A = A', B = B'$, and $\gamma = \gamma'$.
(AAS) $\alpha = \alpha', \beta = \beta'$, and $B = B'$.
(AAA) $\alpha = \alpha', \beta = \beta'$, and $\gamma = \gamma'$.

Note that $A = A'$ means that the hyperbolic length of the segment denoted by A is the same as that of the segment denoted by A'.

Corollary: 13.2.3 *Let B be a non-euclidean segment with* $\cosh B = \frac{1}{2\sin \pi/7}$. *Let p and v be the end points of B. If z is the rotation by $2\pi/7$ fixing v and x the rotation of order two fixing p, then $\langle x, z \rangle$ is discrete and is a $(2,3,7)$ triangle group.*

Proof: Let T be any right triangle with one side B and an angle of $\pi/2$ at p. If α, β and γ are the angles of T and A, B and C, the sides, we have $\cosh B = \cos \beta / \sin \alpha$. Let b' be the point along $\tilde{A}$ where the geodesic through v making an angle of $\pi/7$ with B intersects $\tilde{A}$. The vertices v, p, b' form another right triangle, T', with side B and angle β'. Since $\cosh B = \cos \beta' / \sin \pi/7$, $\beta' = \pi/3$ and T' is a $(2,3,7)$ triangle by (AAA).

By 4.1.5 the group $H = \langle z, x, R_{b'} | z^7 = x^2 = R_{b'}^3 = zxR_{b'}^{-1} \rangle$ is discrete. But this is precisely the same as the group generated by x and z. □

We can now complete the proof of the theorem. After applying an isometry, we may assume that the isosceles triangle Act is the isosceles triangle T_7 constructed as follows: pick any point v and any point p at a distance $D_0(2,7)$ from p. Let z be the counterclockwise rotation by an angle of $2\pi/7$ fixing v. Let $p_1 = p$, $p_2 = z(p)$ and $p_3 = z^4(p)$. Use (SSS) to conclude that $Act = T_7$. Then if $x = E_{p_1}$, $E_{p_2} = zxz^{-1}$ and $E_{p_3} = z^4xz^{-4}$. Whence $\langle x, z \rangle \supset \langle E_{p_1}, E_{p_2}, E_{p_3} \rangle$. To see that the subgroup is discrete, it suffices to show that $\langle x, z \rangle$ is discrete. This follows from the above corollary.

This completes the proof of sufficiency. □

Part IV

The Real Number Algorithm and the Turing Machine Algorithm

Chapter 14

Forms of the Algorithm

The purpose of this chapter is to translate the geometrically based triangle algorithm, the discreteness theorem and the intertwining algorithms into a purely computational algorithm for determining the discreteness of a two-generator group. Since the translated algorithm allows all standard computations with real numbers, we call it the real number algorithm (theorem 14.4.1). We also find certain restrictions on the input to the real number algorithm so that it translates into an algorithm that can be implemented on a computer, a *Turing machine* algorithm, (theorem 14.5.1).

The real number algorithm can be thought of as an outline or abstract of the algorithm. It describes the sequence of computational moves to be made by the algorithm without taking into account how the input is given or whether the required computational operations can be implemented on a computer.

The crucial step in translating the real number algorithm into a Turing machine algorithm is to make a choice of input to the algorithm that will assure that the computational operations the real algorithm requires can be carried out on a computer. The input for the real number algorithm consists of the eight real numbers that are the entries of the two matrices. For the Turing machine algorithm it is assumed that the matrix entries are algebraic over $\mathbf{Q}$ so that each is given by specifying its irreducible polynomial and by specifying an *isolating interval*. An isolating interval for a real algebraic number α is a pair of rational numbers r and s such that $r < \alpha \leq s$ where the interval $(r, s]$ contains no other roots of the minimal polynomial for α.

Minimal polynomials and isolating intervals are appropriate input. They are standard quantities in the field of symbolic computation and there are Turing machine algorithms for performing the standard arithmetic operations in finite extensions of the rationals. These can be found in the article by R. Loos entitled *Computing in Algebraic Extensions* (see [5]).

There are two crucial steps in proving that with this input the real number algorithm translates into a Turing machine algorithm. One is to show that there is an algorithm for comparing the size of two real numbers lying in a finite simple extension of the rationals. This follows from the Loos SIGN algorithm p.175 of [5]. The other is to prove that there is an algorithm for computing the order of an elliptic matrix when the entries of the matrix lie in a finite extension of the rationals. This is theorem 14.2.1.

In this chapter we emphasize the real number algorithm and not the Turing machine algorithm. The reason for this is that there may be more than one way to obtain an algorithm that can be carried out on a computer from the real number algorithm. That is, other choices for the input to the real number algorithm might allow it to be translated into a different Turing machine algorithm. In different settings different choices for the input will be appropriate.

In order to make the distinctions between the different forms of the algorithm more precise, we begin with the question, What is an algorithm?

14.1 What is an algorithm?

Heuristically one can regard an algorithm as a recipe for solving a problem, a recipe that is composed of simple steps and always gives the right answer. Since a recipe that does not stop does not give the right answer, the definition implies that the algorithm always comes to a stopping point. However, the definition leaves a lot of room for deciding what the allowed simple steps are.

In the case of our algorithm to determine the discreteness of a two-generator subgroup of $PSL(2, \mathbf{R})$ it is appropriate to distinguish among

14.1. WHAT IS AN ALGORITHM?

three types of algorithms. The more conceptual forms of the algorithm (i.e. the triangle algorithm given here (section 2.5) and the intertwining algorithm of [15]) are called *geometric* algorithms because the simple steps are geometric in nature. They consist of such operations as finding the intersection of two hyperbolic lines, comparing hyperbolic areas and finding the primitive rotation corresponding to a given elliptic element.

We make the definition of a *Turing machine* algorithm more precise below, but roughly speaking it is an algorithm whose simple steps can be carried out by a computer. In particular, the input must be finite. Since it may require an infinite amount of information to specify a real number from the set of all real numbers, no Turing machine algorithm can deal with the set of all real numbers. Nevertheless, there are reasons to consider *real number* algorithms, algorithms which deal with all real numbers whose allowed simple steps include all ordinary arithmetic operations on real numbers and certain additional operations. The notion of a real number algorithm, a variation of the idea of a BSS machine [3], is defined precisely below.

In addition to ordinary arithmetic operations with real numbers (e.g., $+, -, \times$, and $\div$) and the ability to compare real numbers (e.g., $<$) the real number algorithm (the computational form of our algorithm) requires the algebraic operation of taking square roots of positive numbers, the transcendental operation of computing the inverse cosine of a real number between -1 and 1, and the ability to determine when a real number is rational. The arc cosine computation and the rationality determination are needed in order to compute the order of an elliptic matrix. When we translate this algorithm to the Turing machine algorithm, we eliminate the need for these by producing an elliptic order algorithm which requires only standard arithmetic operations (i.e. we prove: If the entries of an elliptic matrix E lie in a finite extension of the rationals of degree d, then E is of finite order if and only if E^n is the identity for some $n \leq 64d^2$.)

The rest of this chapter is organized as follows. Turing machines and real number algorithms along with BSS machines are defined in sections 14.1.1 and 14.1.2 below. Section 14.2 deals with methods for computing the order of an elliptic element and proves the elliptic order algorithm. Section 14.3 contains preliminary computations and notation dealing with the more pedestrian calculations that the real number algorithm requires. Section 14.4 gives the real number algorithm, listing each computational step (theorem 14.4.1). In section 14.5, it is proved that an appropriate choice of input translates the real number algorithm into a Turing machine algorithm (theorem 14.5.1).

14.1.1 Turing machine Algorithms

Turing machine algorithms are well known to logicians and computer scientists, and a leisurely introduction to Turing machines and their relation to actual computers is given in the first few chapters of *Computability and Logic* [4]. Accordingly we give only a brief account here.

A *Turing machine* is essentially a simple model for computation. It consists of a tape marked off into squares, a finite alphabet, and a finite set of states. Each square of tape is either blank or contains a symbol from the alphabet. We turn the machine on by writing the input onto the tape, putting the machine into a designated initial state and setting it to scan a square of our choice. After the machine is turned on it makes a sequence of moves, each move determined by the contents of the square being scanned and the current state of the machine. The moves to be made in particular situations are given by a finite list of rules (the machine's program). During each move the machine may go to a new state and in addition it may print a new symbol on the tape square being scanned (or erase that square) or transfer its attention to an adjacent square. If in a particular situation no move is specified in the list of rules, the machine halts. The machine never runs out of tape; additional blank tape is added as necessary.

If N denotes the natural numbers, a function $f : N \to N$ may be computed by a Turing machine as follows. The input n is written as a sequence of n 1's on the tape and the machine is started at the leftmost 1. When the machine halts, the number of 1's on the tape is $f(n)$. In particular the machine must halt for all appropriate input for it to compute a function.

There are many variations on the definition of Turing machine given above, but in all cases the class of computable functions is the same. Turing machines do not closely resemble digital computers, probably because they were invented before such computers were built. Nevertheless the class of functions $f : N \to N$ computable by idealized computers with unlimited memory is the same class as computed by Turing machines. In fact all known models of computation give the same class of computable functions from N to N. The upshot of these results is the widely accepted view, known as Church's thesis, that Turing computable functions include all functions $f : N \to N$ which can be effectively computed by any means.

Our discussion of Turing machines has focused on computation of functions from N to N, but the same considerations apply to algorithms where the input and the output may be expressed as finite words over a fixed finite alphabet. In fact one can reduce such computations to the previous case with the aid of appropriate maps (i.e., maps which can be computed by a Turing machine) between the set of all such words and the integers. By Church's thesis any algorithm which consists of a sequence of effective steps and which halts for all inputs can be carried out on a Turing machine.

In the case of our Turing machine algorithm we will be computing in algebraic number fields, and the input will be the eight matrix entries from an algebraic number field. Since each matrix entry is given by specifying its irreducible polynomial and its isolating interval, the input is a finite sequence of rational numbers, or what is the same thing, a finite sequence of integers. The output consists of a simple *yes* or *no* according as the group generated is discrete or not. The steps of our algorithm are for the most part taken from the known techniques of symbolic computation [5].

14.1.2 Real Number Algorithms

Our concept of real number algorithm is a variation of the notion of BSS machine proposed by Blum, Shub, and Smale [3]. One of their motivations was to make the theory of computation based on Turing machines relevant to analysis, geometry and topology.

Roughly speaking a BSS machine is an algorithm that contains four types of simple steps, called nodes: input nodes (only one is allowed), output nodes, computational nodes where rational function are computed, and branch nodes where the branching is governed by deciding whether a given number is positive. To be more precise

Definition: 14.1.1 A *(finite dimensional)* **BSS machine** *over the real numbers* $\mathbf{R}$ *is specified by an input space* $I = \mathbf{R}^l$, *an output space* $O = \mathbf{R}^n$, *a state space* $S = \mathbf{R}^n$ *and a finite directed graph of nodes. There are the following type of nodes.*

1. *Exactly one input node, which has no incoming edge and one outgoing edge. Associated to the input node is a linear injective map from I to S.*

2. *Output nodes each with no outgoing edge and a linear map from S to O.*

3. *Computational nodes each with a single outgoing edge and an associated rational map from S to S.*

4. *Branch nodes with two outgoing edges and a polynomial map $h : S \to \mathbf{R}$. One outgoing edge is associated to the condition $h(x) < 0$ and the other to $h(x) \geq 0$.*

The machine computes in the obvious way. Each computation is described by a path in the graph. The path starts at the input node, where the input is converted to a state x by means of the associated linear map. The next mode is of course the target of the input node's outgoing edge. At a computation node x is replaced by its image under the associated rational map unless this image is undefined, in which case the machine halts without producing output. At a branch node x is unchanged, but the successor node is determined by whether or not $h(x) < 0$. Finally if an output node is reached, the current state x is converted to an output, and the machine halts.

BSS machines with some additional capabilities will be used to specify *real number algorithms*. We allow computational nodes for which the associated maps are algebraic and transcendental, specifically the square root function (of some coordinate of the state) and the inverse cosine. We also allow a branch node in which the choice of outgoing edge depends upon whether or not a particular coordinate of the state is rational. The inverse cosine node and the rationality node are needed in order to compute the order of an elliptic matrix.

As mentioned earlier, when we translate this real number algorithm to the Turing machine algorithm, we eliminate the need for the arc cosine and rationality nodes by producing an elliptic order algorithm which requires only standard arithmetic operations. To complete the translation of the real number algorithm to the Turing machine algorithm, we need to be able to take (a finite number) of square roots and to be able compare sizes of real numbers (a capability built into the BSS machine). We are able to do this by calling upon a body of results from symbolic computation [5]. In a finite simple extension of the rationals there are algorithms for adding, subtracting, and multiplying algebraic numbers and there is an algorithm for finding the inverse of a non-zero algebraic number. In addition, there are algorithms for computing the sign of a real algebraic number and finding the primitive element that exhibits a multiple separable extension as a simple extension.

14.2 The Elliptic Order Algorithm

A matrix E in $SL(2, \mathbf{R})$ is elliptic if $|Tr(E)| < 2$. If E is elliptic, let $ord(E)$ denote its order. It is the smallest integer $\bar{m}$ such that $E^{\bar{m}} = 1$. If there is no such $\bar{m}$, we set $ord(E) = \infty$. Let m be the order of the corresponding transformation (the order of the image of E in $PSL(2, \mathbf{R})$). If $\bar{m}$ is odd, $m = \bar{m}$ and if $\bar{m}$ is even, $m = \frac{\bar{m}}{2}$. We write $o(E)$ to denote the order of the image of E in $PSL(2, R)$.

For any matrix M, let $T(M) = |Tr\, M|$. Recall that if as a transformation E rotates by an angle of 2θ, $(T(E))^2 = 4\cos^2\theta$. If $2\theta = \pm 2\pi/n$ for some integer n, then E is called a (geometrically) *primitive* rotation. If E is of finite order, but not primitive, some power of E is primitive. We let E_0 be the smallest power of E that is primitive. We call it the *primitive rotation corresponding* to E. If E is not primitive, then E rotates by $\pm k2\pi/n$ for some integer k, with $1 < k < n/2$. The integer k is called the *phase* of E which is denoted by $k(E)$.

If we are working over the reals, $o(E)$ can be computed from the trace of E as long as one can compute the arc cosine of a real number between -1 and 1 and determine whether a real number is rational or not.

If we are working in a finite extension of the rationals so that the entries of E lie in an extension of degree d, we show that there is an algorithm for computing $o(E)$.

Theorem: 14.2.1 The elliptic order algorithm (version #1): *If E is a matrix in $SL(2, R)$ with $Tr\ E = \tau$, $|\tau| < 2$, and if the entries of E lie in a finite extension, F, of $\mathbf{Q}$ of degree d, then there is an algorithm for determining $o(E)$. The input to the algorithm is τ and the algorithm only uses the simple arithmetic operations in F of addition, subtraction, and multiplication.*

Proof: We need to decide whether $\beta \pm i\sqrt{1-\beta^2}$ is a root of unity since $\beta = \tau/2$ is the cosine of a rational multiple of π precisely when it is the real part of a root of unity. Let $\rho = \beta + i\sqrt{1-\beta^2}$. Since the complex conjugate of ρ is a root of unity precisely when ρ is, we need only check ρ. If ρ is a root of unity, it is a primitive nth root of unity for some integer n. The degree of its irreducible polynomial is $\phi(n)$ where ϕ is the Euler ϕ-function (see [21] p. 204, theorem 6). Since ρ lies in $F(i, \sqrt{1-\beta^2})$, an extension of F of degree at most 4, we must have $\phi(n) \leq 4d$. If the factorization of n as a product of primes is $n = p_1^{n_1} \cdots p_r^{n_r}$, then $\phi(n) = p_1^{n_1-1}(p_1-1) \cdots p_r^{n_r-1}(p_r-1)$ (see p. 113 of [40]). Verify that $n \leq 2(\phi(n))^2$. Since $\phi(n) \leq 4d$, $n \leq 32d^2$. Thus to determine whether or not E is of finite order, one merely needs to test whether $\rho^m = 1$ for each $m \leq 32d^2$. The condition that $\rho^m = 1$ is actually two polynomial conditions in β (which allows the computations to actually be carried out in F and not in the extension of F). To see this observe that $Re((\beta + i\sqrt{1-\beta^2})^m) = 1$ contains only even powers of $\sqrt{1-\beta^2}$ and thus reduces to a polynomial equation in β. Similarly, each term in $Im((\beta + i\sqrt{1-\beta^2})^m) = 0$ contains a non-zero odd power of $\sqrt{1-\beta^2}$ which can be factored out. The other factor involves only even powers of $\sqrt{1-\beta^2}$ and thus reduces to a polynomial in β alone. Either $\beta = \pm 1$ or β satisfies the polynomial given by the second factor. If $\rho^m \neq 1$ for any $m \leq 32d^2$, then $o(E) = \infty$. □

As a corollary to the proof we obtain a second elliptic order algorithm.

Corollary: 14.2.2 The elliptic order algorithm (version #2): *Let E be a matrix in $SL(2, \mathbf{R})$ with $|Tr\ E| < 2$. If the entries of E lie in a finite extension, F, of $\mathbf{Q}$ of degree d, then E is of finite order if and only if E^n is the identity for some $n \leq 64d^2$.*

14.2. THE ELLIPTIC ORDER ALGORITHM

Remark: 14.2.3 The elliptic order algorithm (version #3): *Version #2 of the elliptic order algorithm has the advantage that it only requires that one know a bound for the degree of the finite extension. The referee has pointed out that when knows in addition $f(x)$, the primitive polynomial for τ, there is a simpler algorithm: If $f(x)$ is not monic, then τ is not an algebraic integer and the order of E is infinite. Suppose $f(x)$ is monic. If all roots of f lie in the open real interval $(-2, 2)$, then by Kronecker's theorem β is a root of unity so E has finite order, else it does not. One can test this condition without computing the roots of f by applying the Sturm theorem (p.220 of Van der Waerden [40]) and computing whether $w(2) - w(-2) = \deg f(x)$. (Here w is as defined on page 220-221.)*

Remark: 14.2.4 *It is important to emphasize that for the purposes of determining the order of an elliptic, the real number algorithm requires the arc cosine function and being able to determine whether or not a real number is rational. Version #1 or #2 of the elliptic order algorithm can be applied in any finite extension of the rationals and by contrast does not require either an arc cosine function or the ability to determine rationality.*

Since the geometric and intertwining algorithms require knowing not just the order of an elliptic, but also its phase and the corresponding primitive transformation, we prove the following lemma:

Lemma: 14.2.5 *If E is elliptic and $o(E)$ is finite, then E_0 and $k(E)$ can be computed using simple arithmetic operations provided the size of two real numbers can be compared.*

Proof: Let $m = o(E)$. Since computing the product of two matrices and computing the trace of a matrix only involve simple arithmetic operations, we can compute $\frac{(T(E))^2}{2} - 1, \frac{(T(E^2))^2}{2} - 1, ..., \frac{(T(E^{m-1}))^2}{2} - 1$. Note that E^t rotates by an angle of $2\theta_t$ where $\cos 2\theta_t = \frac{(T(E^t))^2}{2} - 1$. The larger the cosine in absolute value, the smaller the rotation angle. Since we can compare the sizes of real numbers, we can let $E_0 = E^t$ where $\frac{(T(E^t))^2}{2} - 1$ is maximal. There will be two such integers t (one corresponding to a clockwise rotation and the other to a counterclockwise oration). We always choose the smaller one. If $E \neq E_0$, compute

$E_0^{\pm n}$ for all integers $1 \leq n \leq m/2$. Then $E = \pm E_0^{\pm k}$ for some k and $k = k(E)$. □

14.3 Notation and Preliminary Computations

14.3.1 Fixed points and cross-ratios

If M is a matrix in $PSL(2, \mathbf{R})$, m will denote a preimage in $SL(2, \mathbf{R})$. For any $m \in SL(2, \mathbf{R})$, let $m = \begin{pmatrix} a & b \\ c & d \end{pmatrix}$. Write $a(m), b(m), c(m)$, and $d(m)$ to denote the entries of the matrix m.

$T(m) = |Tr\, m| = |a + d|$. Also define $T(M) = T(m)$.

If M is hyperbolic, let $Fix(m)$ denote the fixed points of m. The fixed points of m, which are also the fixed points of M, are denoted by $Fix(M)$ and are given by the formula

$$Fix(M) = \frac{a - d \pm \sqrt{(a+d)^2 - 4}}{2c}.$$

If m is elliptic or parabolic, $Fix(m) = Fix(M)$ consists of a single point defined as follows. When $T(m) = 2$, $Fix(m) = \frac{a-d}{c}$. When $T(m) < 2$,

$$Fix(m) = \frac{a - d + i\sqrt{4 - (a+d)^2}}{2c}.$$

If M is hyperbolic, we let $A(M)$ (or $A(m)$) denote the attracting fixed point and $R(M)$ (or $R(m)$) denote the repelling fixed point. We can distinguish the two as follows: Pick $z \in Fix(M), z \neq \infty$. If $0 \notin Fix(M)$ then $z = A(M)$ if $|z - \frac{b}{d}| < |z|$ and $z = R(M)$ otherwise. If $0 \in Fix(M)$, then $0 = A(M)$ if $1 \notin Fix(M)$ and $|\frac{a+b}{c+d}| < 1$. Otherwise, $0 = R(M)$. If $1 \in Fix(M)$, then $-1 \notin Fix(M)$. Then $0 = A(M)$ if $|\frac{-a+b}{-c+d}| < 1$ and $0 = R(M)$ otherwise.

The cross ratio of g and h, $C(g, h)$ is defined by

$$C(g, h) = \frac{(R(g) - R(h))(A(g) - A(h))}{(R(g) - A(h))(A(g) - R(h))}.$$

14.3. NOTATION AND PRELIMINARY COMPUTATIONS

The Jørgensen number of g and h, denoted $J(g,h)$, is defined by $J(g,h) = |Tr([g,h]) - 2| + |Tr^2(g) - 4|$.

Lemma: 14.3.1 *Given $M, N \in PSL(2, \mathbf{R})$ and the corresponding matrices $m, n \in Sl(2, \mathbf{R})$, let r be an integer, then M^r, $T(m) = T(M)$, $Tr\, m$, $Tr([M, N])$, and $J(g, h)$ can be computed using simple arithmetic operations. $Fix(m) = Fix(M)$, $A(M) = A(m)$, $R(M) = R(m)$, and $C(g, h)$ can be computed using simple arithmetic operations and taking square roots. If g and h are hyperbolic transformations, it can be determined whether or not $A(h) = A(g)$, $A(h) > R(h)$, or $C(g, h) \geq 0$ using simple arithmetic operation and taking square roots.*

Proof: The assertions follow immediately from the definitions and the calculations above. Complex numbers are thought of as ordered pairs of real numbers so that all ordinary operations with complex numbers can also be allowed including finding the real and imaginary parts and taking absolute values. □

Remark: 14.3.2 *It can be shown that the equalities and inequalities involving the fixed points of transformations reduce to other simple arithmetic conditions on the matrix entries that do not involve square roots.*

14.3.2 Computation of p_2 and γ

For hyperbolic transformations g and h in $SL(2, \mathbf{R})$ whose axes are distinct, but not disjoint, let p_2 be the point of intersection of the axes and let E_{p_2} be the half-turn about p_2. As in chapter 2 let $E_{p_1} = gE_{p_2}$, $E_{p_3} = hE_{p_2}$, and $\gamma = E_{p_1}E_{p_2}E_{p_3}$. Note that $\gamma = gE_{p_2}$ and $\gamma^2 = [g, h]$.

Lemma: 14.3.3 *For hyperbolic transformations g and h in $SL(2, \mathbf{R})$ with distinct but intersecting axes the coordinates of p_2, the point of intersection of their axes, the matrix of E_{p_2}, the half-turn about p_2, γ, $o(\gamma)$, and $k(\gamma)$, can be computed using ordinary arithmetic operations and taking one square root.*

Proof: For $g \in SL(2, \mathbf{R})$, the axis of g is the intersection with the upper-half-plane of the Euclidean circle with center at the point on the real axis with coordinates $(C_g, 0)$ where $C_g = \frac{A(g)+R(g)}{2}$ and radius $Rad_g = |\frac{A(g)-R(g)}{2}|$. Note that if the matrix of g is given by $\begin{pmatrix} a & b \\ c & d \end{pmatrix}$, then $C_g = \frac{a-d}{2}$ and $Rad_g^2 = \frac{(a+d)^2-4}{c^2}$. One can compute that p_2 has coordinates (r, s) where

$$r = \frac{(C_h^2 - C_g^2) + (Rad_g^2 - Rad_h^2)}{2(C_h - C_g)} \text{ and } s = \sqrt{Rad_g^2 - (r - C_g)^2}.$$

Finally note that the matrix of the half-turn with fixed point $r + si$ is $E_{p_2} = \frac{1}{s}\begin{pmatrix} -r & s^2 + r^2 \\ -1 & r \end{pmatrix}$ and $\gamma = g E_{p_2}$. Once the matrix of γ has been computed, its order and phase can also be computed (lemma 14.2.5). □

14.3.3 Positive and Negative Rotations

The transformation that sends z to $e^{it}z$ has *positive rotation* about the origin if $0 < t < \pi$ and *negative rotation* about the origin for $\pi < t < 2\pi$. Elliptics of order two do not have a positive or negative rotation. For an arbitrary elliptic element of order other than 2 define positive and negative rotation about its fixed point by conjugation. The parabolic transformation with fixed point at ∞, has positive rotation if $g(0) > 0$ and negative rotation otherwise. For an arbitrary parabolic element, define positive and negative rotation by conjugation. Write $Rot(g) = 1$ if g has positive rotation about its fixed point and $Rot(g) = -1$, if the rotation is negative.

Lemma: 14.3.4 *If g is parabolic or elliptic of finite order greater than 2, then $Rot(g)$ can be computed using simple arithmetic operations that do not require taking square roots.*

Proof: If g is parabolic, conjugate g by the matrix

$$q = \frac{1}{\sqrt{Fix(g)}}\begin{pmatrix} -1 & 0 \\ 1 & -Fix(g) \end{pmatrix}.$$

If $qgq^{-1}(0) > 0$, then $Rot(g) = 1$. Otherwise $Rot(g) = -1$. Note that if g is parabolic $F(g)$ is in the field and that when we *conjugate* by

$\sqrt{w}M$ where w is in the field and M is a matrix, then the entries are all actually multiplied by w and thus remain in the field. $qgq^{-1}(0) > 0$ reduces to the condition that $\frac{bc}{1-d^2} > 0$

If g is elliptic, compute $Fix(g)$. Conjugating g by

$$q = \frac{1}{\sqrt{Fix(g) - \overline{Fix(g)}}} \begin{pmatrix} 1 & -Fix(g) \\ 1 & -\overline{Fix(g)} \end{pmatrix}.$$

moves the fixed point of g to 0. If $Im\ qgq^{-1}(1) > 0$, then $Rot(g) = 1$. Otherwise, $Rot(g) = -1$.

Note that all arithmetic operations involved in computing with complex numbers are carried out by computing with ordered pairs of real numbers. Again, as with the parabolic case, when g is elliptic, $Im\ qgq^{-1}(1) > 0$ reduces to an arithmetic condition not involving square roots that the entries of g must satisfy. $\square$

14.4 The Real Number Algorithm

We are now in a position to translate the triangle algorithm, the geometric discreteness theorem and the intertwining algorithm into a real number algorithm.

The steps of the algorithm below are to be followed in the order given except when otherwise indicated. This means that one performs the operation indicated at step n. If the step ends with the word *Stop*, the algorithm outputs *G is discrete* or *G is not discrete* as indicated. (Technically the algorithm could output *G is elementary*, but since the hypothesis of the theorem is that G is non-elementary, this will not happen.) If the algorithm says *go to step q*, one proceeds to step q. In the absence of either a *Stop* or a *go to* instruction, the algorithm proceeds to the next step listed (usually step $n + 1$ in the numbering).

Occasionally a name has been attached to a step or a sequence of steps (e.g., **division step** or **hyperbolic-parabolic**). These names are not part of the algorithm, but are mnemonic devices to help the reader keep track of what the algorithm is doing. The terms usually refer to part(s) of the more conceptual geometric algorithm.

Theorem: 14.4.1 The Real Number Algorithm: *If A and B are elements of $PSL(2,\mathbf{R})$, let g and h be elements of $SL(2,R)$ whose images are A and B respectively. Let $G = \langle A, B \rangle$. Assume that G is non-elementary. Then the procedure below determines whether or not G is discrete. The procedure stops after a finite number of steps. In addition to ordinary arithmetic operations the procedure assumes that one can compute square roots and the order of an elliptic matrix and compare sizes of real numbers.*

1. **First computations**

    (a) *If $Tr\ g < 0$, replace g by $-g$.*

    (b) *If $Tr\ h < 0$, replace h by $-h$.*

    (c) *If $Tr\ g > Tr\ h$, replace the pair (g,h) by the pair (h,g).*

    (d) *If $Tr\ g = 2$ and $Tr\ h > 2$, go to step 4 (hyperbolic-parabolic).*

    (e) *If $Tr\ g = 2$ and $Tr\ h = 2$, go to step 5 (parabolic-parabolic).*

    (f) *If $Tr\ g < 2$ and $Tr\ h > 2$, go to step 6 (elliptic-hyperbolic).*

    (g) *If $Tr\ g < 2$ and $Tr\ h = 2$, go to step 7 (elliptic-parabolic).*

    (h) *If $Tr\ h < 2$, go to step 8 (elliptic-elliptic).*

    (i) *If $C(g,h) = 0$ or ∞, G is either elementary or not discrete. (Note we now have $2 < Tr\ g \leq Tr\ h$.)*

        i. *If $A(h) = A(g)$ and $R(h) = R(g)$, then G is elementary. Stop.*

        ii. *If $A(h) = R(g)$ and $A(g) = R(h)$, then G is elementary. Stop.*

        iii. *If $A(h) = R(g)$ but $A(g) \neq R(h)$, then G is not discrete. Stop.*

        iv. *If $A(h) = A(g)$ but $R(h) \neq R(g)$, then G is not discrete. Stop.*

        v. *If $A(g) = R(h)$, but $A(h) \neq R(g)$, then G is not discrete. Stop.*

    (j) *If $Tr\ g > 2$ and $C(g,h) > 0$, go to step 3 (hyperbolic-hyperbolic with disjoint axes).*

14.4. THE REAL NUMBER ALGORITHM

(k) If $T(g) > 2$ and $C(g,h) < 0$, go to step 2, (hyperbolic-hyperbolic with intersecting axes).

2. **Hyperbolic-Hyperbolic with intersecting axes.**

   (a) If $|Tr\,[g,h]| \geq 2$, G is discrete. Stop.

   (b) If $Tr\,[g,h] > 0$, then G is not discrete. Stop.

   (c) If $o([g,h]) = \infty$, then G is not discrete. Stop.

   (d) If $o([g,h])$ is finite and $k(\gamma) = 1$, then G is discrete. Stop.

   (e) If $o([g,h])$ is finite, but $k(\gamma) \neq 2$ or 3, then G is not discrete. Stop.

   (f) **First normalization step:** We have $o([g,h])$ is finite and $k(\gamma) = 2$ or 3.

      i. If $T(g) \leq T(hg^{-1}) \leq T(h)$, replace (g,h) by (g^{-1}, hg^{-1}) and go on to the division step (step 2g).

      ii. If $T(h) \leq T(g) \leq T(hg^{-1})$, replace (g,h) by (h,g) and go to the division step (step 2g).

      iii. If $T(h) \leq T(hg^{-1}) \leq T(g)$, replace (g,h) by (h^{-1}, gh^{-1}) and go to the division step (step 2g).

      iv. If $T(hg^{-1}) \leq T(g) \leq T(h)$, replace (g,h) by (hg^{-1}, g^{-1}) and go on to the division step (step 2g).

      v. If $T(hg^{-1}) \leq T(h) \leq T(g)$, replace (g,h) by (gh^{-1}, h^{-1}) go on to the division step (step 2g).

   (g) **Division step**

      i. If $T(hg^{-1}) \leq T(hg)$, go to the acute triangle step (step 2h).

      ii. If $T(gh^{-1}) > T(gh)$, go to the general replacement step (step 2i).

   (h) **Acute triangle step :** $T(hg^{-1}) \leq T(hg)$ and the triangle is an acute triangle.)

      i. If $T(g) = T(h) = T(hg^{-1})$, G is discrete. Stop.

      ii. If $T(g) = T(h)$ and $T(hg^{-1}) = T(gh)$, G is discrete. Stop.

iii. If $o([g,h]) \neq 7$ or $k(\gamma) \neq 2$, G is not discrete. Stop.
iv. If $T(h) \neq T(hg^{-1})$, G is not discrete. Stop.
v. Set $\tau = T(\gamma)$. If $\frac{1}{2}T(g) = \frac{\tau+1}{2}$ and $\frac{1}{2}T(h) = \frac{1}{2}T(hg^{-1}) = \frac{1}{2-\tau}(1 + \frac{\tau-1}{2}\sqrt{\tau+2})$, then G is discrete. Stop.
vi. If none of the above hold, but $T(gh^{-1}) \leq T(gh)$, then G is not discrete. Stop.

(i) **The general replacement step:** $T(gh^{-1}) > T(gh)$

i. If $T(g) \leq T(h) \leq T(gh)$, replace (g,h) by the pair (g^{-1}, h). Then return to the division step (step 2g).
ii. If $T(g) \leq T(gh) \leq T(h)$, replace (g,h) by (g, gh). Then return to the division step (step 2g).
iii. If $T(gh) \leq T(g) \leq T(h)$, replace (g,h) by the pair (gh, g). Then return to the division step (step 2g).

3. **Hyperbolic-Hyperbolic with Disjoint Axes**

(a) If $Tr\, g > Tr\, h$, replace the pair (g,h) by the pair (h,g).

(b) If $A(g) = A(h)$, $R(g) = R(h)$, $A(g) = R(h)$, or $R(g) = A(h)$, then $C(g,h) = 0$ or ∞ and G is either not discrete or elementary.

   i. If $A(h) = A(g)$ and $R(h) = R(g)$, then G is elementary. Stop.
   ii. If $A(h) = R(g)$ and $A(g) = R(h)$, then G is elementary. Stop.
   iii. If $A(h) = R(g)$ but $A(g) \neq R(h)$, then G is not discrete. Stop.
   iv. If $A(h) = A(g)$ but $R(h) \neq R(g)$, then G is not discrete. Stop.
   v. If $A(g) = R(h)$, but $A(h) \neq R(g)$, then G is not discrete. Stop.

(c) If $C(g,h) < 0$, go to step 2, (hyperbolic-hyperbolic with intersecting axes).

(d) If $C(g,h) > 1$, replace h by h^{-1}.

14.4. THE REAL NUMBER ALGORITHM

(e) If $J(g,h) < 1$, G is not discrete. Stop.

(f) If $Tr\,(gh) < -2$, G is discrete (and free). Stop.

(g) If $Tr\,(gh) = \pm 2$, gh is parabolic. Replace (g,h) by (g,gh) and go to step 1.

(h) If $-2 < Tr\,(gh) < 2$, then gh is elliptic. Replace the pair (g,h) by the pair (g,gh) and go to step 1.

(i) If $Tr\,(gh) > 2$, replace (g,h) by the pair (g,gh) if $Tr\,(gh) > 0$ and by the pair $(-gh,g)$ if $Tr\,(gh) < 0$. Return to the beginning of this step (step 3, hyperbolic-hyperbolic with disjoint axes).

4. Hyperbolic-Parabolic

(a) If $Tr\,g > Tr\,h$, replace the pair (g,h) by the pair (h,g).

(b) If $Fix(g) = A(h)$ or $Fix(g) = R(h)$, G is not discrete. Stop.

(c) If $c(g) \neq 0$, conjugate g and h by

$$\begin{pmatrix} 0 & -1 \\ 1 & -\frac{a(g)-d(g)}{2c(g)} \end{pmatrix}.$$

Then g becomes $\begin{pmatrix} 1 & \tau \\ 0 & 1 \end{pmatrix}$ where $\tau = -c(g)$.

(d) If $\tau < 0$, replace g by g^{-1}.

(e) If $A(h) > R(h)$, replace h by h^{-1}.

(f) Conjugate g and h by

$$\frac{\sqrt{R(h) - A(h)}}{\sqrt{2}} \cdot \begin{pmatrix} \frac{2}{R(h)-A(h)} & \frac{R(h)+A(h)}{A(h)-R(h)} \\ 0 & 1 \end{pmatrix}.$$

(g) If $|b(g)b(h)| < 1$, G is not discrete. Stop.

(h) If $Tr\,(gh) < -2$, then G is discrete (and free). Stop.

(i) If $-2 < Tr\,(gh) < 2$, then gh is elliptic. Replace the pair (g,h) by the pair (g,gh) and go to step 1.

(j) *If $Tr(gh) = 2$, then gh is parabolic. Replace the pair (g,h) by the pair (g,gh) and go to step 1.*

(k) *In all other cases, replace the pair (g,h) by the pair (g,gh) and return to the beginning of this step (step 4, hyperbolic-parabolic).*

5. **Parabolic-Parabolic**

    (a) *If $Tr\, g < 0$, replace g by $-g$.*

    (b) *If $Tr\, h < 0$, replace h by $-h$.*

    (c) *If $F(h) = F(g)$, G is elementary. Stop.*

    (d) *Compute*

    $$CR = \frac{(F(g) - h(F(h))) \cdot (F(h) - g(F(h)))}{(F(g) - g(F(h))) \cdot (F(h) - h(F(g)))}.$$

    If $CR > 0$, replace h by h^{-1}.

    (e) *If $-2 < Tr(gh) < 2$, then gh is elliptic. Replace (g,h) by the pair (g,gh) and go to step 1.*

    (f) *If $Tr(gh) \leq -2$, G is discrete (and free). Stop.*

6. **Elliptic-Hyperbolic**

    (a) *If $Tr\, g > Tr\, h$, replace (g,h) by the pair (h,g).*

    (b) *If $o(g) = \infty$, then G is not discrete. Stop.*

    (c) *If $o(g) < \infty$, replace g by g_0.*

    (d) *If $Rot(g) = -1$, replace g by g^{-1}.*

    (e) *Conjugate g by t to obtain $\bar{g}$ where t is given by the matrix*

    $$\frac{1}{\sqrt{R(h) - A(h)}} \cdot \begin{pmatrix} 1 & -R(h) \\ 1 & -A(h) \end{pmatrix}.$$

    If $|\bar{g}(i|Fix(\bar{g})|)| > |Fix(\bar{g})|$, replace h by h^{-1}.

14.4. THE REAL NUMBER ALGORITHM

(f) If $Tr\ g < 0$, replace g by $-g$.

(g) If $Tr\ h < 0$, replace h by $-h$.

(h) If $Tr\ (gh) \leq -2$, G is discrete. Stop.

(i) If $Tr\ (gh) = 2$, replace (g, h) by (g, gh) and go to step 1.

(j) If $-2 < Tr\ (gh) < 2$, replace (g, h) by (g, gh) and go to step 1.

(k) If $Tr\ (gh) > 2$, replace (g, h) by (g, gh) and return to the beginning of this step, (step 6, elliptic-hyperbolic).

7. **Elliptic-Parabolic**

    (a) If $|Tr\ g| < 2$, but $o(g) = \infty$, G is not discrete. Stop.

    (b) If $|Tr\ g| < 2$, $o(g) < \infty$, replace g by g_0.

    (c) If $Rot(g) = -1$, replace g by g^{-1}.

    (d) If $Rot(h) = -1$, replace h by h^{-1}.

    (e) If $Tr\ g < 0$, replace g by $-g$.

    (f) If $Tr\ h < 0$, replace h by $-h$.

    (g) If $-2 < Tr\ (gh) < 2$, replace (g, h) by (g, gh) and go to step 1.

    (h) If $Tr\ (gh) \geq 2$ or $Tr\ (gh) \leq -2$, G is discrete. Stop.

8. **Elliptic-Elliptic**

    (a) If $F(g) = F(h)$, then either G is elementary or G is not discrete. Stop.

    (b) If $|Tr\ g| < 2$, but $o(g) = \infty$, G is not discrete. Stop.

    (c) If $|Tr\ h| < 2$, but $o(h) = \infty$, G is not discrete. Stop.

    (d) If $o(g) < \infty$, replace g by g_0.

    (e) If $o(h) < \infty$, replace h by h_0.

    (f) If $Rot(g) = -1$, replace g by g^{-1}.

(g) If $Rot(h) = -1$, replace h by h^{-1}.

(h) If $Tr(gh) \geq 2$ or $Tr(gh) \leq -2$, then G is discrete. Stop.

(i) If $-2 < Tr(gh) < 2$ and $o(gh) = \infty$, G is not discrete. Stop.

(j) If $k(gh) = 1$ and $Rot(gh) = -1$, G is discrete. Stop.

(k) If $1 - \frac{1}{o(g)} - \frac{1}{o(h)} - \frac{k(gh)}{o(gh)} < \frac{1}{84}$, G is not discrete. Stop.

(l) Compute $o(g(gh)_0)$, $o((gh)_0 h)$ and $k(g(gh)_0)$.

(m) If $o(g(gh)_0) = \infty$ or $o((gh)_0 h) = \infty$, G is not discrete. Stop.

(n) If $1 - (\frac{1}{o(g)} + \frac{1}{o(gh)} + \frac{k(g(gh)_0)}{o(g(gh)_0)}) < \frac{1}{2}(1 - \frac{1}{o(g)} - \frac{1}{o(h)} - \frac{k(gh)}{o(gh)})$, replace (g, h) by $(g, (gh)_0)$ and return to the beginning of step 8 (elliptic-elliptic).

(o) Otherwise, replace (g, h) by $(h, (gh)_0)$ and return to the beginning of step 8 (elliptic-elliptic).

Proof: The proof consists of two parts: (1) translating the triangle algorithm and the discreteness theorem into purely computational steps and (2) translating the intertwining algorithm of [15] into purely computational steps. As we do this we keep track of the computational operations involved.

Translating the intersecting axes case: We follow the triangle algorithm of chapter 2 in particular section 2.5. Begin with g, h and gh. Compute $T(g)$, $T(h)$ and $T(hg^{-1})$. Recall that p_2 is the point where the axes of g and h intersect and that p_1 and p_3 are defined by the requirement that $g = E_{p_1} E_{p_2}$ and $h = E_{p_3} E_{p_2}$. The generators g and h determine the triangle with vertices p_1, p_2 and p_3. However, the ordered triangle and the ordered vertices and the ordered pair of generators depends upon the ordering of the absolute values of the three traces. That is:

1. If $T(g) \leq T(h) \leq T(hg^{-1})$, the triangle is $\triangle(p_1, p_2, p_3)$ and the triple of generators is $(E_{p_1} E_{p_2}, E_{p_3} E_{p_2}, E_{p_3} E_{p_1})$ so that the pair of generators is (g, h).

2. If $T(g) \leq T(hg^{-1}) \leq T(h)$, the triangle is $\triangle(p_2, p_1, p_3)$ and the triple of generators is $(E_{p_2} E_{p_1}, E_{p_3} E_{p_1}, E_{p_3} E_{p_2})$ so that the pair of generators is (g^{-1}, hg^{-1}).

14.4. THE REAL NUMBER ALGORITHM

3. If $T(h) \leq T(g) \leq T(hg^{-1})$, the triangle is $\triangle(p_3, p_2, p_1)$ and the triple of generators is $(E_{p_3}E_{p_2}, E_{p_1}E_{p_2}, E_{p_1}E_{p_3})$ so that the pair of generators is (h, g).

4. If $T(h) \leq T(hg^{-1}) \leq T(g)$, the triangle is $\triangle(p_2, p_3, p_1)$ and the triple of generators is $(E_{p_2}E_{p_3}, E_{p_1}E_{p_3}, E_{p_1}E_{p_2})$ so that the pair of generators is (h^{-1}, gh^{-1}).

5. If $T(hg^{-1}) \leq T(g) \leq T(h)$, the triangle is $\triangle(p_3, p_1, p_2)$ and the triple of generators is $(E_{p_3}E_{p_1}, E_{p_2}E_{p_1}, E_{p_2}E_{p_3})$ so that the pair of generators is (hg^{-1}, g^{-1}).

6. If $T(hg^{-1}) \leq T(h) \leq T(g)$, the triangle is $\triangle(p_1, p_3, p_2)$ and the triple of generators is $(E_{p_1}E_{p_3}, E_{p_2}E_{p_3}, E_{p_2}E_{p_1})$ so that the pair of generators is (gh^{-1}, h^{-1}).

We next consider $T(hg^{-1})$ and $T(hg)$. If $T(gh^{-1}) < T(hg)$, we apply the tests of the discreteness theorem. The acute triangle is equilateral if $T(g) = T(h) = T(hg^{-1})$. It is right isosceles if $T(g) = T(h)$ and $T(hg^{-1}) = T(gh)$.

To test the last case, determine that $o([g, h]) = 7$ and $k(\gamma) = 2$, so that $T(\gamma) = 2\cos(2\pi/7)$. If this is not the case, then the group is not discrete. If $T(h) \neq T(hg^{-1})$, G is not discrete.

We have $o([g, h]) = 7$ and $k(\gamma) = 2$. If γ rotates by $2 \cdot \frac{2\pi}{7}$ and $\tau = |Tr(\gamma)|$, then $\tau = 2\cos(\frac{2\pi}{7})$ and $\frac{\tau}{2} = 2\cos^2\frac{\pi}{7} - 1$. Whence $\sin^2\frac{\pi}{7} = \frac{2-\tau}{4}$. Since $\cosh D_0 = \frac{1}{2\sin\frac{\pi}{7}}$, $\cosh^2 D_0 = \frac{1}{2-\tau}$, and $\sinh^2 D_0 = \frac{\tau-1}{-(\tau-2)}$. Compute that $\cos\frac{6\pi}{7} = -\cos\frac{\pi}{7} = -\sqrt{\frac{\tau+2}{4}}$. Thus to decide whether or not $\frac{1}{2}T(g) = \cosh^2 D_0 - \sinh^2 D_0 \cdot \cos\frac{2\pi}{7}$ and whether or not $\frac{T(h)}{2} = \frac{T(hg^{-1})}{2} = \cosh^2 D_0 - \sinh^2 D_0 \cdot \cos\frac{6\pi}{7}$, check whether or not $\frac{1}{2}T(g) = \frac{\tau+1}{2}$ and whether or not $\frac{T(h)}{2} = \frac{T(hg^{-1})}{2} = \frac{1}{2-\tau} + \frac{\tau-1}{2-\tau}\sqrt{\frac{\tau+2}{4}}$.

We then proceed with the general replacement step. If $T(hg) < T(hg^{-1})$, then we replace the triangle with sides $T(g)$, $T(h)$ and $T(hg^{-1})$ by the triangle with sides $T(g)$, $T(h)$ and $T(gh)$, replacing the generating pair (g, h) by the pair (g^{-1}, h) when $T(g) \leq T(h) \leq T(gh)$, by the pair (g, gh) when $T(g) \leq T(gh) \leq T(h)$, and by the pair (gh, g) when $T(gh) \leq T(g) \leq T(h)$. Again, with the new pair if $T(hg^{-1}) \leq T(gh)$, we have an acute triangle and we can test for discreteness. Otherwise, we return to the general replacement step. The acute triangle algorithm assures that we only return to the general replacement step a finite number of times before we obtain an acute triangle.

Note that in steps f(ii), (iii) and (v), we actually have $T(h) = T(g)$ since by assumption we have $T(g) \leq T(h)$ and we also have $T(h) \leq T(g)$.

Translating the proof for the intertwining cases: For the most part the statements of [15] translate in a straightforward manner. In some places there are obvious ways in which to make the statements more computational. Occasionally the translation requires some extra work. For example, the case of elliptic-elliptic requires some modification since area computations need to be eliminated. We give the details of two cases. They are step IV-3 (elliptic-hyperbolic) of [15] and the entire elliptic-elliptic case.

To obtain Step 6 (elliptic-hyperbolic): We first conjugate by the transformation that sends z to $\frac{z-R(h)}{z-A(h)}$ so that the axis of h is the imaginary axis. After conjugation we have the transformations $\bar{g}$ and $\bar{h}$. We compute the fixed point of $\bar{g}$ and $|Fix(\bar{g})|$. We let L be the line through $Fix(\bar{g})$ perpendicular to the imaginary axis. Since L is perpendicular to the imaginary axis, the ends of L are at $-q$ and q where $q = |Fix(\bar{g})|$. If Q is the point where L intersects the imaginary axis, $Q = iq$. Let L' be the segment of L between Q and $Fix(\bar{g})$. Q divides the imaginary axis into two pieces, A^-, the segment containing 0, and A^+, the segment containing ∞. L divides the upper half-plane into two half-planes. The condition of [15] that $\bar{g}(L')$ and A^- lie in the same half-plane is equivalent to $\bar{g}(Q)$ lying inside the circle $|z| < q$. Thus it suffices to determine whether $|\bar{g}(i|Fix(\bar{g})|)| < |Fix(\bar{g})|$. If this is not the case, replace h by h^{-1} and continue. (Note that if $Fix(g)$ lies on the axis of h, we leave things as they are.) Note that if a matrix M is multiplied by i, the i disappears when we conjugate another matrix by iM. At the end of this we have finished using $\bar{g}$ and have replaced the original pair (g, h) with the pair (g, h^{-1})

To obtain step 8 (elliptic-elliptic): This requires reworking the original algorithm in [15]. The difficulty is in computing the areas of T and T_1 and T_2. Recall that the fixed points of g and h are x and y respectively. We let L be the hyperbolic line through x and y and choose

14.4. THE REAL NUMBER ALGORITHM

hyperbolic lines L_g passing through x and L_h passing through y so that $g = r_{L_g} r_L$ and $h = r_L r_{L_h}$ where r_H denotes reflection in the hyperbolic line H. Now L_g and L_h intersect in a point z interior to the upper half-plane precisely when gh is elliptic. Compute $o(gh)$, $k(gh)$, $Rot(gh)$, and $(gh)_0$. Assume that $o(gh)$ is finite. If $k(gh) = 1$, then apply the Poincaré Polygon Theorem to $T \cup r_{L_g}(T)$ where T is the triangle with vertices x, y and z, to conclude that G is discrete. The area of T is $\pi - \pi \frac{1}{o(g)} - \pi \frac{1}{o(h)} - \pi \frac{k(gh)}{o(gh)}$. If the area of T is less than $\frac{\pi}{84}$, G is not discrete. If $k(gh) \neq 1$ or $Rot(gh) \neq -1$, construct T_1 and T_2 as follows: S_1 is the hyperbolic line passing through z making a counterclockwise angle of $\frac{\pi}{o(gh)}$ with L_g and S_2 is the hyperbolic through z making a clockwise angle of $\frac{\pi}{o(gh)}$ with L_h. S_1 intersects L at a point w and S_2 intersects L at a point v. S_1 and S_2 both pass through the interior of T. T_1 is the triangle with vertices x, z, and w. T_2 is the triangle with vertices y, z, and v. Since L_g and S_1 intersect at w and since $g(gh)_0 = r_{L_g} r_{S_1}$, the area of T_1 is equal to $\pi - \pi(\frac{1}{o(g)} + \frac{1}{o(gh)} + \frac{k(g(gh)_0)}{o(g(gh)_0)})$. If the area of T_1 is less than half of the area of T, replace (g,h) by $(g,(gh)_0)$ and return to the beginning of step 7 (elliptic-elliptic). Otherwise, the area of T_2 is less than half the area of T and we replace (g,h) by $(h,(gh)_0)$ and return to the beginning of step 7. Since the area of the triangle under consideration is reduced in half at each step and the algorithm ends if the area if the triangle under consideration is less than $\frac{\pi}{84}$, the algorithm stops. We remark that in [15], the justification for this area inequality stopping the algorithm was omitted. The justification is that one can apply Knapp's theorem to $T \cup r_{L_g}(T)$ to conclude that if G is discrete, then the area of this region is a multiple of the area of a fundamental region for the group, which cannot be less than $\frac{\pi}{42}$. Finally we remark that none of the area inequalities (e.g. steps 8k and 8n) actually require computations with π since the factors of π from both sides of the inequalities cancel. □

Remark: 14.4.2 *As in [15] we restrict the algorithm to non-elementary groups. The reason for this that if g and h are hyperbolics with integral entries and a common axis, it is not clear if there is an effective procedure to determine whether or not G is discrete.*

Remark: 14.4.3 *The need to use square roots can be actually elimi-*

nated. A detailed analysis shows that square roots arise in three situations: in conjugating matrices, in determining fixed points of transformations, and in computing E_{p_2}. When a transformation is conjugated by $\sqrt{w}M$ where M is a matrix and w is a positive real number, the square root drops out after conjugation. When square roots arise in relation to fixed points, they are used in the determination of various equalities and inequalities (e.g. whether $A(h) = A(g)$ or $A(h) = R(g)$, or $C(g,h) > 0$). One can check that the equality or inequality reduces to simple arithmetic conditions on the original entries in the matrices that do not involve square roots. Finally, the square root that is taken in computing E_{p_2} only plays a role in computing the phase of γ. The algorithm can be reworked to replace this by a computation of the phase of $[g,h]$ which is the same as γ^2. This just makes the list of steps slightly more cumbersome.

14.5 The Turing Machine Algorithm

In translating the real number algorithm into a Turing machine algorithm one calls upon the standard algorithms for addition, subtraction, multiplication and division in algebraic extension given by Loos [5]. Then one needs to show that one is working in a setting where three additional operations can be carried out. One needs to be able to (1) compare sizes of elements, (2) take the square root of a positive element, and (3) compute the order of an elliptic matrix be it finite or infinite. The proof of the Turing machine algorithm consists of showing that the input has been chosen so that all three can be done.

Theorem: 14.5.1 The Turing Machine Algorithm: *Let A and B be elements of $PSL(2, \mathbf{R})$. Let $G = \langle A, B \rangle$. Assume that G is non-elementary. Then the real number algorithm (theorem 14.4.1) can be implemented on a computer. The input will be the eight minimal polynomials, M_{α_i} and the eight isolating intervals, $Isol_{\alpha_i} = (r_i, s_i]$ corresponding to $\alpha_1, ..., \alpha_8$, the eight entries in the matrices A and B. The output will be one of two statements: G is discrete or G is not discrete.*

Proof: The entries of the two matrices lie in $F = \mathbf{Q}(\alpha_1, ..., \alpha_8)$. Call F the field of operations. We will go through the real number algorithm

14.5. THE TURING MACHINE ALGORITHM

step by step and notice that we can carry out the algorithm as long as our field of operations F allows in addition to the operations of ordinary arithmetic the three additional operations (1), (2) and (3) listed above.

Step 1. comparing sizes: Being able to compare the size of two elements of F is the same as being able to determine the sign of their difference. There is an algorithm for determining the sign of a number lying in a simple algebraic extension of the rationals (p. 175 of [5]). Namely, if α is given by its minimal polynomial M_α and isolating interval I_α and if $\beta \in \mathbf{Q}(\alpha)$ is given by its representing polynomial B, then there is an algorithm whose input is M_α, $Isol_\alpha$ and B and whose output is $s = sign(\beta)$. (The representing polynomial for β is the polynomial B with $\beta = B(\alpha)$.) Thus there will be a sign algorithm in F if we can exhibit F as a simple extension and compute the minimal polynomial and isolating interval for its primitive element.

It is classical that a separable multiple extension is a simple extension. Since minimal polynomials are square free, F is separable. Thus $F = \mathbf{Q}(\alpha)$ for some α. It is not classical, but nevertheless true that the existence of α is proved constructively. That is, using theorem 11 and algorithm 2 SIMPLE p. 184 of [5] one sees that there is an algorithm whose input is M_{α_i} and $Isol_{\alpha_i}, i = 1, ..., 8$, and whose output consists of the minimum polynomial for α, M_α; an isolating interval for α, $Isol_\alpha$; and the representing polynomials for the α_i, C_i. That is, the C_i are polynomials in α with $\alpha_i = C_i(\alpha)$.

Thus we can compare sizes in the field of operations.

Step 2. taking square roots: There are algorithms for carrying out all of the simple arithmetic operations (addition, subtraction, multiplication and finding inverses) in $\mathbf{Q}(\alpha)$ using the representing polynomials (see page 174 of [5]). In addition these algorithms for algebraic number arithmetic (Algorithm 1, page 180 of [5]) include in the output the isolating interval and a primitive square free polynomial corresponding to the sum, product, etc. Thus one can carry out all of the simple arithmetic operations keeping track of the representing polynomials, the minimal polynomials and the isolating intervals of the elements that arise. Thus if the algorithm requires taking the square root of $w > 0$, we may assume that the minimal polynomials and the isolating intervals for w and $\sqrt{w}$ are know. We can, therefore, apply the algorithm SIMPLE that finds the primitive element to obtain β,

M_β, and $Isol_\beta$ where $F(\sqrt{w}) = \mathbf{Q}(\alpha, \sqrt{w}) = \mathbf{Q}(\beta)$. We pass to the new extension $\mathbf{Q}(\beta)$. Because this is again a simple extension and M_β and $Isol_\beta$ are given, there is still a sign algorithm and one can still carry out all of the simple arithmetic operations.

Step 3. computing elliptic orders: If the degree of each α_i is d_i and the degree of $\mathbf{Q}(\alpha)$ is d, then $d \leq \prod_{i=1}^{8} d_i$. The elliptic order algorithm 14.2.2 assures that we can compute the order of an elliptic element just by computing its first $32d^2$ powers and seeing if any of them are $\pm$ the identity.

Since all three operations can be carried out, the theorem follows. □

Part V

Appendix

Appendix A

Verifying the Matelski-Beardon cases

Knapp's theorem allows one to calculate precisely when one can have a set of generators that do not satisfy the cycle condition at the vertices. Such a calculation or its equivalent appears in [20] as well as in both [2] and [27]. The calculation given here is a modification of that in [27]. We show

Theorem: A.0.2 *Let k and n be an integers with $1 < k < n/2$. If A and B are hyperbolics with intersecting but distinct axes that generate a discrete group G and if $[A, B]$ is the square of a (non-primitive) rotation by an angle $\pm k \cdot 2\pi/n$, then either*

- *$t = 3$, $k = 3$ and G^* is a $(2, 3, n)$ triangle group with $n > 4$, or*

- *$t = 2$, $k = 2$ and G^* is a $(2, 4, n)$ triangle group with $n > 3$, or*

- *$t = 9$, $k = 2$ and G^* is a $(2, 3, 7)$ triangle group.*

Proof: We know that the area of $\mathbf{U}/(G^*) = 2\pi[2(g-1) + \sum_{j=1}^{m}(1-\frac{1}{v_j})]$. Here g is the genus of the quotient and the v_i give the orders of the m conjugacy classes of elliptic and parabolic elements G^*. The area of the pentagon is $\pi - k \cdot 2\pi/n$. Equating the area of P with $t \cdot$ Area $(\mathbf{U}/(G^*))$ (7.1) and using the fact that $t \geq 1$, we obtain

$$1 - 2k/n \geq 2(2(g-1) + \sum_{j=1}^{m}(1 - \frac{1}{v_j})) \qquad (A.1)$$

or
$$-k/n \geq 2g - 5/2 + \sum_{j=1}^{m}(1 - \frac{1}{v_j}). \tag{A.2}$$

We proceed to treat various cases.

If $g \geq 2$, the right hand side is positive and the left hand side is negative. Thus $g \leq 1$. If $g = 1$, the right hand side is at least $-1/2 + 1 - 1/v_1$ which is positive since $v_1 \geq 2$.

- *Thus we may assume that $g = 0$.*

We know that $m \geq 3$ if $g = 0$. Further for each j, $1 - 1/v_j$ is positive. We compute that

$$-\frac{k}{n} = -\frac{1}{v_1} + -\frac{1}{v_2} + \text{ a series of positive terms.}$$

Since $1 \geq \frac{1}{v_1} + \frac{1}{v_2}$, we can conclude that

$$1 > \frac{1}{v_1} + \frac{1}{v_2} - \frac{k}{n} \geq (m-2)\frac{1}{2} \geq 0.$$

Thus $-\frac{k}{n} + \frac{1}{v_1} + \frac{1}{v_2}$ is some number between 0 and 1 that is greater than or equal to $(m-2)/2$. If $m \geq 4$, $(m-2)/2 \geq 1$.

- *Thus we must have $m = 3$.*

Since $t \geq 2$, $2 \cdot \text{Area}(\mathbf{U}/(G^*)) \leq \text{Area}(P)$, compute that $\frac{k}{2n} \leq (\frac{1}{v_1} + \frac{1}{v_2} - \frac{3}{4}) + \frac{1}{v_3}$. Since each $v_i \geq 2$,

$$(\frac{1}{v_1} + \frac{1}{v_2} - \frac{3}{4}) \leq \frac{1}{4}$$

. • *Assume now that $(\frac{1}{v_1} + \frac{1}{v_2} - \frac{3}{4}) \leq 0$*

Then $\frac{k}{2n} \leq \frac{1}{v_3}$. Since $k \geq 2$, $v_3 \leq n$. At the same time we see that $n \leq v_3$ as follows. G^* has an element of order n and, therefore, n divides v_i for some i. Since we may assume that $v_1 \leq v_2 \leq v_3$, we have $n \leq v_3$. Thus in this case we must have $v_3 = n$ and $k = 2$ so that $\frac{1}{v_1} + \frac{1}{v_2} = \frac{3}{4}$. Compute that if $v_1 = 2$, $v_2 = 4$. If $v_1 \geq 3$, calculate that $\frac{1}{v_2} \geq \frac{5}{12}$. Since $v_2 \geq v_1 \geq 3$, $\frac{1}{v_2} \leq \frac{1}{3}$ which is a contradiction. Thus we must have $k = 2$, $v_1 = 2$, $v_2 = 4$, $4 = v_2 \leq v_3 = n$.

If $n = 4$, the area of P is zero. Thus $n > 4$. Finally use $n > 4$, to compute that $2t(n-4) = 4(n-4)$, so that $t = 2$.

- *Thus if* $(\frac{1}{v_1} + \frac{1}{v_2} - \frac{3}{4}) \leq 0$, *conclude that* $k = 2$, $t = 2$, $n > 4$, $v_1 = 2$, $v_2 = 4$, *and* $v_3 = n$. Thus we have $k = 2$, $t = 2$ and a $(2, 4, n)$ triangle group.
- *Next we assume that* $(\frac{1}{v_1} + \frac{1}{v_2} - \frac{3}{4}) > 0$.

Since $\frac{1}{v_1} + \frac{1}{v_2} < 1$, we have $\frac{1}{4} > (\frac{1}{v_1} + \frac{1}{v_2} - \frac{3}{4}) > 0$.

If $v_1 = 2$, compute that $2 < v_2 < 4$, whence $v_2 = 3$.

To rule out $v_1 \geq 3$ argue as follows: If $v_1 \geq 3$, $v_2 \geq 3$, whence $\frac{1}{3} - \frac{3}{4} - \frac{1}{v_2} \geq \frac{1}{v_1} - \frac{3}{4} + \frac{1}{v_2} > 0$ or $-\frac{5}{12} + \frac{1}{v_2} > 0$ so that $\frac{12}{5} > v_2$, which contradicts $v_2 \geq 3$.

- *In what follows we may assume that* $v_1 = 2$, $v_2 = 3$.

Return to equation 7.1 to compute that in this case

$$2t\left(\frac{v_3 - 6}{6v_3}\right) = 1 - \frac{2k}{n}.$$

Recall that n divides v_3 and set $d = \frac{v_3}{n}$. Compute that $\frac{t}{3}(v_3 - 6) = v_3 - dk$. If $n = 2$, then $v_3 - 6$ is negative whence $v_3 \leq 6$.

Because G^* is a discrete triangle group, we must have $1/2 + 1/3 + 1/v_3 < 1$ or $6 < v_3$. Thus we cannot have $n = 2$.

If $n = 3$, $1/2 + 1/3 + 1/3 > 1$.

Thus we may assume that $n > 3$. Thus n divides v_3. We consider the possibilities for t.

- First we rule out $t = 2$ as follows.

If $t = 2$, $\frac{2}{3}(v_3 - 6) = v_3 - 2dk$. So that $6(dk - 2) = v_3$. Note that $d = v_3/n$ and $n > 3$ implies $v_3/3 > v_3/n$. Since we also have $k \geq 2$, $v_3 = 6(dk - 2) > 6(\frac{v_3}{3} \cdot 2 - 2) > 4v_3 - 12$. Thus $4 > v_3$. But discreteness requires that v_3 be greater than 6. Thus it cannot be that $t = 2$.

- *Assume next that* $t \geq 3$.

Then $t/3 \geq 1$ so that $v_3 - 2dk = \frac{t}{3}(v_3 - 6) \geq v_3 - 6$. Conclude that $3 \geq dk$. Since $k \geq 2$ and d is an integer, $d = 1$ and $k = 2$ or 3. Since $d = 1$, $n = v_3$.

- *Assume that* $k = 2$.

If $k = 2$, $t = 3\frac{v_3 - 4}{v_3 - 6} = 3 + \frac{6}{v_3 - 6}$. Now $\frac{6}{v_3 - 6}$ is an integer.

When $6 < v_3 - 6$, then $12 < v_3$ and the fraction is not an integer. Thus we may assume that $v_3 < 12$. We also know by discreteness that $v_3 > 6$.

We compute $t = 3 + 6/(v_3 - 6)$ for the various values of v_3.

If $v_3 = 12, t = 4$.
If $v_3 = 11$ or $v_3 = 10$, t is not an integer.
If $v_3 = 9$, $t = 5$; if $v_3 = 8$, $t = 6$, and if $v_3 = 7$, $t = 9$.

Since $k = 2$ and k and n are relatively prime, we rule out $v_3 = 12$ or 8. We will rule out $t = 5$ by looking at the corollary of the extended Knapp count. Namely corollary 7.4.3 of theorem 7.4.2 implies that $5 - 2$ must be divisible by 9. (Note that we could also use this corollary to rule out $v_3 = 12$ or 8.)

- We have seen that *either* $t = 3$ *and* $k = 3$ *and we have a* $(2,3,n)$ *group or* $t = 9$ *and* $k = 2$ *and we have a* $(2,3,7)$ *group, or* $k = 3$.
- Finally we consider $k = 3$.

If $k = 3$, then $\frac{t}{3} \cdot (v_3 - 6) = v_3 - 6$. Since $v_3 \neq 6$, $t = 3$. □

We can also obtain the following corollary which can be stated in various forms (see [31] or [27]).

Corollary: A.0.3 *If G^* is a $(2,4,n)$ triangle group, then n is odd and $G = G^*$. If G^* is a $(2,3,n)$ triangle group, then $G = G^*$ if and only if n is odd and G is a proper subgroup of G^* if and only if n is even in which case G is a $(3,3,n/2)$ triangle group.*

Proof: If n is odd, then γ and $[A, B]$ have the same order. A subgroup of index two in a triangle group T generated by x, y and z, with $x^2 = y^3 = z^n = xyz = 1$ or with $x^2 = y^4 = z^n = xyz = 1$ corresponds to the kernel of a homomorphism ϕ of T onto Z_2. Such a homomorphism is determined by its action on the generators. It is easy to verify that there is no such homomorphism if T is the $(2,4,n)$ triangle group and n is odd and that there is such a homomorphism is T is a $(2,3,n)$ triangle group precisely when n is even. In that case, x is not in the kernel. Since x corresponds to E_{p_1} in our case, G is then a proper subgroup of G^*.

Use Singerman's list [38] of all containment relations among triangle groups to see that in this case G must be a $(3,3,n/2)$ group. □

Remark: A.0.4 *We remark that a careful analysis of the geometry shows that when γ rotates by $\pm 2k\pi/n$, $2k\pi/n$ is the interior angle of the pentagon for otherwise the interior angle would be greater than π, meaning that there was no pentagon (i.e. γ was not elliptic).*

Appendix B
A Summary of Notation

Notation and conventions about terminology are introduced through out the course of these notes as it is needed. However, many of the results of the various sections are independent of each other. A reader may choose to skip reading one section and be confronted in a later section by notation established in a skipped section. The purpose is to provide a partial summary of notation and conventions used throughout the paper.

- An *acute* triangle is one in which all angles are *less than or equal* to $\pi/2$. *Acute* angles include angles of $\pi/2$.

- **U** denotes the upper-half plane or the unit disc. It will be clear from the context which.

- $d(x,y)$ denotes the distance in the hyperbolic metric between points x and y in **U**.

- Let x and y be any two points of **U**, $[x,y]$ denotes the geodesic segment connecting x and y; $(x,y]$ and $[x,y)$ respectively represent the half open geodesic segment between x and y and $\widetilde{[x,y]}$ the complete geodesic containing $[x,y]$.

- If S is any geodesic arc, $\tilde{S}$ is the complete geodesic containing S.

- If S is any geodesic segment, its hyperbolic length is denoted by S_d.

- Intersecting axes means axes that intersect but are *distinct*.

Bibliography

[1] A.F. Beardon, in *Holomorphic Functions and Moduli*, Springer-Verlag, (1988).

[2] A.F. Beardon, The Geometry of Discrete Groups, Springer-Verlag, (1983).

[3] L. Blum, M. Shub, and S. Smale, On a Theory of Computation and Complexity over the Real Numbers: NP-Completeness, Recursive Functions and Universal Machines, *Bulletin of the AMS*, **21(1)**, (1989), 1-46.

[4] G. Boolos, R. Jeffrey, *Computability and Logic*, 2nd edition, Cambridge University Press, (1980).

[5] B. Buchberger, G.E. Collins, R. Loos (w. R. Albrecht) editors, Computer Algebra Symbolic and Algebraic Computations, second edition, Springer+Verlag, N.Y., (1983).

[6] C. Doyle and D. James, Discreteness criteria and high order generators for subgroups of $SL(2,\mathbf{R})$, *Ill. J. Math* **25** (1981), 191-200.

[7] W. Fenchel, Elementary Geometry in Hyperbolic Space, de Gruyter Studies in Mathematics, 11, Berlin-New York, (1989).

[8] F. Gehring and G. Martin, Stability and extremality in Jørgensen's inequality, to appear.

[9] F. Gehring and G. Martin, Iteration theory and inequalities for Kleinian groups, to appear.

[10] J. Gilman, Inequalities and discrete groups, *Canadian J.* **XL(1)** (1988), 115-130.

[11] J. Gilman, On the existence of elliptic elements in discrete groups, in *Holomorphic Functions and Moduli, II*, Springer-Verlag, N.Y. (1988), 23-27.

[12] J. Gilman, A geometric approach to Jørgensen's inequality, *Advances in Math.*, **85 (2)**, (1991), 193-197.

[13] J. Gilman, A geometric approach to the hyperbolic Jørgensen inequality, *Bull. A.M.S.* **16(1)**, (1987), 91-92.

[14] J. Gilman, On the complexity of the $PSL(2, \mathbf{R})$ discreteness algorithm, in preparation.

[15] J. Gilman and B. Maskit, An algorithm for two-generator discrete groups, *Mich. Math. J.*, **38 (1)**, (1991), 13-32.

[16] Sa'ar Hersonsky, A generalization of the Shimizu-Leutbecher and Jørgensen inequalities to Möbius transformations in $\mathbf{R}^N$, *Proceedings of the AMS*, (1994).

[17] T. Jørgensen, On discrete groups of Mobius transformations, *Amer. J. Math* **98** (1976), 739-749.

[18] R.N. Kalia and G. Rosenberger, automorphisms of the Fuchsian groups of type (0;2,2,2,q;0), *Comm. Algebra (6)* **11** (1978), 1115-1129.

[19] G. Kern-Isberner and G. Rosenberger, Uber Diskretheitsbedingungen and die diophantische Gleichung $ax^2 + by^2 + cz^2 = dxyz$, *Arch. Math.*, **34** (1980), 481-493.

[20] A.W.Knapp, Doubly generated Fuchsian groups, *Michigan Math. J.* **15** (1968), 289-304.

[21] S. Lang, *Algebra*, Addison-Wesley publ., Reading, Mass. (1965).

[22] R.C. Lyndon and J.L. Ullman, Pairs of real 2-by-2 matrices that generate free products, *Mich. Math. J.* **15** (1968), 161-166.

BIBLIOGRAPHY

[23] W. Magnus, Noneuclidean Tesselations and their Groups, Academic press, N.Y. (1974).

[24] W. Magnus, Collected Papers, ed. G. Baumslag and B. Chandler, Springer-Verlag, N.Y. (1984).

[25] B. Maskit, On Poincaré's theorem for fundamental polygons, *Advances in Math.* **7** (1971), 219-230.

[26] B. Maskit, Kleinian Groups, Springer-Verlag, Berlin, (1988).

[27] J.P. Matelski, The classification of discrete 2-generator subgroups of PSL(2,**R**) *Israel J. Math.* **42** (1982), 309-317.

[28] Magnus, Karass and Solitar, Combinatorial Groups Theory, Wiley & Sons, N.Y. (1966).

[29] N. Purzitsky, Two generator discrete free products, *Math. Z.* **126** (1972), 209-23.

[30] N. Purzitsky, Real two-dimensional representations of two-generator free groups, *Math. Z.* **127** (1972), 95-104.

[31] N. Purzitsky, All two-generator Fuchsian groups, *Math. Z.* **147** (1976), 87-92.

[32] N. Purzitsky and G. Rosenberger, Two generator Fuchsian groups of genus one, *Math. Z.* **128** (1972), 245-251. Correction: *Math. Z.* **132** (1973), 261-262.

[33] R. Riley, Applications of a Computer Implementation of Poincaré's Theorem on Fundamental Polyhedra, *Math. Computation* **40** (1983), 633-646.

[34] G. Rosenberger, Fuchssche Gruppen, die freies Produkt zweier zyklischer Gruppen sind, un die Gleichung $x^2 + y^2 + z^2 = xyz$, *Math. Ann.* **199** (1972), 213-228.

[35] G. Rosenberger, Von Untergruppen der Triangelgruppen. *Illinois J. Math* **22** (1978), 404-413.

[36] G. Rosenberger, Ein Bemerkung zu einer Arbeit von T. Jørgensen, *Math. Z.* **165** (1919), 261-265.

[37] G. Rosenberger, All generating pairs of all two-generator Fuchsian groups, *Arch. Math.* **46** (1986), 198-204.

[38] D. Singerman, Finitely maximal Fuchsian groups, *Journal London Math. Soc.* **(2), 6** (1972), 29-38.

[39] A. Tarski, A Decision Method for Elementary Algebra and Geometry, 2nd rev. edition (Berkeley and Los Angeles), (1951).

[40] B. L. Van der Warden, Modern Algebra, Frederick Ungar Pub., (1953).

[41] Wada, Thesis, Columbia University (1986).

[42] P. L. Waterman, Mobius transformations in several dimensions, to appear.

Editorial Information

To be published in the *Memoirs*, a paper must be correct, new, nontrivial, and significant. Further, it must be well written and of interest to a substantial number of mathematicians. Piecemeal results, such as an inconclusive step toward an unproved major theorem or a minor variation on a known result, are in general not acceptable for publication. *Transactions* Editors shall solicit and encourage publication of worthy papers. Papers appearing in *Memoirs* are generally longer than those appearing in *Transactions* with which it shares an editorial committee.

As of May 31, 1995, the backlog for this journal was approximately 5 volumes. This estimate is the result of dividing the number of manuscripts for this journal in the Providence office that have not yet gone to the printer on the above date by the average number of monographs per volume over the previous twelve months, reduced by the number of issues published in four months (the time necessary for preparing an issue for the printer). (There are 6 volumes per year, each containing at least 4 numbers.)

A Copyright Transfer Agreement is required before a paper will be published in this journal. By submitting a paper to this journal, authors certify that the manuscript has not been submitted to nor is it under consideration for publication by another journal, conference proceedings, or similar publication.

Information for Authors and Editors

Memoirs are printed by photo-offset from camera copy fully prepared by the author. This means that the finished book will look exactly like the copy submitted.

The paper must contain a *descriptive title* and an *abstract* that summarizes the article in language suitable for workers in the general field (algebra, analysis, etc.). The *descriptive title* should be short, but informative; useless or vague phrases such as "some remarks about" or "concerning" should be avoided. The *abstract* should be at least one complete sentence, and at most 300 words. Included with the footnotes to the paper, there should be the 1991 *Mathematics Subject Classification* representing the primary and secondary subjects of the article. This may be followed by a list of *key words and phrases* describing the subject matter of the article and taken from it. A list of the numbers may be found in the annual index of *Mathematical Reviews*, published with the December issue starting in 1990, as well as from the electronic service e-MATH [**telnet e-MATH.ams.org** (or **telnet 130.44.1.100**). Login and password are **e-math**]. For journal abbreviations used in bibliographies, see the list of serials in the latest *Mathematical Reviews* annual index. When the manuscript is submitted, authors should supply the editor with electronic addresses if available. These will be printed after the postal address at the end of each article.

Electronically prepared manuscripts. The AMS encourages submission of electronically prepared manuscripts in $\mathcal{A}_\mathcal{M}\mathcal{S}$-TeX or $\mathcal{A}_\mathcal{M}\mathcal{S}$-LaTeX because properly prepared electronic manuscripts save the author proofreading time and move more quickly through the production process. To this end, the Society has prepared "preprint" style files, specifically the amsppt style of $\mathcal{A}_\mathcal{M}\mathcal{S}$-TeX and the amsart style of $\mathcal{A}_\mathcal{M}\mathcal{S}$-LaTeX, which will simplify the work of authors and of the production staff. Those authors who make use of these style files from the beginning of the writing process will further reduce their own effort. Electronically submitted manuscripts prepared in plain TeX or LaTeX do not mesh properly with the AMS production systems and cannot, therefore, realize the same kind of expedited processing. Users of plain TeX should have little difficulty learning $\mathcal{A}_{\mathcal{M}}\mathcal{S}$-TeX, and LaTeX users will find that $\mathcal{A}_{\mathcal{M}}\mathcal{S}$-LaTeX is the same as LaTeX with additional commands to simplify the typesetting of mathematics.

Guidelines for Preparing Electronic Manuscripts provides additional assistance and is available for use with either $\mathcal{A}_{\mathcal{M}}\mathcal{S}$-TeX or $\mathcal{A}_{\mathcal{M}}\mathcal{S}$-LaTeX. Authors with FTP access may obtain *Guidelines* from the Society's Internet node e-MATH.ams.org (130.44.1.100). For those without FTP access *Guidelines* can be obtained free of charge from the e-mail address guide-elec@math.ams.org (Internet) or from the Customer Services Department, American Mathematical Society, P.O. Box 6248, Providence, RI 02940-6248. When requesting *Guidelines*, please specify which version you want.

At the time of submission, authors should indicate if the paper has been prepared using $\mathcal{A}_{\mathcal{M}}\mathcal{S}$-TeX or $\mathcal{A}_{\mathcal{M}}\mathcal{S}$-LaTeX. The *Manual for Authors of Mathematical Papers* should be consulted for symbols and style conventions. The *Manual* may be obtained free of charge from the e-mail address cust-serv@math.ams.org or from the Customer Services Department, American Mathematical Society, P.O. Box 6248, Providence, RI 02940-6248. The Providence office should be supplied with a manuscript that corresponds to the electronic file being submitted.

Electronic manuscripts should be sent to the Providence office immediately after the paper has been accepted for publication. They can be sent via e-mail to pub-submit@math.ams.org (Internet) or on diskettes to the Publications Department, American Mathematical Society, P. O. Box 6248, Providence, RI 02940-6248. When submitting electronic manuscripts please be sure to include a message indicating in which publication the paper has been accepted.

Two copies of the paper should be sent directly to the appropriate Editor and the author should keep one copy. The *Guide for Authors of Memoirs* gives detailed information on preparing papers for *Memoirs* and may be obtained free of charge from the Editorial Department, American Mathematical Society, P. O. Box 6248, Providence, RI 02940-6248. For papers not prepared electronically, model paper may also be obtained free of charge from the Editorial Department.

Any inquiries concerning a paper that has been accepted for publication should be sent directly to the Editorial Department, American Mathematical Society, P. O. Box 6248, Providence, RI 02940-6248.

Editors

This journal is designed particularly for long research papers (and groups of cognate papers) in pure and applied mathematics. Papers intended for publication in the *Memoirs* should be addressed to one of the following editors:

Ordinary differential equations, partial differential equations, and applied mathematics to JOHN MALLET-PARET, Division of Applied Mathematics, Brown University, Providence, RI 02912-9000; e-mail: am438000@brownvm.brown.edu.

Harmonic analysis, representation theory, and Lie theory to ROBERT J. STANTON, Department of Mathematics, The Ohio State University, 231 West 18th Avenue, Columbus, OH 43210-1174; electronic mail: stanton@function.mps.ohio-state.edu.

Ergodic theory, dynamical systems, and abstract analysis to DANIEL J. RUDOLPH, Department of Mathematics, University of Maryland, College Park, MD 20742; e-mail: djr@math.umd.edu.

Real and harmonic analysis and elliptic partial differential equations to JILL C. PIPHER, Department of Mathematics, Brown University, Providence, RI 02910-9000; e-mail: jpipher@gauss.math.brown.edu.

Algebra and algebraic geometry to EFIM ZELMANOV, Department of Mathematics, University of Wisconsin, 480 Lincoln Drive, Madison, WI 53706-1388; e-mail: zelmanov@math.wisc.edu

Algebraic topology and differential topology to MARK MAHOWALD, Department of Mathematics, Northwestern University, 2033 Sheridan Road, Evanston, IL 60208-2730; e-mail: mark@math.nwu.edu.

Global analysis and differential geometry to ROBERT L. BRYANT, Department of Mathematics, Duke University, Durham, NC 27706-7706; e-mail: bryant@math.duke.edu.

Probability and statistics to RICHARD DURRETT, Department of Mathematics, Cornell University, White Hall, Ithaca, NY 14853-7901; e-mail: rtd@cornella.cit.cornell.edu.

Combinatorics and Lie theory to PHILIP J. HANLON, Department of Mathematics, University of Michigan, Ann Arbor, MI 48109-1003; e-mail: phil.hanlon@math.lsa.umich.edu.

Logic and universal algebra to GREGORY L. CHERLIN, Department of Mathematics, Rutgers University, Hill Center, Busch Campus, New Brunswick, NJ 08903; e-mail: cherlin@math.rutgers.edu.

Algebraic number theory, analytic number theory, and automorphic forms to WEN-CHING WINNIE LI, Department of Mathematics, Pennsylvania State University, University Park, PA 16802-6401; e-mail: wli@math.psu.edu.

Complex analysis and complex geometry to DANIEL M. BURNS, Department of Mathematics, University of Michigan, Ann Arbor, MI 48109-1003; e-mail: burns@gauss.stanford.edu.

Algebraic geometry and commutative algebra to LAWRENCE EIN, Department of Mathematics, University of Illinois, 851 S. Morgan (MIC 249), Chicago, IL 60607-7045; email: u22425@uicvm.uic.edu.

All other communications to the editors should be addressed to the Managing Editor, PETER SHALEN, Department of Mathematics, Statistics, and Computer Science, University of Illinois at Chicago, Chicago, IL 60680; e-mail: shalen@math.uic.edu.

Other Titles in This Series

(*Continued from the front of this publication*)

530 **Y. S. Han and E. T. Sawyer,** Littlewood-Paley theory on spaces of homogeneous type and the classical function spaces, 1994

529 **Eric M. Friedlander and Barry Mazur,** Filtrations on the homology of algebraic varieties, 1994

528 **J. F. Jardine,** Higher spinor classes, 1994

527 **Giora Dula and Reinhard Schultz,** Diagram cohomology and isovariant homotopy theory, 1994

526 **Shiro Goto and Koji Nishida,** The Cohen-Macaulay and Gorenstein Rees algebras associated to filtrations, 1994

525 **Enrique Artal-Bartolo,** Forme de Jordan de la monodromie des singularités superisolées de surfaces, 1994

524 **Justin R. Smith,** Iterating the cobar construction, 1994

523 **Mark I. Freidlin and Alexander D. Wentzell,** Random perturbations of Hamiltonian systems, 1994

522 **Joel D. Pincus and Shaojie Zhou,** Principal currents for a pair of unitary operators, 1994

521 **K. R. Goodearl and E. S. Letzter,** Prime ideals in skew and q-skew polynomial rings, 1994

520 **Tom Ilmanen,** Elliptic regularization and partial regularity for motion by mean curvature, 1994

519 **William M. McGovern,** Completely prime maximal ideals and quantization, 1994

518 **René A. Carmona and S. A. Molchanov,** Parabolic Anderson problem and intermittency, 1994

517 **Takashi Shioya,** Behavior of distant maximal geodesics in finitely connected complete 2-dimensional Riemannian manifolds, 1994

516 **Kevin W. J. Kadell,** A proof of the q-Macdonald-Morris conjecture for BC_n, 1994

515 **Krzysztof Ciesielski, Lee Larson, and Krzysztof Ostaszewski,** $\mathcal{I}$-density continuous functions, 1994

514 **Anthony A. Iarrobino,** Associated graded algebra of a Gorenstein Artin algebra, 1994

513 **Jaume Llibre and Ana Nunes,** Separatrix surfaces and invariant manifolds of a class of integrable Hamiltonian systems and their perturbations, 1994

512 **Maria R. Gonzalez-Dorrego,** $(16,6)$ configurations and geometry of Kummer surfaces in $\mathbb{P}^3$, 1994

511 **Monique Sablé-Tougeron,** Ondes de gradients multidimensionnelles, 1993

510 **Gennady Bachman,** On the coefficients of cyclotomic polynomials, 1993

509 **Ralph Howard,** The kinematic formula in Riemannian homogeneous spaces, 1993

508 **Kunio Murasugi and Jozef H. Przytycki,** An index of a graph with applications to knot theory, 1993

507 **Cristiano Husu,** Extensions of the Jacobi identity for vertex operators, and standard $A_1^{(1)}$-modules, 1993

506 **Marc A. Rieffel,** Deformation quantization for actions of R^d, 1993

505 **Stephen S.-T. Yau and Yung Yu,** Gorenstein quotient singularities in dimension three, 1993

504 **Anthony V. Phillips and David A. Stone,** A topological Chern-Weil theory, 1993

503 **Michael Makkai,** Duality and definability in first order logic, 1993

502 **Eriko Hironaka,** Abelian coverings of the complex projective plane branched along configurations of real lines, 1993

501 **E. N. Dancer,** Weakly nonlinear Dirichlet problems on long or thin domains, 1993

500 **David Soudry,** Rankin-Selberg convolutions for $SO_{2\ell+1} \times GL_n$: Local theory, 1993

(See the AMS catalog for earlier titles)